WAR POETRY

War Poetry is a new anthology of the diverse poetry of the two world wars. It challenges the dominance of English officer poets in the canon of war poetry and, through contextual material and a comprehensive introduction, suggests new ways of reading the genre.

The anthology contains substantial selections not only from established war poets such as Wilfred Owen, Isaac Rosenberg and Keith Douglas, but also incorporates lesser-known works such as ballads by Derbyshire miners, modernist poetry by Herbert Read and H.D., and the Gaelic elegies of Sorley MacLean. The poems are annotated and accompanied by biographical and bibliographical information. The prose section of the anthology contains extracts from essays, articles and letters – some reproduced for the first time – which allow the poems to be read within the wider intellectual, cultural and political debates of the first half of the century. The in-depth introductory chapters discuss the poems and extracts at length, seeking to answer questions and discuss issues such as the development of the canon of war poetry and the relationship between war poetry and 'Englishness' and other nationalisms.

War Poetry reveals a diversity of voices, many of which until now have not been heard, and all of which participated in the major cultural and intellectual arguments of their times. It was collected with the student in mind but will also make fascinating reading for any poetry lover.

Simon Featherstone is Senior Lecturer in English at Anglia Polytechnic University.

Critical Readers in Theory and Practice

GENERAL EDITOR: Rick Rylance, *Anglia Polytechnic University*

The gap between theory and practice can often seem far too wide for the student of literary theory. *Critical Readers in Theory and Practice* is a new series which bridges that gap: it not only offers an introduction to a range of literary and theoretical topics, but also *applies* the theories to relevant texts.

Each volume is split into two parts: the first consists of an in-depth and clear introduction, setting out the theoretical bases, historical developments and contemporary critical situation of the topic. The theory is then applied to practice in the second part in an anthology of classic texts and essays.

Designed specifically with the student in mind, *Critical Readers in Theory and Practice* provides an essential introduction to contemporary theories and how they relate to textual material.

Bakhtinian Thought: An introductory reader *Simon Dentith*

War Poetry: An introductory reader *Simon Featherstone*

WAR POETRY

An introductory reader

SIMON FEATHERSTONE

LONDON AND NEW YORK

First published 1995
by Routledge
11 New Fetter Lane, London EC4P 4EE

Simultaneously published in the USA and Canada
by Routledge
29 West 35th Street, New York, NY 10001

Typeset in Janson by
Ponting–Green Publishing Services, Chesham, Bucks

Printed and bound in Great Britain by
Clays Ltd, St Ives PLC

British Library Cataloguing in Publication Data
A catalogue record for this book is available from
the British Library

Library of Congress Cataloging in Publication Data
War Poetry: An introductory reader /
[edited by] Simon Featherstone.
p.   cm. – (Critical Readers in Theory and Practice)
Includes bibliographical references and index.
1. World War, 1914–1918 – Poetry.
2. English poetry – 20th century – History and criticism.
3. World War, 1914–1918 – Literature and the war.
4. World War, 1939–1945 – Literature and the war.
5. War poetry, English – History and criticism.
6. World War, 1939–1945 – Poetry   7. English poetry – 20th
century.   8. War poetry, English.
I. Featherstone, Simon.   II. Series.
PR1195.W65P63   1995
821'.91080358–dc20   94–16861

ISBN 0–415–07750–8 (hbk)
ISBN 0–415–09570–0 (pbk)

For Helen

Contents

General Editor's Preface

The interpretation of culture never stands still. Modern approaches to familiar problems adjust our sense of their importance, and new ideas focus on fresh details or remake accepted concepts. This has been especially true over recent years when developments across the humanities have altered so many ideas.

For many this revolution in understanding has been exciting but difficult, involving the need to integrate advanced theoretical work with attention to specific texts and issues. This series attempts to approach this difficulty in a new way by putting together a new balance of basic texts and detailed, introductory exposition.

Each volume in the series will be organised in two parts. Part One provides a thorough account of the topic under discussion. It details important concepts, historical developments and the contemporary context of interpretation and debate. Part Two provides an anthology of classic texts or – in the case of very recent work – essays by leading writers which offer focused discussions of particular issues. Commentary and editorial material provided by the author connect the explanations in Part One to the materials in Part Two, and in this way the reader moves comfortably between original work and enabling introduction.

The series will include volumes on topics which have been of particular importance recently. Some books will introduce specific theoretical ideas; others will re-examine bodies of literary or other material in the light of current thinking. But as a whole the series aims to reflect, in a clear-minded and approachable way, the changing ways in which we understand the expanding field of modern literary and cultural studies.

Rick Rylance

Acknowledgements

I would like to thank the following for their permission to reprint copyright material:

For Ivor Gurney: 'First Time In', 'The Silent One', 'Strange Hells', 'Swift and Slow', 'The Mangel-Bury' and 'While I Write', Robert Haines, Sole Trustee of the Gurney Estate 1982. Reprinted from *Collected Poems of Ivor Gurney* by permission of Oxford University Press.

For Wilfred Owen: 'Strange Meeting', the Estate of Wilfred Owen. Reprinted from *The Complete Poems and Fragments* by permission of Chatto & Windus.

For Thomas Beardsley: 'This is My Story', George Shipstone: 'My Little Grey Home in the West', C. Butters: 'Send 'Em Along', *The Ilkeston Advertiser*.

For David Jones: Preface and extracts from *In Parenthesis*, Faber & Faber Ltd.

For H.D.: 'After Troy', and extracts from 'The Tribute' and *The Walls Do Not Fall*, the Estate of Hilda Doolittle. Reprinted from *Collected Poems 1912–1944* by permission of Carcanet Press Ltd. and New Directions Publishing Corporation.

For Herbert Read: 'To a Conscript of 1940' and extracts from 'My Company', 'Ode', 'Sorel, Marx, and the War.', and 'To Hell with Culture', David Higham Associates.

For Sorley MacLean: 'Going Westwards', 'Alasdair MacLeod', 'Heroes', and 'Death Valley' from *From Wood to Ridge*, Carcanet Press Ltd.

For Hamish Henderson: extracts from *Elegies for the Dead in Cyrenaica*, 'Victory Hoe-Down', 'The 51st Highland Division's Farewell to Sicily', 'Ballad of Anzio' and 'The Blubbing Buchmanite', the author.

For Keith Douglas: 'Simplify me when I'm dead', 'Mersa', 'Cairo Jag', 'Sportsmen', 'Dead Men', 'How to Kill' and extract from 'Vergissmeinnincht', copyright Marie J. Douglas 1978. Reprinted from *The Complete Poems of Keith Douglas* (1979) by permission of Oxford University Press. From a letter to J. C. Hall: Mr J. C. Hall.

For Terence Tiller: 'Lecturing to Troops' and 'Big City', the Estate of Terence Tiller. Reprinted from *Unarm, Eros* by permission of The Hogarth Press.

For G. S. Fraser: 'Egypt', extracts from 'Exile's Letter' and 'Recent Verse: London and Cairo', Mrs Paddy Fraser.

For Bertrand Russell: extract from *Principles of Social Reconstruction*, Unwin Hyman/HarperCollins Publishers.

For Edgell Rickword: extract from 'Notes on Culture and the War' and 'Poetry and Two Wars', Carcanet Press Ltd.

For Arthur Koestler: from *The Yogi and the Commissar and Other Stories*, (1945) Peters Fraser & Dunlop Ltd.

For Sir Stephen Spender: from *Citizens in War – and After*, the author.

For Siegfried Sassoon: extract from 'Silent Service', George Sassoon.

Every effort was made to clear permission of all pieces reprinted in the anthology, and the publisher would be very happy to hear from the copyright holders whom we are unable to trace.

I am indebted to a number of people who have given me invaluable advice and help. Chief among these is the series editor, Rick Rylance, who has been unstinting in his careful attention to the project, and in his reading and rereading of several drafts. I also owe a great deal to the support of Peter Cattermole with whom I discussed many of the ideas contained here, and to Ann Featherstone who first told me about the war poets of Ilkeston and painstakingly made copies of their poems. Others who have given advice, provided information and saved me from error include Dennis Featherstone, Kate Haywood, Hamish Henderson, Dominic Hibberd, Karen Iles, Peter Jackson, Tony Kirby, Kim Landers, Claire Richards, Michael Schmidt, Nikky Twyman, Don Watts, Nigel Wheale and Mike Woodhouse. I would also like to acknowledge the efficiency and goodwill of the library staff at Anglia Polytechnic University, Cambridge University Library, the Imperial War Museum and the British Library.

Introduction

Of all twentieth-century literatures, war poetry seems in many ways the least open to the intrusion of any kind of literary theory. The direction of much contemporary theory, based on versions of Saussurean linguistics, has been towards the divorce of literature and life, and the sign and its referents. But war poems seem to insist on the closeness of writing to often appalling personal experience, and confront readers with what the critic Paul Fussell has termed 'actual and terrible moral challenges' (Fussell 1992). To do anything other than acknowledge that experience and those challenges can seem recklessly improper. Jean Baudrillard's notorious analysis of the Gulf War as a series of rhetorical performances unattached to any material reality suggests in extreme form the dangers of theory effacing individual suffering and moral questioning in a display of intellectual finesse (Baudrillard 1991; Norris 1992).

Whilst it is clearly true that a reading of war poetry which followed Baudrillard's approach and did not acknowledge an experiential base would damage the writing and its purposes, the view of war poetry as the expression of extreme experience alone is also limiting. In this reading war poetry is largely separated from the literary and intellectual cultures of the society which produced it and seems to come from what Keith Douglas terms 'another place', unaffected by the historical and social forces of peacetime. Its authors then become icons of suffering rather than participants in the complex and changing cultures that preceded, affected and were affected by, the wars. Even major writers like Wilfred Owen, Isaac Rosenberg and Keith Douglas tend to be fixed within what David Jones calls the 'parenthesis' of wartime, and their work is read in terms of the exceptional circumstances of its production, rather than its relationship to the mainstream of British literature.

The concentration by many critics on war poetry as a special case of twentieth-century literary history (a fuller discussion of the criticism will be given in Chapter 1) has had a number of consequences: the variety of its forms have been reduced; the variety of responses to war have been reduced correspondingly, and, ironically, access to the variety of experiences of war has also been limited. In this book I want to argue that both the theory and practice of war poetry and critical responses to it need to be rethought. I shall argue that we need to consider not just the immediate personal concerns of the poetry, but also a range of issues which come into play when we think about the First and Second World Wars, such as how and when the category of 'war writing/poetry' emerged, what place war writing has in contemporary culture, and what critical methods are most appropriate to its understanding. Such theorizing does not diminish the importance of extreme experience in the creation of war poetry, but instead emphasizes the intellectual, cultural and linguistic resources which allowed such experience to be transformed into poetry.

The development of a theory of war poetry is best done through a practical revision of the category and the canon, and so this book contains an anthology of poetry and prose material from the two wars as well as critical essays. Together they form a textbook for studying the poetry of the First and Second World Wars in its intellectual and historical contexts rather than as two isolated movements. The anthology material stresses the continuities and revisions of pre- and inter-war writing and the work provoked by the two major conflicts of the twentieth century. It focuses on the importance of war poetry for an understanding of British culture rather than just the British experience of war, and for this reason the selection of poets and writers, and the themes of the essays, emphasize other issues than front-line experience of battle.

The poetry collected here contains a wider range of writers than usually appears in selections of war poetry. Alongside the work of well-established war poets such as Owen and Douglas there are substantial selections from writers who are normally seen as marginal figures in the canon. The dominant Englishness which underlies the selection in many war poetry anthologies has led to the exclusion of writers like the Gaelic poet Sorley MacLean and the Highland Scot Hamish Henderson (both included here) who offer distinctly Scottish versions of the Second World War. There is also a substantial selection of Ivor Gurney's work which presents a radical revision of conventional ideas about English war poetry, as do the poems by working-class soldier poets, taken from local newspapers of the First World War. H.D.'s work, which is hardly ever read as war poetry, suggests the importance of feminist perspectives on war, and, with the poetry of the neglected champion of English modernism,

Herbert Read, shows the link between war writing and the avant garde during the First World War. In the selections from Read and H.D. I have included work from both wars, indicating the strong link between the writing of the two periods, and in the selection as a whole I have given equal weight to Second World War writing, a body of work which has been overshadowed by the more celebrated poetry of the First War.

The selection of prose texts provides an intellectual and theoretical context for the poetry. It is drawn mainly from wartime writings on politics, culture and literature, and many of the pieces have not previously been reprinted or are difficult to find. The prose passages contribute to continuing debates about such issues as national identity, the influence of the state on national culture, the influence of non-English cultures on British writing, and the significance of popular culture. Their concerns relate directly and indirectly to the issues and contexts of war poetry and enable the reader to place the poetry within a wider view of wartime culture than that offered by anthologies which concentrate on military experience alone.

In the first part of the book, the seven chapters provide analyses of many of the poems and examine the relationship of the poetry to the issues developed in the prose selections. They focus on six main areas: the place of war poetry in the wider culture of the representation of war; ideas of Englishness; popular cultures; politics; non-English cultures (two chapters explore the influence of provincial, Scottish, Jewish and Eastern cultures on the writing of the war); and gender. All of these issues relate to current debates in critical theory, and the essays demonstrate the application of these debates to an interpretation of the poetry. They show not only the use of theory in thinking about war poetry, but also reveal the relevance of war poetry to a study of issues that go beyond the 'parenthesis' of the wars and which are part of contemporary literary and cultural debates.

For a reader who wishes to approach the material from the viewpoint of single authors, the headnotes to the selections and the index will guide him or her to the appropriate chapter. The anthology material is prefaced by short introductions and biographical information, and for each of the poets there is information on standard editions and selections, and suggestions for secondary reading. There are also textual notes to the poems, and a guide to other anthologies and general reading is provided in the Further Reading section.

Part I

DISCUSSIONS

I
War and British Culture
1914–82

Wartime and the post-war age

The First and Second World Wars remain a vital part of British cultural life. Anniversaries of battles and other events of the wars bring TV documentaries, reappraisals and debates, recorded reminiscences and the transmission of old feature films. In any public library there will be a substantial section of scholarly and popular studies of the two wars, war memoirs and biographies, and there is a whole subliterary genre of paperbacks and comic books on war themes, sold and resold on market stalls. In the midst of this diverse culture of war is another subgenre, war poetry. There are currently some twenty-two anthologies of war poetry in print, more than on any other single subject, and with a much larger audience than twentiety-century poetry normally attracts. War poetry is taught on school and higher-education English Literature courses, and its influence is also felt in the teaching of history and social studies. But although war poetry is undoubtedly popular, its relationship with the other forms of the popular culture of war mentioned above is problem- atic. War poetry, as it is now generally presented and interpreted in the anthologies, is the poetry of 1914–18. Its purpose is seen to be telling the truth about war, and its prevailing attitudes as pacifist. The central figures are Wilfred Owen, who wrote of the poet's duty to warn future generations of the consequences of war, and Siegfried Sassoon, satirist and rebel against the war's conduct. In other forms of recent popular culture, however, the focal point is the Second World War, and a far more positive view of its purpose and conduct is presented. I want to explore the relationship between these different representations of war in order to suggest the complex contemporary context for any study of war writing. I will concentrate on one important area and period for the diffusion of both the poetry and other war-related material: the culture of adolescence in the thirty years after the Second World War.

From 1945 until well into the 1970s, the popular narratives aimed at male children and adolescents were obsessed with the Second World War. The world-view of D. C. Thomson (the major British publisher of comics for this market) did not acknowledge the development of a European Community or dominant German and Japanese economies. In the *Valiant*, one of the long-running Thomson comics, Italians were still cowardly 'spaghetti-eaters', the Japanese were cunning and cruel in the jungles of Burma, and the Germans remained the arch-villains, appearing to be defeated time after time by British military heroes like Captain Hurricane. The history was wildly inaccurate and the violence wholly unrealistic, but in the *Valiant*, its competitors like the *Victor* and the *Rover*, and in the little A5 comic books with titles like *Commando*, there was never any doubt about what would interest its readership: the war in Europe, Africa and Burma in the early 1940s. Although there were occasional stories about the First World War, these concerned peripheral activities to the main slaughter on the Western Front – primitive submarines, air aces, secret agents and the like. The only large-scale war to be consistently represented was 'the last war' and, within the conventions of the Second World War narrative, the activity was never questioned and its political contexts never considered.

The obsession with a war that was at least a generation removed from its audience is also apparent in many of the adventure/action feature films that were made in the 1950s, 1960s and 1970s, again with a youthful, male audience in mind. Simple stories of stereotyped action, nationalist politics and racist characterization remained the standard fare of high-budget war films throughout this period. There are too many to enumerate, but *The Dam Busters* (1954), *The Guns of Navarone* (1961), *Where Eagles Dare* (1969), *Battle of Britain* (1969) and *A Bridge Too Far* (1977) are characteristic examples of the genre. The novels of writers like Alistair Maclean and Douglas Reeman were the literary equivalent of such films, war/adventure stories, produced in cheap paperback editions, with an enormous readership. Subgenres of the standard Second World War adventure narrative were also created and these were developed in comics, film and TV drama. A notable example of these is the prison-camp escape story which became a popular classroom text in Eric Williams' *The Wooden Horse* (1949) and a best seller in Pat Reid's memoir *The Colditz Story* (1952). Both were filmed (in 1950 and 1954 respectively) and the latter formed the basis of the popular TV series *Colditz* (1972–3). Hollywood made its own blockbuster version of the genre with *The Great Escape* (1963).

The Second World War remained an active element in the popular culture of young males when its politics and technology had become hopelessly old-fashioned. Its narratives and images became an important part of the construction of the idea and experience of masculinity in the post-war period. Although the process by which this happened has only recently begun to be explored (see Dawson 1990), an analogous experience was described in relation to the First World War by writers in the 1930s. Christopher Isherwood's comments on the influence of that war in his autobiographical work *Lions and Shadows* (1938) apply in many ways to the experience of post-Second World War adolescents:

> Like most of my generation, I was obsessed with the idea of 'War'. 'War,' in this purely neurotic sense, meant The Test. The test of your courage, of your maturity, of your sexual prowess: 'Are you really a man?' Subconsciously, I believe, I longed to be subjected to this test; but I also dreaded failure.
>
> (Isherwood 1979: 46)

If the intensity of masculine obsession in the 1950s and 1960s was not as great as that described by Isherwood, the concern with war in male childhood fantasies was certainly persistent, and this is demonstrated by the treatment of the theme of war, as well as by the number of war-related stories. The narratives and imagery of the mass culture of war are remarkably stable over a period of thirty years, with little or no acknowledgement of the changing political circumstances of Britain or of the different kinds of conflict in which the post-war British army became involved. The Korean War, the prolonged anti-colonialist wars in Kenya, Cyprus, Malaya and Aden, the beginning of the British army's longest campaign in Northern Ireland, and the development of Britain's nuclear weaponry were not only unacknowledged, but had no effect upon the dominant heroic and militarist ideology of the comics and films. This continuity of representation in mass culture is in marked contrast to the changes that took place in the presentation of war in another component of adolescent culture, the school textbook.

War was always a popular subject in schools. It went with national and imperial history as a staple of both public-school and state-school curricula from the end of the nineteenth century (see Mangan 1986). The survival of this kind of education after the Second World War is apparent in the persistence of the stirring poems of military heroism in English literature textbooks of the period. The sections on war in W. M. Smyth's

Poems of Spirit and Action (1957) (aimed at 'boys and girls in their teens') contain such nineteenth-century favourites as 'The War Song of Dinas Vawr' and 'The Burial of Sir John Moore at Corunna'. The First World War is represented not by the poetry of Wilfred Owen or Siegfried Sassoon but by a sonnet of Herbert Asquith (a friend of Rupert Brooke and a very minor poet in a lyrical nationalist mode), and by Laurence Binyon's 'For the Fallen', a popular elegy written early in the war.

Such a selection, however, was a last gasp of an old order. The poetry of Owen and Sassoon, well-known to writers and intellectuals since the 1920s, achieved some academic respectability with D. S. R. Welland's full-length study of Owen in 1960 (Welland 1960). Soon the influence of Owen's and Sassoon's anti-militarist stance permeated the secondary sector of education. New emphases on relevant modern material, the encouragement of classroom discussions and interdisciplinary study, along with a strong examination bias towards the methods of practical criticism, led to changes in the kind of poetry taught in schools. The old-style patriotic ballads were exchanged for poems which provoked argument and encouraged students to take up social and political issues.

Many English Literature textbooks of the 1960s and 1970s have a section on war, and in these sections by far the most popular poets are Owen and Sassoon. Their criticisms of war and nationalism had made them inappropriate for school reading before this time, but in the increasingly liberal educational climate of the 1960s, their concerns became those of a newly radical teaching establishment. Owen and Sassoon wrote about youth and war, and these were issues that educational theory saw as relevant and appealing to adolescents (with some justification). They also appealed to those teachers recently qualified from higher education, who had been involved in the Campaign for Nuclear Disarmament and later in the anti-war campaigns concerning US involvement in Vietnam. The link between modern and historical issues is made in many of the textbooks. A common strategy is to juxtapose poems by Owen and Sassoon and a post-1945 poem about atomic weapons (James Kirkup's 'No More Hiroshimas' is a favourite, as is Peter Porter's 'Your Attention Please'), or to put a photograph of the trenches alongside that of a nuclear explosion, then ask pupils to 'discuss together some of the questions raised about who in the end is responsible for war and about what can be done about it' (Adams 1968: no page numbers). Sometimes the poetry is explicitly used to counter the kind of images of war prevalent in the comic books and films mentioned earlier.

In the same collection, the editor presents the poetry as a corrective to films such as *The Guns of Navarone*, and in *Touchstones 3*, a textbook for 14-year-olds, the editors suggest that reading war poetry prevents war becoming an unreal fiction on the TV screen, equivalent to a Western or a thriller (Benton and Benton 1969: 165).

On a more traditional pedagogical level, the poetry of both Owen and Sassoon is suited to the demands of 'practical criticism', the dominant post-war critical method for the close reading of poems. What is required is a short poem, preferably with a regular form, a vivid subject-matter, some, but not too many, semantic difficulties, and plenty of identifiable metrical and technical features. A poem like Owen's 'Anthem for Doomed Youth' is perfectly suited. The meaning is relatively straightforward, but there are things that need explaining (passing-bells, orisons, what is meant by 'The pallor of girls' brows shall be their pall'); the sonnet structure needs some comment, and many 13-year-olds have had their first experience of alliteration with 'the stuttering rifles' rapid rattle'.

The presence of war poetry in school anthologies is significant, not only because it was an important means of popularizing the poetry in this period, but also because it indicates the place of war poetry in a wider culture of war. It is part of a range of competing representations, many of which are in opposition to the perceived anti-war purpose of the poetry. The growth in popularity of Owen and Sassoon in the 1960s was part of a shift in political outlook in education in the period. But in recent years, the political context for reading war poetry and interpreting the popular culture of war has changed, particularly after the Falklands War of 1982.

The political shift to the Right after 1979 caused a revaluation and revival of nationalist feelings and rhetorics in England, and these found a popular focus in the war with Argentina. In an editorial in *PN Review*, a literary journal which reflected some aspects of the new conservatism in British culture in the early 1980s, the poet and critic Donald Davie wrote that during the Falklands War there returned 'the recognition, by the nation at large, of martial valour as indeed a value, and one that we have giggled about for too long' (Davie 1983). This kind of argument, aimed, like many of Davie's polemics, against a liberal/Left educational establishment, was part of a more general realignment of values in Britain. The triumphalist rhetoric of much of the tabloid press was one obvious manifestation of a reversion to pre-First-World-War jingoism, but a book like David Tinker's *A Message from the Falklands* (1982) is perhaps an even more startling example.

Tinker was a young Royal Navy lieutenant, and his book is a collection of letters written in the period leading up to his death in an attack on HMS *Glamorgan*. He is an educated, thoughtful witness of the war, liberal in outlook and with a taste for reading and writing poetry. His father's account of his early life stresses his interest in the First World War and its poets, particularly Wilfred Owen. According to his father, Hugh Tinker, he 'cherished Owen's longing for peace instead of war. And in his own writing – whether or not he consciously took Owen as his model – he adopted the same bleak, spare, stripped-down mode of expression' (Tinker 1982: 6). Yet his letters on the outbreak of the war include a rhetoric more usually associated with the naïve patriotism (and racism) of 1914:

> We are off to the Falkland Islands as you have probably heard to do a bit of Wog-Bashing! There's a terrific force of ships assembling … sixteen British warships steaming south across the Atlantic at a great rate of knots – terrific!
>
> (Tinker 1982: 155)

This kind of writing can, of course, be explained as the special register of an officer cadre, and it certainly reflects the disbelief amongst many servicemen in the early stages of the crisis that a war would be fought. Nevertheless, as the letters progress, it seems more to be part of a fundamental problem of expression. The only way that the Falklands war can be talked about, as it changes from a 'Wog-Bashing' jaunt to what Tinker comes to call cynically 'a war for a flag' (p. 171), is by eclectic historical and literary reference – to Owen's poems, A. E. Housman, the duffel coats and cocoa of Second World War navy films, and the atmosphere of 1914. Even his conversion from the description of the 'terrific force' of ships and men in the early letters to the view that the war was 'fought on "principle" by two dictatorships' (p. 179) repeats rather than develops the mental patterns of First World War poetry in its change from idealism to disillusionment.

Tinker's attraction to the poetry and beliefs of Owen reflect the educational experience of a boy brought up in the 1960s and 1970s but, in response to a real war, his language and outlook is not at all straight-forward. His letters accurately reflect the confused reactions to war, past and present, that are part of post-1945 British culture. The reversion to the language of jingoism, the images drawn from popular versions of the Second World War, and the need to repeat the pattern of First World War disillusionment are all elements of a complexity of interpretation and representation that accounts of war poetry, with their concentration on the writing and beliefs of a poet like Owen, can easily overlook.

The populist nationalism provoked by the Falklands, and the revival of military action as an acceptable means of national self-assertion, exemplified once again in the Gulf War of 1991, necessarily affect any reading of war poetry. Several recent popular anthologies, for example, do not give precedence to anti-war writers like Owen and Sassoon, preferring to emphasize the Englishness and self-sacrifice of minor poets (Garnett 1990 provides a good example of this tendency). Rupert Brooke, for a long time the disparaged poet of romantic jingoism, once more became a figure of interest in the 1980s with the publication of two popular accounts of him and his circle (Lehmann 1980; Delany 1987). Thus, although the pre-eminence of Owen and Sassoon remains in the teaching of war poetry in schools and colleges, the discrepancy between their apparent anti-war outlook and a newly nationalist, and at times militarist, popular culture is very marked. The adolescent readers of Owen and Sassoon in the 1980s were not only exposed to the relatively antiquated jingoisms of D. C. Thomson's and Alistair Maclean's versions of the Second World War, but to the revivalist nationalisms of the post-Falklands *Sun*, the popular cult of the Paras and the SAS, and the imported militarism of *Rambo* films.

Definitions and interpretations of war poetry are not just matters of literary taste, but are affected by the volatile politics of nationalism and historical perception. These need to be taken into account in any criticism, and suggest a need for a working theory that defines the processes of the development of war poetry and its place in British culture. In the next section I will examine in detail the figure of the war poet, both as a product of political and commercial influences, and as a popular response to the psychological and cultural pressures of war.

The making of the war poet

Despite attempts to give it a long literary pedigree (see, for example, Johnston 1964; Banerjee 1976), war poetry is a product of a set of particular cultural and historical circumstances that came together in the First World War: the development of a relatively systematic culture of patriotism and imperialism in the late Victorian and early Edwardian era; the resulting change in the perception of the military, from that of mercenaries to representatives of English values; and a policy of mass recruitment, at first voluntary, then compulsory. It was the last factor that was most significant. The role of writers in constructing militarist myths of the army and empire during the nineteenth century had been largely that of interpreter or reporter. Tennyson provided a version of Victorian militarism that distanced itself from the language of trade and economics by a retreat into Arthurian myth. Rudyard Kipling created a voice and persona for the English soldier in his *Barrack Room Ballads* (1892) that was extraordinarily influential on later poetry (see Chapter 3), but was never a soldier himself. By 1914, however, it was the participation of the poet in war that was as important as his writing.

It is worth looking at the creation of the reputation of Rupert Brooke in relation to this change. Brooke is a crucial figure in the history of war poetry, though the general disparagement of his poetry by later poets and critics has tended to obscure his real significance. This is less to do with his writing and more to do with the ways in which he was presented (or marketed) after his death in 1915. Brooke's experience of war was minimal. His military career began through the good offices of Edward Marsh, editor of *Georgian Poetry* and Parliamentary Private Secretary to Winston Churchill who was then First Lord of the Admiralty (for Marsh's influence on Brooke see Hassall 1959). Churchill had a taste for the adventurous and the glamorous, and he welcomed the presence of 'the most beautiful man in England' and his friend, the well-connected Herbert Asquith in the newly founded Royal Navy Division, which acted under his personal supervision. Brooke played a confused part as a wholly untrained sub-lieutenant in the abortive reinforcement of Antwerp in 1914, and died of blood-poisoning in April 1915 on his way to another disastrous campaign in the Dardanelles.

Brooke was a different kind of military hero to the Gordons and Kitcheners of the late Victorian era. He was a non-military soldier, a 'poet-soldier' as Churchill called him in a *Times* memorial that set the tone for the celebration of Brooke as a national war poet. The very amateurishness of his contribution acted as a guarantee of the justice of the political cause for which he died, and allowed the inclusion of a Byronic romanticism of poetic action into the heartiness of public-school militarism. The image of Brooke the poet-soldier put forward by Marsh and Churchill emphasized the sensual and 'poetic' over the military. This is demonstrated by the photographs in the *Collected Poems* (Brooke 1918) which picture him not in uniform, but wearing the loosely-knotted tie of an 1890s aesthete and in a sensuous, bare-shouldered pose. Churchill's obituary, like Brooke's 'War Sonnets' of December 1914, stresses the aesthetics of sacrifice rather than the duties of militarist patriotism, an emphasis given religious sanction by William Inge, the Dean of St Paul's in a sermon delivered two weeks before Brooke's death in April 1915 in which he quoted from the sonnets. Churchill writes:

> He expected to die; he was willing to die for the dear old England whose beauty and majesty he knew; and he advanced towards the brink in perfect serenity, with absolute conviction of the rightness of his country's cause and a heart devoid of hate for fellow-men.
>
> (Brooke 1918: clviii)

The passage integrates the language of patriotism, morality and artistic judgement in its celebration of an ideal soldier. The military hero in Churchill's account is both poet and warrior – 'fearless' *and* 'joyous', 'versatile' *and* 'deeply instructed'.

The change in the role of the poet from encourager of war to participant was crucial to later war writing. In one sense it was a glamorized acknowledgement of a material fact. The regular army was not big enough to fight a war on the scale which developed during the latter part of 1914 and needed volunteers. But this role change also marked the extent to which redefinitions of Englishness in terms of military service and patriotic duty had entered national culture. Brooke's popularity was great and persistent. His *1914 and Other Poems* (1915), went through twenty-five impressions between 1915 and 1918, and was read by soldiers and civilians alike. The *Collected Poems*, published in 1918, ran through eleven impressions in the next five years. Although his audience was limited mostly to a middle-class readership (there is no echo of Brooke in the Ilkeston poems, for example [Poetry Anthology, pp. 135–41]), it was nevertheless considerable. Critics have tended to stress the rejection of Churchill's version of Brooke as the war went on, basing this on the comments of other poets, but there is no evidence of a wide-scale distaste for what he represented in the period up to 1920. It is true that some writers reacted against Brooke when the true nature of the war became clear; as early as 1915 Charles Sorley accused Brooke of taking the 'sentimental attitude' (Silkin 1972: 76). But it is easy to exaggerate the extent of such opposition. The post-war pre-eminence of Sassoon and Owen has tended to obscure the fact that many poets went on writing in the manner of Brooke throughout the war. A poet of the stature of Ivor Gurney classed Brooke's sonnet 'The Soldier' as one of the 'best and most interesting' poems in Charles Osborn's anthology *The Muse in Arms* in March 1918, even as he suggested the inclusion of more work by Sassoon and Robert Graves (Gurney 1991: 412).

The literary reputation of Brooke collapsed in the inter-war period under the influence of a generation of poets of the left who saw themselves, in Stephen Spender's words, as 'the inheritors of the task of the war poets which had been broken off with the death of Wilfred Owen' (Spender 1944: 13). John Heath-Stubbs, a poet of a generation younger than Spender, commented that Brooke 'stood for all the attitudes to war which we detested' (Hewison 1977: 96). However, despite the rejection of Brooke's work and reputation, the means by which Brooke was made into a war poet through his own willingness to act as a spokesman, by the patronage of influential public figures and by a publishing industry eager for relevant war material, became a model for the creation of war poets in the Second World War. Alun Lewis, one of the major poets of the war, came to prominence in much the same way as Brooke.

Lewis's poem 'All Day It Has Rained ...' (Poetry Anthology p. 000) was published in 1941 in *Horizon*, the leading metropolitan literary periodical of the Second World War, where it received praise from the editor Cyril Connolly as an accurate expression of the atmosphere of the 'phoney war' period. After this Lewis enthusiastically took on the role of 'war poet'. His first collection, published in the following year, has the dramatic title *Raiders' Dawn and Other Poems* and opens with a section called 'Poems in Khaki'. The 'Author's Note' emphasizes his military activity, claiming that 'two-thirds of [the poems] have been written on active service' (Lewis 1942: no page number), though the active service had, in fact, been in Hampshire, Gloucestershire and Morecambe. Lewis also shows himself aware of the demands for an appropriate 'war poet' image. His biographer, John Pikoulis, quotes a letter in which Lewis suggests the use of a wood-engraved portrait for the front cover of *Raiders' Dawn*: 'I feel it makes the whole thing rather Rupert Brooke-ish, which may or may not be a good thing from a commercial point of view' (Pikoulis 1984: 150). The intense image of the poet certainly was a good thing, for *Raiders' Dawn* was into its fourth impression within eighteen months of publication. The war-poet role enabled Lewis to enter the established poetry world with remarkable swiftness. Even before the publication of his first collection, he was portrayed alongside William Empson, Cecil Day-Lewis and Dylan Thomas as one of the poets of the day in the popular magazine *Lilliput* (the article proved a cause of annoyance because his portrait 'appeared alongside the photographs of poets who were still in civilian life, the feature apparently having very little to do with war poets at all' [John 1970: 34]).

The marketing of Lewis was, then, very similar to that of Brooke. Though their outlooks were different (see discussion of Lewis in Chapter 6), the definition of their social role was the same. Like Brooke, Lewis was represented as a spokesman for a generation (more accurately, a male generation), and it is in this role that the war poet has remained vaguely, but seemingly permanently, fixed in popular consciousness. War poetry always had a social function before it had a literary one, and this is reflected in the unusual popularity of poetry during both world wars. Sales of poetry rose and so did the amount of poetry being written and published. A cursory glance at the bibliographies of First and Second World War poetry compiled by Catherine Reilly suggests that there was a genuine need to write and a ready market for the writing (Reilly 1978, 1986). Any theory of war poetry must take into account the popularity of different kinds of war poetry, not only that published in books and anthologies and written by established poets. Reilly's research has revealed thousands of pamphlets, broadsheets and postcard poems, and to these can be added thousands more poems reproduced in local newspapers (see the Ilkeston poems in this Poetry Anthology). People who might not have written verse at other times began to do so during the war, and this suggests that commercial and propaganda interests were exploiting, rather than creating, a popular need. Poetry has always been deeply ingrained as a cultural marker for the formal expression of grief, through which the bereaved can express themselves in a medium that is at once both private and public. This impulse, along with more straightforward patriotic motives, might explain the production of many of the poems of both wars. Poetry can enable people to express other kinds of extraordinary experience and to work out that experience in a kind of therapy. Robert Graves's essay 'Secondary Elaboration' (1925) (extract in Prose Anthology, pp. 228–32) gives a rare first-hand account of the way that extreme personal experiences of the war directly affected the writing of poetry. Graves analyses the effect of his war experience on the writing and rewriting of a poem that seemingly has nothing to do with the war. He calls the process 'secondary elaboration', a Freudian term which links poetic creation and the mind's transformation of experience into dreams and fantasies. In Graves's account, the poem transforms, and is then later transformed by, the experience of war in a process that he relates to Freudian psychoanalysis (Graves's essay is indebted to the work of the innovative psychiatrist W. H. R. Rivers who treated both Siegfried Sassoon and Wilfred Owen at Craiglockhart hospital and who encouraged their poetry – see Showalter 1987).

'Secondary Elaboration' shows vividly that the poetry of war is concerned with personal experience of a particularly dramatic and harrowing kind, but the peculiarity of war poetry is that it represents a negotiation between that personal experience and the public role of the war poet. As the case of Rupert Brooke demonstrates, war poetry is political as well as experiential. Whether it is pro- or anti-war, it inevitably engages with public issues of nationalism, patriotism, class and history. The public role of the war poet is also implicated in strategies of state propaganda and commercial marketing. Such a combination of personal expression and public iconography poses the question as to how we turn such a theory of war poetry into a critical practice of describing and interpreting the texts. In the next section I will consider the ways in which such questions of definition and interpretation have been dealt with in recent studies of war poetry.

Reading war poetry

The place of war writing in literary studies has always been problematic. Much of the material that is designated war poetry doesn't fit with the dominant version of early-twentieth-century literary history and its emphasis on the modernism of Ezra Pound, T. S. Eliot, and their successors. The major poets of the First World War seem peripheral to such a movement and there is apparently little to connect the technique of Owen's Shelley-derived 'Strange Meeting' or Sassoon's demotic lyrics with the experimental strategies of Eliot's *The Waste Land* or Pound's *Hugh Selwyn Mauberley*. The dominant influence on most British war poetry, as it tends to be represented in anthologies, comes not from America or Europe but from the English ruralism of Thomas Hardy and the Georgians, traditions which modernism supplanted in the aftermath of the war. As F. R. Leavis wrote in his influential study *New Bearings in English Poetry* (1932), 'Edward Thomas, Owen, and Rosenberg alone could hardly have constituted a challenge to the ruling poetic fashions' (Leavis

1963: 64), with the clear implication that the necessary challenge came from the two contemporaries that are the subject of separate chapters in his survey, Pound and Eliot.

Leavis's judgement was a critical orthodoxy until the 1970s; for while war poetry was a popular poetry and had become influential within schools, its importance was largely determined by its subject-matter and its documentary value rather than its relationship to a wider literary culture. In the 1970s, however, there appeared two books which argued for the cultural importance of war poetry and developed coherent strategies for reading war writing: Jon Silkin's *Out of Battle* (1972) (the arguments of which are summarized and developed in the Introduction to his *Penguin Book of First World War Poetry* [1979]) and Paul Fussell's *The Great War and Modern Memory* (1975); the work of Silkin and Fussell needs to be seen not just as excellent criticism of individual poems and poets, but also as part of the continuing arguments about how we think about the two world wars. Both books are powerfully polemical, and both pose crucial questions of strategy for the study of war poetry.

In many ways Jon Silkin's work provides a forceful synthesis of post-Second-World-War critical views on war poetry. Silkin concentrates on the poetry of the First World War, dividing it into four 'stages of consciousness': Patriotism, represented by poets such as Rupert Brooke; Anger and Protest against the war, represented by Sassoon; Compassion, represented by Owen; and Desire for social change, represented by Rosenberg (Silkin 1979: 26–30). Leaving aside Silkin's advocacy of Rosenberg, which was still unusual in the early 1970s, his idea of the development of war poetry is similar to that of Robert Graves and Edgell Rickword, both poets of the First World War who wrote important essays on war poetry during the Second War (see Graves's 'The Poets of World War II' and Rickword's 'Poetry and Two Wars', both in Prose Anthology, pp. 232, 247). Rickword and Graves also suggest a developing consciousness of the realities of war as a determining factor in the poetry. However, Silkin is more concerned than either of his precursors to include First World War poetry within a wider poetic tradition, particularly that of Romanticism.

Silkin offers many illuminating readings of individual poems in *Out of Battle* and his sense of the complex interaction of the poetry with Romantic precursors was important for the development of a critical approach that concentrated on the linguistic resources and strategies of the poets rather than their biographies. Yet, as his conclusion makes clear,

Silkin's reading of First World War poetry as essentially late Romantic writing does affect significantly both his interpretative strategy and the canon of war poetry that he established in the very influential Penguin anthology. Silkin eschews what he terms 'social and historical' or 'political' approaches in favour of a reading that 'consider[s] the poems for their response to the values they evolved in relation to the experiences they recreated' (Silkin 1972: 341). Such an approach necessarily emphasizes an autonomy of poetic creation which to some degree transcends the circumstances of a poem's production, a process which Silkin himself acknowledges in the conclusion. Although, like Rickword, he is very sensitive to the importance of social class in a poet's development, as for example in his writing on Rosenberg, he is unlike Rickword in his presentation of other historical, social and political contexts as 'an inescapable impingement' on poetry rather than a determining force (Silkin 1972: 1). Silkin maintains a firm commitment to a literary canon which establishes a moral and political 'advance' through the war (a view spelled out in the introduction to the Penguin anthology), and this movement is underpinned by a direct literary analogy to the Romantic poets and their responses to the Napoleonic wars of the late eighteenth and early nineteenth centuries.

Silkin's model is orderly and illuminating, particularly in its argument for the importance of Rosenberg as a political poet drawing on Jewish and Romantic sources. However, that very orderliness and Silkin's commitment to a literary tradition of representative poets, mirroring 'stages' of Romantic poetry, pose problems for establishing a canon of war poetry which includes other writers than the now standard list of Brooke, Owen, Sassoon and Rosenberg. It is difficult to fit some major poets of the war into such a scheme; although Silkin writes with insight about both Ivor Gurney and David Jones, for example, neither poet fits with an over-arching scheme of politico-moral development. The numerous 'amateur' poems of the war, represented in this anthology by the Ilkeston poems, cannot be included at all, for they do not acknowledge a change of consciousness in the way that Silkin suggests. Their outlook remains relatively stable, with few signs of a straightforwardly patriotic approach early in the war, but no clearly defined change to an anti-war stance later on (see discussion in Chapter 3). Women writers are similarly excluded from a canon predicated upon a canon of 'major writers' whose moral and literary development is dependent upon the pressure of war experience on literary sensibility.

Paul Fussell's *The Great War and Modern Memory* (1975) breaks away from the trend of interpretation of war poetry represented by Silkin. Fussell rejects the notion of a straightforward 'movement of consciousness' from patriotic illusion to embittered reality, suggesting a more varied literary and social context for the poetry. Unlike Silkin, who largely ignores anything but an established literary canon, Fussell locates war writing within a wider culture of minor poets, magazines and personal documents. He also widens the customary focus of First World War poetry by stressing the formative influence of that poetry on writing in the Second World War and beyond. Fussell argues forcefully for war poetry to be read as richly mythologizing and fantasy-driven culture of sexuality, pastoral landscapes, superstition and rhetorical invention. Using a quotation from Bernard Bergonzi's *Heroes Twilight* (1965) as an example of the standard view of war poetry that he rejects, Fussell writes:

> 'The dominant movement in the literature of the Great War was … from a myth-dominated to a demythologised world.' No: almost the opposite. In one sense the movement was towards myth, towards a revival of the cultic, the mystical, the sacrificial, the prophetic, the sacramental, and the universally significant. In short, towards fiction.
>
> (Fussell 1975: 131)

Fussell's sense of war poetry as fiction is very different to Silkin's appeal to a Romantic tradition, yet at the heart of *The Great War and Modern Memory*, as with *Out of Battle*, there is a difficult theoretical problem about the relationship of war writing to its social and intellectual context.

For Fussell, the First World War is a wholly exceptional event; it represents *the* crucial turning-point of twentieth-century consciousness, and demands from both poet and critic a radically different historical sense to that which might be applied to other periods. 'The war will not be understood in traditional terms', he writes, 'the machine gun alone makes it so special and unexampled that it simply can't be talked about as if it were one of the conventional wars of history. Or worse, of literary history' (p. 153). Unlike Silkin, Fussell's only recourse to literary or political history is to illustrate the ironic difference between the First World War and the pre-war culture, a strategy that, for Fussell, is a fundamental strategy of First World War writing: the only way a poet – or a critic – can write about the unexampled is to refer ironically to the 'normal' or traditional. Yet even as he celebrates this rhetorical strategy and appeals to the complex and ironic mythologies of war writing which require the critic to move beyond traditional historiography and acknowledge the wholly exceptional nature of what occurred, Fussell affirms a much more traditional view of what he terms in a later essay the 'importance of experience, sheer vulgar experience' (Fussell 1990: 14). In one sense Fussell affirms and celebrates the literariness of war writing, calling one of the chapters 'Oh, What a Literary War' and suggesting that 'reading the national literature is what the British did a great deal of in the line' (Fussell 1975: 161); however, alongside this is a belief in the primacy of front-line experience. For Fussell, beyond the mesh of allusion and irony constructed in *The Great War and Modern Memory* are not determining historical and social forces, but the experience and endurance of the individual fighting soldier.

Fussell's work, then, veers between an analysis of war writing as a complex set of rhetorical strategies for expressing the inexpressible and a celebration of the literature as a special kind of experiential writing. The latter purpose carries the weight of Fussell's own experience as a soldier in the Second World War, a personal involvement in the subject-matter which is never made explicit in *The Great War and Modern Memory*, although it is undoubtedly the emotional core of the work. Fussell's war experience does openly inform some of the essays in his later collection *Killing in Verse and Prose* (1990) and greatly influences the argument of *Wartime* (1989), a study of the culture of the Second World War, and it is in this later work, rather than the rhetorically more powerful *Great War* (1975), where the limitations of an otherwise creative tension become more apparent.

The argument for a special authority of experience, by which military experience is normally implied in the context of war poetry, can result in a distortion of historical and cultural analysis as well as allowing insight and sympathy. An example of the former result can be traced back to Sassoon and Owen themselves, whose front-line experience made them extremely hostile to civilians (particularly women) who they believed to be ignorant of the realities of war. Later anthologies and criticism of war writing, taking their bearings from the outlook of Sassoon and Owen, frequently emphasized military experience over civilian experience, even when the latter was potentially as extreme (as during the Second World War). Vernon Scannell's book on Second World War poets, *Not Without Glory* (1976), for example, excludes consideration of the work of any writer who wasn't in the forces, as does Ian Hamilton's anthology of poetry from the same period (Hamilton 1965). Fussell's writing on both wars has a similar bias and virtually ignores women writers. Such selectivity in the exploration of the 'vulgar experience' of war is understandable if we wish to see war in terms of a soldier's experience alone, but it can only distort our sense of a wider culture of war which includes the experience of women, for whom the period of the war marked enormous social changes (see Chapter 7), and the political and cultural arguments of a range of non-combatant intellectuals.

Fussell's view of the First World War as an 'unexampled' event which can be explored only through irony, also needs to be viewed critically. As I argued in the first section of this chapter, post-1945 readers have been exposed to representations of both wars which tend to fix and simplify their significance. Wars are removed from the complexities of continuing historical and cultural processes by such representations to become David Jones's parentheses – periods of immense historical and personal significance which lie, nevertheless, beyond the norms of historical and cultural interpretation. While there is every reason for participants in the extremities of war to view their experiences in such a way, an account of the writing of the wars needs to be alert to the historical continuities as well as divergences. To treat wartime as a parenthesis of history is to depoliticize it, blur the social and cultural complexities of its literature and thought and ultimately make it mythical rather than historical. While mythologizing is one process by which a writer like David Jones seeks to makes sense of his experiences on the Western Front, to accept it as a principle for the study of First World War writing runs the risk of ignoring the persistent issues of social division and ideological argument that underlie the myth-making.

The historian John Terraine has pointed to one aspect of such elision in Fussell's work, suggesting that Fussell views the First World War as 'a private contest between the literate British middle class and the German Empire' (Terraine 1980: 36). Such a summary does not do justice to the complexity of Fussell's description of wartime literary culture, but it does draw attention to the lack of a sense of social and cultural diversity within British writing in *The Great War and Modern Memory*, and in *Wartime*. Not only are women writers barely mentioned in either book, but neither are Hamish Henderson and Sorley MacLean, two Scottish poets of the Second World War who offer a distinctly un-English approach to their experience of desert warfare (see Chapter 6), nor the vast number of writers who drew on 'non literary' sources such as ballads and music-hall songs. The exclusion of such voices from most considerations of war writing, as I will argue in later chapters, is the result of cultural and political factors which are not peculiar to wartime. However, the social crisis that the wars represented offers a good opportunity to examine the ways in which different aspects of British culture reacted to historical change, and to mythologize wars as periods outside history denies the possibility of such a study.

Fussell and Silkin, in their different ways, reflect the possibilities and problems that the writing of the two wars pose for post-1945 readers. Their readings make sense of a literature of extreme experience and rapid change, but also suggest the difficulties of dealing with such a diverse and challenging body of work. The issues that they confront are not only those of establishing a canon and developing a working method, but also of dealing with the still potent social, political and cultural implications of the poetry. Ivor Gurney posed a scathing, unanswerable question for critics of war poetry in his poem 'War Books' which begins, 'What did they expect of our toil and extreme/Hunger – the perfect drawing of a heart's dream?' Without offering any 'theory' of war poetry that might suggest such a perfect drawing, the chapters that follow will concentrate on the ways in which the poetry of Gurney's extreme hunger contributed to the arguments and expressions of a diverse British culture in the first half of the century.

2
Englishness

Militarism and patriotism

The elevation of Rupert Brooke to the status of national war poet was both an innovation and a continuation of a process of national self-representation. The crisis of the First World War demanded new ways of defining and communicating national identity and purpose. Brooke's sacrificial militarism and aesthetic nationalism formed one response to this demand. In another way, though, Brooke represents part of a continuing debate about the nature of Englishness which has its origins in the latter part of the nineteenth century. In this chapter I will describe the main lines of this debate and suggest the ways in which it influenced the writing of the two wars.

The history of 'Englishness' in the thirty or so years before the First World War is one of assertion and crisis. In popular memory, the period is the golden age of nation and Empire; in reality, as recent studies of English and British culture have suggested, it was a time of serious questioning of the nature and meaning of English nationhood (Nairn 1981; Wiener 1985; Colls and Dodd 1986). This sense of disquiet is by no means limited to the retrospective interpretations of historians. Cecil Sharp, the founder of the English Folk Dance and Song Society, was impelled to lobby for English folk music to be taught in schools because of a perceived threat to national identity from abroad. 'It cannot be said,' he wrote in 1907, 'that at the present moment, the English people are remarkable for their love or pride of country' (Sharp 1907: 135). The poet Edward Thomas expressed a similar unease. 'I wonder how many others feel the same,' he writes in *The Country* (1913), 'that we have been robbed … of the small intelligible England of Elizabeth and given the word Imperialism instead' (Thomas 1981: 198). The uncertainty was at once disguised and expressed in two dominant discourses of national representation that developed in the period, one militarist and imperialist, the other essentially ruralist.

Militarist patriotism was connected with the growth of imperialism abroad and an increasing uniformity and control of communications at home, through such media as education and mass entertainment. One example of this connection is the jingoistic culture that grew up in the urban music-halls of the last quarter of the nineteenth century. It was in the music-halls that the first and most famous 'jingo' song became popular amongst a working-class audience which, in Gareth Stedman Jones's words, had become 'actively and self-consciously Tory' (Jones 1974: 494). G. W. Hunt's 'The Dogs of War' (1877) became a model for the popular representation of brash patriotic confidence:

> We don't want to fight, but by Jingo if we do,
> We've got the ships, we've got the men, and got the
> money too,
> We've fought the Bear before, and while we're Britons
> true,
> The Russians shall not have Constantinople.

The trick of the song is to implicate the listener into identification with the actions of the British state. 'We' is used six times, and each time it is linked to qualities of good conduct and assertiveness, and to wealth and material power. An obscure threat to invade Turkey thus becomes a test of the manhood of nation and state, and, by extension, of the audience. The influence of this kind of populist politics is identifiable in some of the working-class writing of the First World War, as well as in the commercial popular songs of the war (see, for example, 'Tribute to the 11th Division' in the Ilkeston poems (Poetry Anthology, p. 137); for discussion of patriotic songs of the First World War see Murdoch 1990; for studies of the politics of the nineteenth-century music-hall see Diamond 1990; Summerfield 1986).

Militarist nationalism depended upon the soldier being perceived as a representative of national values. Hunt's song distances the soldier as a tool of an abstract nation, and this probably reflects an earlier distrust of the army which remained in popular consciousness the 'adventurous desperadoes, lumpen proletariat roughs, looters [and] rapers' that A. L. Lloyd describes as the regular army of the early nineteenth century (Lloyd 1975: 237). In the years between Hunt's song and Brooke's volunteer heroism, soldiers were transformed from mercenaries to symbols of national character. This was achieved, in part, by the propagation of personality cults of leaders like Gordon of Khartoum, but more effectively by the growth of the myth of Tommy Atkins, the archetypal English soldier and the salt of the imperial earth. Rudyard Kipling's *Barrack Room Ballads* (1892) made the case for the common soldier as embodying firmly-established English values. In so doing, he also created an eloquent demotic discourse for the soldier which both drew upon and informed nationalist popular culture. If the public-school mythology of duty and fair play has often been used to explain the ready recruitment of officers in 1914, it was in part Kipling and his imitators' translation of nationalist abstractions into a language readily assimilable by a mass audience that allowed a popular war to begin in 1914 (for discussion of the influence of Kipling on working-class poetry of the First World War see Chapter 3).

In the late nineteenth century the model of militant Englishness was present in both literary and popular cultures, even if it was refracted through barriers of class. Algernon Swinburne or Alfred Austin could write in the same terms as Jingo Hunt and be printed in *The Times*, and Kipling could be printed in *The Times* and have his work recited in the music-hall. The militarist and imperialist ethos formed part of both public-school and state-school curricula (see Mangan 1981; Roberts 1973: 140–4). There was thus a complex alliance of interests that allowed a common discourse of nationalism. Yet, as I indicated above, this remarkable alliance, based upon new technologies and mass cultural forms, was threatened by a crisis within the idea of Englishness itself. The foci of this crisis became the South African War of 1899–1902 and the rise of Germany as an industrial and imperial competitor.

Boers and peasants: the crisis of Englishness

The formation of what we now tend to call war poetry, that is, oppositional, anti-war poetry, has its roots in the Boer War. The South African campaign spanned two symbolic events – the turn of the century and the death of Queen Victoria – and called into question the base of late-Victorian nationalism. The latter version of Englishness was underpinned by the successes of military and imperial policy, and an accompanying commercial pre-eminence, but in the early years of the twentieth century the nation was faced with the consequences of military defeat and serious economic competition.

The Boer War broke a consensus on Empire formed in the previous twenty years and caused a questioning of the idea of English destiny. The struggle could not be represented as one to civilize 'savage' territories, but involved fellow Caucasian Christians. What is more, the Boers won, and the charm of British military invincibility was broken. As M. van Wyk Smith suggests, poetic reactions to the Boer War can be seen to rehearse the responses to the greater European war to follow (van Wyk Smith 1978: 306–10). Some poets, like Sir Henry Newbolt, wrote of the war in the language of public-school militarist enthusiasm; others, such as Sir William Watson and Sir Alfred Noyes, who are now only cited as jingoists in relation to the First World War, were critical of the purpose and conduct of the campaign (van Wyk Smith 1978: 133–4, 171–2). Kipling himself, in poems which are notable for their unease rather than their jingoism, saw the war as a warning, indicating the need for a reassessment of England's place in the world. 'The peace is gone and the profit is gone, with the old sure days withdrawn,' he writes in 'The Dykes' (1902), and images in his poems of the period reflect this uncertainty, as in the dyke wall in the poem just quoted, and the 'Few, forgotten and lonely' troops in 'Bridge-Guard in the Karroo' (1901). The dominant mood is elegiac, as in the epitaphs to Cecil Rhodes and 'The Settler'. Kipling's work can be compared to that of Thomas Hardy, another poet deeply affected by the Boer War. A similar unease can be traced in his work of this period. There are no patriotic poems as such, but instead the troubled meditation on the new century 'The Darkling Thrush' and the 'War Poems' of *Poems of the Past and Present* (1901) which emphasize individual grief and apprehension, and look forward to the death of the 'sick god' of war.

It was in the aftermath of the Boer War that Hardy's *The Dynasts* was conceived. This vast epic-drama can seem like an aberration in Hardy's work today, but its story of military crisis and the threat of invasion during the Napoleonic Wars is a response to perceived contemporary dangers. Its themes are those of the popular novels of the turn of the century, such as *When England Slept*, *The Invasion of 1910* and *Starved into Surrender*, all of which project national unease on to a threat of invasion from an aggressive European power, usually France or Germany (for a detailed account of these stories see Clarke 1966). Charles Doughty expresses a similar sense of foreboding in his strange epics *The Cliffs* (1909) and *The Clouds* (1912). Like *The Dynasts*, they seek to redefine Englishness in the face of national uncertainty and foreign threat. The eccentricity of Hardy's and Doughty's poems is one sign of the difficulty of writing about the nation without resorting to the clichés of imperialism in this period. However, the popularity of *The Dynasts*, which was the only new

West End theatrical production of 1914 after war had been declared, suggests how pressing the issue of national identity had become.

Both Hardy and Doughty look to England's political history and literary and linguistic heritage to recast its national identity. Hardy's epic drama attempts to revive the method and political scope of Shakespeare's history plays, yet the part of the play that proved most memorable was not a scene of high political drama or nationalist rhetoric, but the one in which the Wessex villagers are on watch for an expected French invasion. It is a vivid rural scene, reminiscent of Hardy's novels and without the rather turgid blank verse of the rest of the play. Writers as diverse as Siegfried Sassoon and George Orwell refer to it during the Second World War (Sassoon 1942; Orwell 1942), and it was also the source of one of the influential radio broadcasts made by J. B. Priestley in the weeks after the Dunkirk evacuation in 1940 (Priestley 1940: 9–13). The power of the scene lies in the use of a rural community to represent the nation in its opposition to an outside threat. Such a metaphor illustrates the development of another discourse of national representation in the period between the Boer War and the First World War in which English nationalism became pastoral as well as militarist.

Martin Wiener has argued that the latter part of the nineteenth century marked a movement away from optimism about industrial progress and towards an identification of Englishness with the rural past and, in particular, the history and countryside of southern England (Wiener 1985: 40–64; see also Howkins 1986). This phenomenon, like that of militarist patriotism, crossed class and political boundaries. Wiener notes that the 'myth of an England essentially rural and essentially unchanging appealed across political lines to both Conservatives and Imperialists, and to anti-Imperialists, Liberals and Radicals' (Wiener 1985: 55). English ruralism acted as a counterpoint to the imperialist nationalism described above by providing a defined set of home-grown values to replace those of an imperilled Empire.

Pastoral England was formed in the writing of popular authors like Richard Jeffreys, in the music of Ralph Vaughan Williams, in the mock-Tudor village architecture of the new suburbia, in magazines like *Country Life* (founded in 1897), and in the romanticism of an aspirant working class (the music-hall took note of the latter change; as early as the 1890s Gus Elen was singing his satires of proletarian ruralist pretensions, 'The 'Ouses in Between' and 'Pretty Little Villa Down in Barking'). Strident nationalism was offset by a more introspective vision of a timeless English landscape. Edward Thomas, a writer who earned much of his living from writing rural pieces before the First World War, suggests this change of mood when he excludes 'professedly patriotic writing' from his anthology *This England* (1915) because 'it is generally bad and because indirect praise is sweeter and more profound' (Thomas 1981: 221).

The myth of English ruralism had the advantages of drawing upon purely national resources and being able at once to project and heal the crisis of national identity. The folk-song collector Cecil Sharp, in one of the most powerful versions of the myth, showed how an essential rural Englishness could be rescued from the ruins of industrialism and imperialism. Folk-songs, he argues, 'have sprung like wild flowers from the very hearts of our countrymen, and therefore are as redolent of the English race as its language'. By collecting them from 'the native and aboriginal inhabitants of remote country districts', 'Old England' could still be preserved. Modern methods of scholarship and systems of mass education could then disseminate these products of true Englishness to save twentieth-century England from the disaster of industrialism and mass culture. He presents his national vision thus:

> If every English child be placed in possession of all these race products, he will know and understand his country and his countrymen far better than he does at present ... The introduction of folk-songs into our schools will not only affect the musical life of England; it will also tend to arouse that love of country and pride of race, the absence of which we now deplore.
>
> (Sharp 1907: 135–6)

In the face of national peril, Sharp's England is able to affirm its essential identity by returning to its rural traditions through the truly English culture of its 'folk'.

War poetry and Englishness

The writing of both world wars needs to be read in the context of these ideas of national representation. The First World War did not initiate feelings of national crisis, despite the powerful myth of a pre-war golden age summed up in the line from Philip Larkin's elegy 'MCMXIV', 'Never such innocence again'. Nor did the war alter the basic language of national representation. What is remarkable about the work of writers like Ivor Gurney, Edward Thomas, Wilfred Owen, Siegfried Sassoon and

David Jones is not normally its rejection of previous discourses of nationhood, but rather the way in which it adapts those discourses to the circumstances of the war. I want to look at four First World War poems from the anthology with reference to the ideas of Englishness and national identity outlined above. They are Ivor Gurney's 'Strange Service' and 'The Mangel-Bury', Wilfred Owen's 'Smile, Smile, Smile', and the extract from Part 7 of David Jones's *In Parenthesis*.

Gurney wrote 'Strange Service' in July 1916. It expresses ideas of national duty and rural idealism, and a cursory reading suggests a straightforward patriotic poem. The poet addresses England as Mother and uses a heightened, quasi-religious rhetoric of patriotic service, combined with pastoral imagery of a timeless English landscape in a statement of personal commitment to the war. But the poem is more problematic than this. The title suggests puzzlement rather than enthusiasm, and the poem goes on to explore the discrepancies between a 'dear service' to a rural England and a 'dreadful service' to a military England 'beyond [the] borders' of such a pastoral ideal. The emphasis upon two kinds of 'service' goes against the whole drift of the nationalist languages described above which affirm a unified Englishness, whether it be that of Tommy Atkins or Cecil Sharp's peasant.

'Strange Service' is a war poem concerned with the *perception* of England in wartime. While the commitment of the poem to the English cause is not in doubt, the available language to talk about that cause certainly is. The most striking example of this is in stanza 4. Gurney describes the beauty of England as 'secret', rather than public. It is made up of 'memories only, and [its] skies and rushy sky-pools [are]/Fragile mirrors easily broken by moving airs …'. The language of pastoral Englishness appears fixed in a personal past, rather than in a timeless public present, and it is 'easily broken', vulnerable to the destructiveness of war. For Gurney, the 'service' demanded by a militarist England cannot be celebrated in the easy metaphors of Rupert Brooke's war sonnets; the language of rural nationalism is questioned even as it is deployed.

In this early poem Gurney is already writing in a way which cannot be classified as pro- or anti-war. It doesn't reject the languages of nationalism, but they are never allowed to rest. The urge to explore and, if necessary, distort received images of Englishness is apparent in much of his later poetry. In 'The Mangel-Bury' (written between 1922 and 1925) Gurney returns to the country around Gloucester, 'our old inheritance, our Paradise', as he describes it in 'De Profundis'. The poem begins as a celebration of Edward Thomas's rural vision, with Gurney 'walking by Gloucester musing on such things/As fill his [Thomas's] verse with goodness' and meeting a farmer whom he helps to load mangels on to a cart. However, the rural simplicity is disrupted by the language of the description. The Gloucester field 'looked as part of the earth heaped up by dead soldiers/In the most fitting place', an image either of graves or a landscape created by soldiers now dead. Throughout the poem the war thwarts the intended celebration of the pastoral: Thomas, the poet of 'goodness', 'had fallen at Arras'; the rural work is desired not because of Gurney's connection with the land, but because he remains a 'soldier still' and needs physical exercise; and the expression of the continuity and community of rural life, so strong in *The Dynasts* scene mentioned above, is silenced in the final lines:

> If my luck had so willed
> Many questions of lordship I had heard him tell – old
> Names, rumours. But my pain to more moving called
> And him to some barn business far in the fifteen acre field.

Gurney's compulsive and painful desire to walk (linked throughout his work with the marches of the war) and the farmer's 'barn business' mean that the communication of the values that the poem strives to define cannot be effected.

Gurney's poetry presents a troubled version of rural idealism which at once uses and questions pastoral conventions. In other poets the tradition of nationalist militarism survives in equally tested forms. Wilfred Owen's 'Smile, Smile, Smile' describes crippled veterans reading, in the notoriously jingoistic *Daily Mail*, of those fighting to keep 'this nation in integrity.' The *Mail* persists in identifying the army with the moral force of the nation. As Owen's bleak pun on the physical and moral senses of the word 'integrity' suggests, however, the rhetoric of nationalism pays no attention to the physical and mental maiming of the victims of the war.

The poem is a scathing satire on jingoistic platitudes which are maintained in the face of the appalling destruction of the men who make up the nation. But more than this, Owen develops the Victorian and Edwardian identification of Englishness and military strength to a terrible extreme. If England is represented by its army and that army has been destroyed, then the integrity of the nation has also disappeared:

> (This is the thing they know and never speak,
> That England one by one had fled to France,
> Not many elsewhere now, save under France.)

By the apocalyptic logic of militarist rhetoric, the nation has disappeared with its army under Brooke's 'foreign field'. The verb 'fled' here seems to suggest a willing, desperate act to get away from the land of the *Daily Mail* in which only the company of crippled veterans share the knowledge of the destruction of the 'real' England.

The most radical consideration of the idea of nation and Englishness to come from the First World War is David Jones's *In Parenthesis* (1937). In this long poem Jones reconstructs the idea of Britain, rather than England. His reference point is not the Napoleonic Wars or the Elizabethan age (the favoured nineteenth-century analogues of national resilience and self-confidence), but the Britain of the sixth-century Welsh epic poem *Y Gododdin* which describes the defeat of Welsh forces at the Battle of Catraeth. Lying behind the apparently eccentric link between a Dark Age skirmish and the Battle of the Somme is Jones's sense of a distorted national culture. For Jones, as for Sharp and Thomas, England (or Britain as Jones always refers to his nation) has lost its identity in the turmoils of industrialism and imperialism, and the war only reveals the extent of a deeper national crisis. However, war also provides him with the raw material to recreate national identity. In the Welshmen and Londoners who made up his battalion, Jones sees 'the genuine tradition of the Island of Britain, from Bendigeid Vran to Jingle and Marie Lloyd' ('Preface' to *In Parenthesis*, Prose Anthology, pp. 239–41). The difference between Jones's version of the 'genuine tradition' of Britishness and that of Cecil Sharp and other enthusiasts for national rediscovery lies in his recognition that identity has to be remade rather than recovered, and that such a process poses great linguistic and formal difficulties. It is this need to reconstruct identity that accounts for the unusual poetic practice of *In Parenthesis*.

The poetic techniques of David Jones are based upon a principle of the simultaneous disjunction and association of images and ideas. With Ivor Gurney and Edward Thomas, he is one of the few war poets who does not use irony consistently in his representation of the link between the past and the war. The reader is supposed to take seriously the link between the Battle of the Somme and the battle at Catraeth. At the same time, though, one is meant to see the problems in accepting such a connection. The obscurity of many of the references and the tenuousness of many of the comparisons are part of the deliberate effect of the poem. For the reader's difficulty in making sense of the connections is not just a personal puzzlement but that of a culture which, in Jones's terms, is no longer able to understand or interpret its own history. The task of reading and making sense of *In Parenthesis* becomes an act of recreating national history and redefining national identity.

The following extract from Part 7 of *In Parenthesis* provides a characteristic example of Jones's poetic techniques (a longer extract from this section is provided in the Poetry Anthology):

> No one to care there for Aneirin Lewis spilled there
> who worshipped his ancestors like a Chink
> who sleeps in Arthur's lap
> who saw Olwen-trefoils some moonlighted night
> on precarious slats at Festubert,
> on narrow foothold on le Plantin marsh –
> more shaved he is to the bare bone than
> Yspaddadan Penkawr.
>   Properly organised chemists can let make more riving
> power than ever Twrch Trwyth;
> more blistered he is than painted Troy Towers
> and unwholer, limb from limb, than any of them fallen at
> Catraeth …
> And the little Jew lies next him
> cries out for Deborah his bride
> and offers for stretcher-bearers
>   gifts for their pains
> and walnut suites in his delirium
>   from Grays Inn Road.

Jones is describing two of those killed or wounded in the moments before the beginning of an attack during the Somme offensive of 1916. The men are ignored by the other soldiers in the tension of the moment, but, characteristically, Jones provides an elegy for them even as he notes this neglect. Lewis's Welshness and his adherence to Welsh traditions are first noted in the demotic language of the soldiers (he 'worshipped his ancestors like a Chink'), but this comment is immediately followed by a different elegiac register: the dead man 'sleeps in Arthur's lap'. There is no irony here. Lewis's sense of his Welsh identity was strong in his life and Jones takes it seriously in death. The Welsh soldier of the First World

War is connected to the Welsh soldier of antiquity by his sense of his own place in an ancient culture. Such an identification, Jones suggests, can make sense of the experience of modern war. The 'precarious slats' are the duckboards of the trenches, but Jones affirms Lewis's link with his cultural heritage. He was still able to see in the trenches Olwen-trefoils, the magical flowers that sprang up wherever the mythical heroine Olwen trod in the ancient Welsh story *Kulhwch ac Olwen*.

Jones's sense of the continuity of the experience of war, however, is never romanticized. He acknowledges that this is a war of 'properly organised chemists' rather than Dark Age swords, and that Lewis is 'unwholer' – more brutally injured – than the soldiers at Catraeth. The final part of the extract suggests that an appeal to the past can be pathetic as well as heroic, as the delirious cries of the Jewish soldier attempt to recapture the sureties of home. Jones's technique forces the reader to consider historical congruities and incongruities in his interpretation of war, and we are never allowed to settle into any sure perspective of ironic contrast or spurious nationalism. Nevertheless, the passage celebrates the particular cultures and histories of the soldiers that made up the British army (here Jewish and Welsh) and this is part of a wider purpose of reconstructing and re-evaluating English history.

The point of making the battle of Catraeth the historical reference point of *In Parenthesis* is both to defamiliarize 'English' history by returning to Celtic rather than Anglo-Saxon precursors, and to evoke a period when, as he says in a footnote, 'the fate of the Island was as yet undecided' (Jones 1937: 191). The instability of the years of the First World War, imagined as a historical parenthesis in the poem's title, is projected through the Dark Age interregnum between Roman and Anglo-Saxon dominance, when 'north Britain was still largely in Celtic posses-sion' (p. 191). This period of English history is largely unknown, and certainly formed no part of the conventional nationalist/imperialist histories of England which dominated English culture before the First World War (see MacDougall 1982). For Jones, the bringing together of two historical parentheses, the sixth century and the First World War, offers the possibility of an escape from the dominant ideologies of English nationalism and imperialism. It allows a different historical vision of what he terms 'an ancient unity and mingling of races; with the Island as a corporate inheritance, with the remembrance of Rome as a European unity' (Jones 1973: 192). Englishness then becomes no longer a domin-ant ideology which marginalizes other cultures, but an acknowledgement of cultural and historical plurality. Only through such an acknowl-edgement, Jones implies, can any sense be made of the events of the First World War.

The effect of Jones's radical experiment in historical reference, poetic technique and national discourse can be seen in the closing passages of *In Parenthesis* (Poetry Anthology, pp. 151–61). He describes the after-math of the bitter fighting in Mametz Wood in terms which are wholly unrealistic in comparison with Sassoon's war poetry, for example. In the sleeve-notes to the recording of Jones reading the poem (RG-520), he summarizes the passage as follows:

> The tutelary spirit of the wood is bestowing garlands of varying floriation upon those Germans and Welshmen and Londoners whose bodies lay scattered where they had fallen in the tangle of the wood and on the open approaches to it.

As a fantasy of reconciliation, it can be compared with Owen's 'Strange Meeting', but Jones's version has none of the ironies of the earlier poem. The tutelary spirit of the woods and the pastoral garlands that she awards mark a return to a common mythology – Anglo-Saxon and Celtic, German and English, English and Welsh – that bypasses the ideology of modern nationalisms. Only in the extravagance of such a conflation of industrial destruction and ancient belief, Jones suggests, can a re-generative meaning be affirmed.

The closing passages of *In Parenthesis* show clearly Jones's attempt to create a ceremonial, public language which avoids the sentimental or aggrandizing rhetoric of nationalism. For all its eccentricity, his version of the pastoral elegy admits a diversity of judgements and voices quite unavailable to more conventional war poems and renders its roll of honour a human record rather than a state function. An unpopular officer remains in death 'That swine Lillywhite'; each award is appraised by the voice of a soldier-narrator ('that's fair enough', 'you'd hardly credit it'); and the tone is carefully modulated to acknowledge both the propriety and absurdity of the scene. As in the passage examined earlier, Jones does not allow a settled perspective on the events he describes. The Battle of the Somme, the great turning-point of modern industrial warfare, is shown as a confused and confusing fragment of history. Yet the poet consistently attempts to find the appropriate discourses to make sense of its events.

The great project of *In Parenthesis* is to create a poetic language adequate not only to record the extremity of personal experience (as in the vivid description of the troops before an attack in the first extract from *In Parenthesis* in the anthology, pp. 151–7), but also to understand the war historically. It aims to connect the details of the experience of the ordinary soldiers to a new construction of national and historical identity. Like Owen and other writers of the war, Jones has a powerful sense of a different kind of community created in the extreme conditions of the Western Front, but he presents this within a continuity of historical experience. He finds in the trenches an essential Britishness which had been displaced in England itself by industrialism, imperialism and a debased public rhetoric. The trenches contained 'a folk-life ... a people, a culture already developed, already venerable and rooted' (Jones 1937: 49). Unlike other English nationalists, Jones recognizes such a culture as a present reality rather than a historical remnant, and his poetry creates a discourse through which to express its complexity.

3
Popular Culture

In Parenthesis sets the complex and intimate society created and maintained by the soldiers in the trenches against what Jones terms the 'relentless mechanical affair' of the war ('Preface' to *In Parenthesis* in Prose Anthology, pp. 239–41). The imagery of mechanism used by Jones and other writers to describe the conduct of the war acknowledges their involvement in the first major conflict between great industrial and commercial powers. The First World War was the first war to control many aspects of everyday life on a mass industrial scale, and its organizations and technologies developed and exploited the systems of production and social control of nineteenth-century civilian industrialism. It consumed men and materials as never before and it also quickly became an object for commercial consumption as the production of goods was geared towards and often promoted by reference to the war (for examples of the numerous commercial advertisements alluding to the war see Rickards and Moody 1975). The alliance of industry and commerce with the state war effort was reflected in all aspects of the market, including that of literature where the increase in the number of books of war poetry was a result of the commercial exploitation of a demand for war-related material. As Catherine Reilly's bibliography of First World War poetry suggests, the bulk of this poetry was written by amateur poets who willingly contributed to national propaganda, and was published by companies which recognized the profitability of such material.

War poetry is still identified with a relatively small canon of writers and this inevitably distorts our view of the genre and its relationship with the mainstream commercial and ideological demands of the period. The pre-eminence of Owen, for example, when his work was largely unpublished until the 1920s, has frequently led to an overemphasis on the opposition to war in war poetry when the great bulk of contemporary material remained unshakeably patriotic throughout. Some recent anthologies have sought to acknowledge the great amount of non-canonical war poetry published during the two wars by including selections from unknown verse writers alongside the customary list of war poets (see, for example, Hibberd and Onions 1986; Selwyn 1989; Selwyn *et al.* 1980, 1983), and Paul Fussell emphasizes the importance of considering this writing in *The Great War and Modern Memory* (1975). Even in these anthologies and criticism, though, there is a good deal of selectivity in the presentation of British culture. Fussell marvels at the literariness of much war writing and suggests that many of the ordinary soldiers were familiar with the great tradition of English poetry; they had 'no feeling that literature is not very near the center of normal experience', he writes (Fussell 1975: 157–8). Many of the poems printed in wartime anthologies support this argument, yet there is a danger of overstatement. The poems that Fussell refers to and which have been reprinted as examples of a 'popular' culture of wartime are frequently the work of officers or people from a social class which gave them access to a dominant literary culture and to metropolitan publishers. Reilly's bibliography confirms the officer rank of the majority of published poets. In this chapter I want to explore further Jones's sense of an oppositional popular culture in war by looking at two areas which have received relatively little critical attention: working-class poetry and soldiers' songs. These texts suggest a very different sense of cultural tradition to that defined by Fussell and offer a different perspective on the relationship of writing to the dominant political ideologies of the two wars. I will also consider the influence of popular culture on the work of three writers of the Second World War, Hamish Henderson, Stephen Spender and Edgell Rickword.

Working-class war poetry

The Poetry Anthology in this book contains five poems written during the First World War by volunteers or conscripts from Ilkeston, a town in the industrial Midlands. They first appeared in the traditional medium of publication for working-class poets, the local newspaper. Wartime anthologies of 'amateur' poetry, particularly those of the First World War, were metropolitan and middle class in outlook and distribution, and these factors tended to exclude provincial, working-class poets. Poetry, though, was seen as an appropriate response to war by all classes and the newspaper poems suggest an alternative literary tradition existing alongside the more visible metropolitan mainstream.

The Ilkeston poems draw on two sources which are rarely mentioned in studies of war poetry: ballad traditions and the work of Rudyard Kipling. Broadsheet ballads on military subjects were commonly sold by itinerant singers and ballad-mongers in the nineteenth century and before (see Palmer 1988: 271–300), and Reilly's bibliography provides some evidence for the persistence of broadsides in the First World War (Reilly 1978). The formulaic phrasing of J. C. Johnson's 'Tribute to the 11th Division' (Poetry Anthology, p. 137) in which 'Every man there was a hero/Who was facing the Turkish shot' suggests the influences of this kind of work. The experience of the writers is conveyed through the narrative and linguistic conventions of the ballad which organize and interpret that experience in thoroughly traditional ways. Despite the apparent dominance of lyric writing in the canon of war poetry, the ballad retained its imaginative hold in working-class culture, and continued to be an important form of popular writing in the Second World War, as the work of Hamish Henderson demonstrates (see below).

Kipling's importance to the debates about Englishness in the years before the First World War has already been noted (see Chapter 2), and, contrary to conventional critical wisdom, he remained popular throughout the war. He was one of the writers most frequently borrowed from service libraries during the war (Fuller 1990: 133) and his work continued to be influential in schools, particularly elementary schools. As several of the Ilkeston poems suggest, his poetic method provided a valid model for interpreting war experiences. Kipling's characteristic metre and rhyme scheme are used in W. Lloyd's 'On the Red Road to Hooge' and C. Butters' 'Send 'Em Along' (both in Poetry Anthology, pp. 138, 140), and in both poems the imitation of Kipling's method enables the poets to present a realistic account of their experiences. The subject of 'On the Red Road to Hooge' is the drudgery of night repairs to defences, and the writer successfully imitates Kipling's way of offsetting the commonplace with a rhythmically and rhetorically powerful refrain. The contrast between the journalistic glamorization of the war and its grinding reality is effectively achieved:

> Not a deed for the paper man to write,
> No glorious charge in the dreary night,
> 'The Daily Mail' won't tell the tale
> Of the night work at Hooge.

'Send 'Em Along' is another poem with a clear sense of the realities of war in its description of entraining wounded soldiers. The 'trouser legs are blood-stained bags', Butters writes, the wounded have the 'honours of thick trench mud', and the 'vacant look' of shell-shocked victims is recorded. In these poems Kipling's poetic model allows a controlled communication of an often grim reality.

In both 'Send 'Em Along' and 'On the Red Road to Hooge', however, there are elements which conflict with the dominant realism. Both end with seemingly anomalous sections. 'The Red Road to Hooge' notes a general's pleasure at the Sherwoods' work and makes a seemingly unironic reference to 'The Charge of the Light Brigade', and in 'Send 'Em Along' the poet affirms that the wounded have won 'a glorious name'. Such tonal inconsistencies can be explained by the difficulties of ending poems for inexperienced poets, leading to the resort of tagging on a formulaic phrase or two borrowed from the conventions of patriotic poetry. But the use of conventional endings also marks a discrepancy between language and outlook, and an overlap of popular and literary culture. For these poets, the way to end a poem is with a conclusion whose language and sentiment mark poetic and ideological propriety even though it counteracts the main argument of the piece. The newspaper poems are rarely consistently imitative of received 'literary' styles, however, and, as I will argue below, use of a particular style doesn't necessarily imply acceptance of the ideology that produced it.

Another influence upon the Ilkeston poems which can be added to those of the ballad tradition and Kiplingesque narratives is that of an oral tradition of collective improvisation. George Shipstone's 'My Little Wet Home in the Trench' (Poetry Anthology, p. 136), is one of a number of recorded parodies of 'My Little Grey Home in the West', and is almost certainly a version heard on the Western Front, rather than one written by Shipstone. Parody and improvisation played a major part in the production of popular songs and rhymes in the First World War and there is some interesting evidence for the process of such production in Thomas Beardsley's poem (Poetry Anthology, p. 135). The song is set to the tune of 'This Is My Story', one of the many uses of hymn tunes for secular purposes during the war, and, Beardsley notes, it was communally written: 'me and 5 pals made this up'. The poem consists of five stanzas employing a mixture of music-hall jingoism (the Kaiser saying 'I'll make one Empire, I'll rule the globe'), Derbyshire idiom ('But not while this Bull-dog stands in my road') and a fairly random use of the vocabulary and slang of the war (Jack Johnsons, limbers, Mons, Marne, Ypres and so on). What is relevant for the interpretation of other uses of conventional and stylized material is the song's comment on its own production: 'The boys that composed this they sit in the dark,/And they've only composed it just for a lark'. The use of patriotic poeticisms can thus mark the deployment of literary conventions and does not necessarily indicate acceptance of their values. While some parts are serious, some are 'a lark'.

Tommy's tunes

The communal description of the parody 'This Is My Story' suggests a link between the popular poetry of the newspapers and the oral culture of the war. Several collections of soldiers' songs appeared during the war, and some versions of the songs have become familiar from the letters and novels of the period and from Joan Littlewood's celebrated Theatre Workshop production *Oh! What a Lovely War* (1963), later filmed by Richard Attenborough (1969). Soldiers' songs have a long history (see Dallas 1972; Palmer 1990), but the First World War, with its new type of volunteer and conscript, provoked different kinds of songs to the insulated repertoire of the regular army or the nationalism and sentiment of mass commercial productions.

Marching Songs, a tunic-pocket-sized collection published in 1914, gives the official version of what soldiers' songs should be like. Its introduction uses Cecil Sharp's argument for national music, noting the shallowness of contemporary popular music and arguing for the need for a revival of true English songs:

> There are plenty of capital marching tunes and songs in existence, but the tired soldier cannot call them to mind on the spur of the moment. What happens on the march is that some musical spirit strikes up a familiar song which goes with a swing; others join in, and success is established ... In this way, the popular Music Hall effusions have lost their freshness, and for this reason we have not included in the present collection any songs of this class. We have depended upon the sterling, undying National Melodies of England, Scotland, Ireland and Wales – melodies which bring with them memories of home.
>
> (anon 1914: no page numbers)

'John Peel', 'Killarney', 'Coming Thro' the Rye' and 'Where Are You Going My Pretty Maid' represent the editor's ideal, and there is a supplement containing the national anthems of Allied nations, including that of Japan.

By 1917, tastes had changed. In that year Second-Lieutenant F. T. Nettleingham published *Tommy's Tunes*, a collection of songs created by the soldiers themselves. It purports to represent that aspect of British humour which tends to be 'derogatory to its own dignity, to wipe itself in the mud, to affect self-satire to an alarming extent' (Nettleingham 1917: 14). The collection is necessarily bowdlerized, but it contains a good range of songs, including several that remain firmly identified with the First World War: 'When This Ruddy War is Over', 'Après la guerre fini', 'The Moon Shines Bright on Charlie Chaplin', 'Old Soldiers Never Die', 'I Want to Go Home' and 'Whiter Than the Whitewash on the Wall'. Nettleingham's collection sold well enough for a follow up, *More Tommy's Tunes*, to be published in the following year. This marked the first appearance of 'The Bells of Hell'. Again, the introduction celebrates the irony rather than the patriotic value of popular song, and, in a remarkable development of the argument, criticizes the British national anthem in the light of them: 'the words [are] futile and out of touch with popular sentiment, and, are, further, incongruous with the ideals of a true democracy' (Nettleingham 1918: 12).

Soldiers' songs remained (and remain) curiosities. They do not fit into the category of war literature, but neither are they folk-songs in Cecil Sharp's purist terms – their indiscriminate use of tin-pan-alley and music-hall tunes, hymns, unclassifiable rhymes and the obscene traditions of the regular army put them outside the definitions of the English Folk Dance and Song Society. Yet it is that very mongrel quality that makes them part of the popular, rather than the mass, culture of the war. The songs transform the musical and lyrical idioms of an established culture – whether it be that of the church, professional song writers, music-hall or army tradition – into an expression of the specific social circumstances of the war. The rigorous obscenity of the mess hall is tempered by the conscript's influence; 'I Want to Go Home' is not a song that could have come from the regular army. John Brophy who, with Eric Partridge, edited the first post-war collection of soldiers' songs, *Songs and Slang of the British Soldier 1914–18* (1930), called them 'songs of homeless men, evoked by exceptional and distressing circumstances; the songs of an itinerant community, continually altering within itself under the incidence of death and mutilation' (Brophy and Partridge 1965: 4).

For Brophy, himself a veteran of the war, the songs were 'genuine "folk-songs"' (*ibid.*). They were produced and consumed collectively in extreme circumstances for the purposes of comfort and survival. 'The

very knowledge of such songs', he writes, 'reduced the emotional disorganization caused by fear, and aided [the soldier], after the experience, to pick his uncertain way back to sanity' (p. 8). Brophy's introduction to *Songs and Slang*, which was retitled *The Long Trail* on its republication in a revised version in 1965, gives a good summary of the subjects of the songs and a sense of their importance to the soldiers. However, the essay, particularly the 1930 version, also indicates the difficulties of discussing this kind of material in the context of wartime culture. While emphasizing the 'plain speaking' and 'animal spirits' demonstrated by the songs, Brophy is also emphatic in his rejection of lewd songs, which, he claims are not 'essentially soldiers' songs'. Swearing was a fact of army life, but Brophy is keen to distance the true effects and motives of such linguistic usage. 'The obscenity satisfied,' he writes, 'because the words blasphemed sex, even as war blasphemed life' (p. 18). Even more unconvincingly, he argues that 'always it must be remembered that the English pay little attention to the meanings of words, and rarely use them with any precision' (p. 12).

The issue here is not really one of bowdlerism or censorship, but of the reception and interpretation of popular culture. For Brophy, the songs represent a collective affirmation of the values found in the war and denied by 'this industrial civilization of ours', the experience of

> the simplification of [the soldier's] life, the hard use of his body, the sense of a tangible, immediate and valuable task, the sense of being a member of a vast society organised to an ethical end, comradeship, uncertainty of the morrow, the possibility of adventure and an enhanced awareness of the mystery and precariousness of life.
>
> (Brophy and Partridge 1965: 19–20)

This sense of value is close to that expressed in such post-war poems as Ivor Gurney's 'The Mangel-Bury' and 'First Time In' (Poetry Anthology, pp. 124, 122) and David Jones's *In Parenthesis*, but it also recalls the anti-industrial idealism of Cecil Sharp's original folk-song project (see discussion in Chapter 2). Brophy boldly moves folk-song beyond Sharp's pastoral and into the war, but, although he celebrates the oral culture of the war, he refuses to acknowledge important features of its political and social meanings. In his account, the songs become, like Sharp's folk-songs, relics of an essential Englishness only barely perceptible from a debased present.

The adaptation of the soldiers' songs of the First World War into a version of moral Englishness was first questioned by Montagu Slater, writing in 1941. His essay 'Bless 'em All' (extract in Prose Anthology, pp. 252–4) suggests a significant change in the way popular culture was conceived during the ten years since Brophy published his collection of songs. Slater argues that the popular culture of the war was created through a struggle with the mass culture of official and semi-official propaganda. A commercial song like 'Tipperary', Slater suggests, was only popular because of the specific interpretation put upon it by the singers. They effectively remade the song, distorting its original meaning to meet their own needs, and a similar practice occurred in the numerous parodies that made up their repertoire. An oppositional culture was created in which there was a constant process of parody, adaptation and subversion of the dominant ideologies of state and army.

Slater's essay compares attempts to control popular expression in the two world wars. In the Second World War, he argues, 'official' popular songs with uplifting messages failed to catch on and tin-pan alley was forced to return to folk-song sources, issuing versions of 'The Quarter-master's Store' and 'Bless 'em All' (one an old regular army song, the other a First World War parody). Slater criticizes the sanitization of the 'official' versions of these songs which, in the former case, plays down the criticism of army mismanagement, and, in the latter, replaces the original dismissive 'fuck 'em all' with an inappropriately cheery euphemism. Such changes, he argues, were part of an attempt to change a radical popular culture into an anodyne mass culture.

The political argument underlying Slater's essay is typical of *Our Time*, the magazine in which it first appeared. *Our Time* has been neglected in studies of the writing of the Second World War, but it provides a fascinating contrast to the more celebrated periodical of the period, Cyril Connolly's *Horizon*. It began in 1938 as a cheaply reproduced booklet called *Poetry and the People*, advertised as 'the first people's magazine of poetry in England'. It had links with the Left Book Club and with a short lived organization 'of Poetry and the People' groups which were devoted to the development of a popular political poetry. In 1941 *Poetry and the People* was renamed *Our Time*, and adopted a larger format and a glossier presentation. By 1942 it had a circulation of 3,000 and after Edgell Rickword became editor in 1944 this increased to 18,000 (*Horizon*'s sales in 1941 were approximately 5,000 [Shelden 1989: 86–7]). Although *Our Time* moved away from its original emphasis upon popular political poetry, it maintained its Leftist politics and its interest in popular culture.

Under Rickword's editorship it pursued a policy of encouraging a broad-based alliance of intellectual and radical popular movements on the model Rickword found in post-liberation France (see account of *Our Time* in Hobday 1989).

'Bless 'em All' suggests one of the ways in which *Our Time* maintained the idea of popular culture as a potentially radical force. In an early contribution to the magazine, when it was still *Poetry and the People*, Rickword himself suggested that the war could provide the conditions for a truly popular culture to be created (see 'Notes on Culture and the War', extract in Prose Anthology, pp. 245–6). The pressure of circumstances – danger, collective involvement, shortages of paper and reading-matter – could 'restore the balance between the written and the spoken word':

> Then the natural story-tellers and poets will come into their own, making conscious the feelings of their group, be it large or small. They are the organisers of emotion, one of the factors directing the collective effort to the common aim ... During the Spanish war it is no exaggeration to say that thousands of ... ballads were composed by amateur poets and circulated in the village or the regiment.

In 1940 Spain usually represented either the defeat of the 1930s Left or the hypocrisy of Stalin who, having supported the Republican cause during the Spanish Civil War, went on to make a non-aggression pact with Nazi Germany. The fact that Rickword makes the Spanish Civil War his point of reference in an argument that otherwise reflects the populism of semi-official propaganda suggests that for him the 1930s did not end up as a 'low, dishonest decade' as W. H. Auden described it in his valedictory poem 'September 1, 1939'. Even in 1940 Rickword sees the war as offering the possibility of the fulfilment of the socialist project of the 1930s, rather than marking its failure. This recovery of 1930s radicalism during the war and the interest in popular culture as an expression of popular radicalism can also be seen in the work of two contrasting writers of the period, Stephen Spender and Hamish Henderson.

Popular culture, popular radicalism

Stephen Spender has often been identified as one of the radical writers of the 1930s who disavowed their political commitments in 1939, and there are some melodramatic pieces by Spender early in the war that give credence to this view (see particularly 'September Journal' in Spender

1985). As the war went on, however, Spender came to see the same kind of possibilities for social and cultural change as those identified by Rickword in 'Notes on Culture and the War'.

In *Citizens in War – and After* (1945) (extract in Prose Anthology, pp. 261–5) Spender uses the Civil Defence organization (which included the National Fire Service and the ARP) as a model for the political and cultural reconstruction of the nation. Post-war Britain, Spender argues, would be based on the Civil Defence principles of erosion of class barriers, local patriotism and participatory local decision-making. The embryo of a truly collectivist society had emerged during the unprecedented crisis of a total war. This collectivism wasn't dependent on the political ideology that motivated the Leftist idealism of the 1930s, but upon local experiences of co-operation and 'the feeling of having been reborn into a new community'. The difficulties of the uneasy application of Soviet political models to British experience in the 1930s, vividly demonstrated in Spender's own *Forward from Liberalism* (1938), are avoided by an appeal to democracy, community and Englishness. In the extract in the Prose Anthology the political argument of *Citizens in War – and After* is pursued through a discussion of the popular culture that Spender observed during his time as a volunteer in the Fire Service.

Spender contrasts the official art of the National Fire Service and Civil Defence in general, which was predicated on Soviet and German models of heroic workers and mythic struggles, with what he sees as the truly collectivist, popular art of the services themselves. In his autobiography, *World Within World* (1951), he describes the fire-station games room, decorated for Christmas, as 'a classic example of something which the writers of the Left had spent so much time discussing during the 1930s: proletarian art, folk art even' (Spender 1951: 277). The same claim is made in *Citizens in War – and After*, but with a significant emphasis on the limitations of such 'folk culture' and the need for an accompanying social and educational programme to develop artistic sensibilities. 'A surprising amount of poetry is read', he writes, '[B]ut it is read under difficult conditions produced by their education'. Spender's reformist argument, which tempers an enthusiasm for popular culture with a sense of a need for further education, feeds into the social programmes of the post-war Labour government, whose Home Secretary, Herbert Morrison, wrote the foreword to Spender's book.

Hamish Henderson's work during the Second World War offers a different perspective on the influence of the political and cultural debates of the 1930s upon the period of the Second World War. His use of popular traditions suggests a less qualified sense of their political and cultural value compared to that of Spender, an attitude that reflects not only the political radicalism of Henderson himself, but also that of the Scottish popular culture that is his main point of reference. Henderson published two works related to his wartime experiences in Africa and Italy, the privately printed *Ballads of World War II* (1950) and *Elegies for the Dead in Cyrenaica* (1948). The *Elegies* demonstrate his debt to the literary culture of the 1930s and to the work of Wilfred Owen (see discussion in Chapter 6), but the *Ballads* show the influence of Scottish folk-song, soldiers' songs and working-class poetry.

Henderson's theory of popular culture is similar to that developed by Rickword and *Our Time*, in which the war is seen to provide the conditions for a new kind of popular culture which is both traditional and radical. In the *Ballads*, Henderson's own works, such as 'The 51st Highland Division's Farewell to Sicily' and 'Ballad of Anzio', are mixed with anonymous British songs and with Italian and German ballads, including 'Lili Marlene', the adopted song of both of the armies in North Africa. The lack of demarcation between traditional and original material reflects Henderson's own sense of his songs emerging from, and then merging back into, an oral repertoire (he comments in an interview that 'Farewell to Sicily' 'was beginning to get sung by people here and there almost as soon as I had written it' [Orr 1966: 78]). However, Henderson demonstrates none of Sharp's nostalgia for a world that has been lost. His view of the place and purpose of such songs acknowledges the new material conditions of production in the Second World War:

> The balladry of World War II developed in conditions quite unlike those of previous major wars. It grew up under the shadow of – and often in competition with – the official or commercial radio of the combatant nations.
>
> The state radio in time of war does not encourage dissidence from the straight patriotic line. It regards most expressions of the human reaction to soldiery as a drag on the national war effort.
>
> (Henderson 1950: iii)

Like Slater, Henderson argues for the political importance of its subversion of official discourses of war. The 'Army balladeer comes of a rebellious house', he writes, and 'his characteristic tone is one of cynicism' (*ibid.*).

The ballads that Henderson includes in his collection represent a culture informed by a more militant political stance than the songs in Brophy and Partridge's anthology. In 'The Blubbing Buchmanite' (Poetry Anthology, p. 200), for example, the debate between a Buchmanite (a supporter of Frank Buchman's evangelical Moral Re-armament movement) and a Greenock communist is decided in a robust flyting of the former. The socialist internationalism, apparent in the inclusion of the German and Italian ballads, draws upon the enthusiasm for Spanish Republican popular culture in the 1930s, something that also informs Rickword's ideas on Second World War culture. Henderson's ballads are also firmly in the Scottish folk tradition of military celebration and lament, and they acknowledge the persistent popular heroic tradition of poetry represented by the newspaper poems of the First World War (see also discussion of Sorley MacLean's work, Chapter 6). These are not pacifist poems. However, like many of the local poems discussed earlier, they mark a difference between celebration of war for patriotic reasons and the celebration of community and courage within war, qualities which, as Henderson's *Elegies* also testify, are not limited to one side in the conflict.

The 'Ballad of Anzio' (Poetry Anthology, p. 198) is a projection of future pride at endurance and participation in the assault on the Anzio beachhead:

> When the M. G.s stop their chatter
> And the cannons stop their roar
> And you're back in dear old Blighty
> In your favourite pub once more;
> When the small talk is all over
> And the war tales start to flow,
> You can stop the lot by telling
> Of the fight at Anzio.

The ballad works as a broadsheet celebration of a contemporary event, in much the same style as J. C. Johnson's 'Tribute to the 11th Division' (Poetry Anthology, p. 137). A more complex use of popular traditions is apparent in 'The 51st Highland Division's Farewell to Sicily' and 'Victory Hoe-Down' (both in Poetry Anthology, pp. 197, 195). Henderson's purpose in these poems is to make a song that celebrates the achievements of military communities without jingoism. This is achieved through his use of Scots vernacular and by an appeal to specifically Scottish traditions of military celebration and lament. 'Victory Hoe-Down' describes the Gordon Highlanders dancing to the tune 'Kate Dalrymple' after the German surrender in Italy. The grotesque description of the men as 'dames fae hell', 'lowpin like a mawkin' is reminiscent of Rosenberg's 'Louse Hunting', but its tone is unambiguously celebratory. The victory is a Scottish victory and the poem remains oppositional within a context of British culture in its refusal to acknowledge any language or culture that might suggest a tradition of English military nationalism. 'Tae hell wi' your oboes', the speaker says, 'Oor pipes/and oor reeds/they supply a' oor needs'. The defeat of Germany is imagined in terms taken directly from Scots ballads ('we'll ding doon Kesselring tae dee in the dykeside'), affirming a continuity of Scottish military prowess and cultural interpretation.

'The 51st Highland Division's Farewell to Sicily' is an ambivalent lament and celebration, marking the withdrawal of a Highland division from Sicily. It expresses both nostalgia for home, and the soldiers' regret at leaving the 'shebeens and bothies' of Sicily. As in 'Victory Hoe-Down', Henderson imbues the lyric with the characteristic strangeness of the Scots ballad repertoire. The sky over Messina is 'unco', strange or foreboding, and the deserted rooms are eerie. Sicily is alien, a place of war and destruction, but it can also be celebrated. In the song, its 'chaulmers', 'shebeens and bothies' and its inhabitants are brought within the local experience and local language of the Scots soldiers. As befits the politics of *Ballads of World War II*, it is an international song, marking both cultural differences and connections, and finally integrating the oppositions of war into a statement of commonality. This complex use of popular forms to create a statement of internationalism and anti-militarism is also apparent in Henderson's finest post-war song, 'The Freedom Come-All-Ye' (1960).

Henderson's ballads demonstrate one way in which popular oral traditions persisted and were adapted to the circumstances of the Second World War. The ballads, the soldiers' songs and the working-class poetry of the First World War show significant deviations in source and outlook from the customary literary examples of wartime culture. This is not to argue for the persistence of a radical popular culture wholly untouched by state ideologies. Popular culture, here as elsewhere, is a complex negotiation of sources and influences which necessarily includes the patriotic and militarist rhetoric current in both wars. Nevertheless, the poems and songs discussed here suggest the existence of cultures outside or on the margins of the literary, which both transform and influence the dominant representations of war in both world wars.

4
Politics

Poetry, politics and two world wars

The nineteenth-century military theorist Clausewitz defined war as politics pursued by other means, but the tendency of modern states is to deny political motivation for wars and to project them instead as ethical or racial struggles. Such displacements are not limited to state propaganda departments. As I argued in earlier chapters, the construction of English patriotism and the ethical propaganda of the First World War involved not just politicians and civil servants, but also writers and artists. The place of the literary establishment in this process of the depoliticization of war was examined by Edgell Rickword during the Second World War, and he was perhaps the first critic to assert that war poetry has political as well as ethical implications.

In his essay 'Poetry and Two Wars' (1941) (extract in Prose Anthology, p. 247), Rickword argues that different standards are applied to writing in wartime than to writing in peacetime, and that this change in judgement is political in motivation. He cites the *Times Literary Supplement*'s appeal for writers to deal realistically with the brutalities of war and notes ironically its pre-war approval of writers who produced the very opposite, what Rickword calls 'elegant vapidities and fatuous experiments'. The reason for this apparent change of heart, he argues, is that in wartime the brutalities that such a war literature would describe could be 'laid by the authors [whom the *TLS*] trusted and boosted, to the charge of the external enemy, whereas in peace time they could not but be laid to a home account'. In other words, social realism is authorised by such periodicals as the *TLS* only when there is no risk of it leading to social change in Britain. Rickword's essay insists upon the identification of the economic conditions of war as the economic conditions of a wider social experience. 'War', he writes, 'is the result of the same human will that condemns the people to [a] low and precarious standard of life whether engaged with an external foe or not'.

'Poetry and Two Wars' is an important corrective to a view of war poetry, and indeed war in general, that has persisted since the First World War; namely that the politics of war are fundamentally different to the politics of peace. Rickword argues the opposite. 'To the *TLS* and its circle of readers,' he writes, 'peace and war may be sharply distinguished, but to the majority of the inhabitants, war only accentuates miseries which are part and parcel of their daily lives'. Such a division between the politics of war and peace has consequences for a reading of war poetry. The very term 'war poetry' risks the isolation of the work within the artificial enclosure of the war years, and suggests a kind of writing relevant only to the extraordinary circumstances of war. Such a definition, as Rickword suggests, can only 'sterilise [its] potentially inflammatory content' (Rickword 1978: 159) so that war writing will only be accepted within established culture when that culture is able effectively to combat it. Thus it might be argued that Wilfred Owen became an established poet after the Second World War partly because his work could then be contained within a distant and mythologized context of the First. Owen then becomes an icon of suffering and protest rather than an author of actively political poetry.

In this chapter and the two that follow I want to argue, with Rickword, that war poetry needs to be read as political poetry. In Chapters 5 and 6 I will look at the wider cultural politics of writers like Isaac Rosenberg and Herbert Read, but in this chapter I will concentrate on what have become the central texts of war poetry, the work of Sassoon and Owen, and suggest that we need to understand the development of both poets by reference to traditions of liberal political thought.

Owen, Sassoon and liberalism

In 'Poetry and Two Wars', Rickword discusses the work of Sassoon and praises the 'indignant pity and keen satire' of his war poetry. However, Rickword also notes Sassoon's failure to maintain the same qualities in his post-war poetry, something he attributes to a lack of political imagination. Sassoon remains the archetypal poet of protest, but, as Rickword suggests, his poetry and his famous statement of 'wilful disobedience' in resigning his commission (Sassoon 1937: 496) are parts of very unstable personal and political experiences which go beyond simple opposition to war. These include not only his brief conversion to socialism after the war and his founding role in the Peace Pledge Union (an influential pacifist organization of the 1930s), but also his return to active service after his protest and his reversion to nationalistic rhetoric in his poetry of the Second World War (for an account of the immediate post-war period see Sassoon 1945, 1981). Sassoon's First World War satires need to be considered alongside his later war poems like 'Silent Service', dated 1940:

> Now, multifold, let Britain's patient power
> Be proven within us for the world to see.
> None are exempt from service in this hour
> And vanquished in ourselves we dare not be.

The diction of 'service' and vanquishing, the elaborate syntax, and the appeal to national unity are precisely the kind of writing that Sassoon's *Counter-Attack* (1918) rejected. The return to such rhetoric is not just a sign of a waning of youthful radicalism, though; it has important implications for an understanding of Sassoon's and Owen's political positions during the First World War.

Sassoon's protest was startling, though not unique (the pacifist Max Plowman also resigned his commission in 1917, and the Scottish Marxist John MacLean had led a campaign against the war from the outset). What made it so potent was his own social position as a member of the landed gentry and his reputation as a gallant officer. Sassoon's change from an unthinkingly patriotic 'fox-hunting man' to a critic of the senseless pursuit of victory at any cost came to represent the drastic consequences of the war for the English social system and the change of mood from patriotism to what C. E. Montague termed 'disenchantment'. However, care needs to be taken in defining the political implications of this change. Sassoon's statement of 'wilful defiance of military authority' is not a protest against war as such, but is a carefully-worded attack on the specific objectives of the latter part of the war:

> I believe that this War, upon which I entered as a war of defence and liberation, has now become a war of aggression and conquest ... I am not protesting about the conduct of the war, but against the political errors and insincerities for which the fighting men are being sacrificed.
>
> (Sassoon 1937: 496)

Such scepticism about the motivation of war was not new, although, in Sassoon's case, the circumstances of its expression were undoubtedly dramatic. In making his criticism of the 'errors and insincerities' of those in command Sassoon is drawing upon a well-established tradition of liberal thought which goes back to the end of the eighteenth century.

Tom Paine, participant in both the American and French revolutions, was the first radical to analyse a 'war system' of political expediency in *The Rights of Man* (1791), arguing that 'the animosity which Nations reciprocally entertain is nothing more than what the policy of their governments excites to keep up the spirit of the system' (cited in Howard 1978: 29–30). The utilitarian philosopher Jeremy Bentham in his *Plan for a Universal and Perpetual Peace* (1798) added colonialism, arms manufacture and secret diplomacy to Paine's analysis of the causes of war and in the middle of the nineteenth century John Stuart Mill argued that bellicose nationalism was a mechanism for the suppression of individual liberty. Mill's argument was taken up by the most immediate liberal influence upon Sassoon, the philosopher and mathematician Bertrand Russell, who maintained a consistent opposition to the First World War.

Russell, with Norman Angell, was the most prominent liberal intellectual to argue against the war. Unlike Angell, though, Russell conducted a vigorous political campaign. He worked for the anti-war pressure group the Union of Democratic Control and, after the passing of the Conscription Act of 1916, for the No Conscription Fellowship (NCF). He was editor of the NCF magazine and a regular speaker at public meetings. Russell's pre-war eminence as a philosopher and mathematician made his opposition to the war a potential embarrassment for the government, and his passport was withdrawn to prevent him lecturing in the USA. He was also dismissed from his post at Trinity College, Cambridge and imprisoned for writing an article adjudged 'insulting to an ally'.

Extracts from one of Russell's numerous wartime publications are included in the Prose Anthology, and they suggest both the intellectual and stylistic verve of his writing of the period, and the strong liberal tradition that lies behind it. *Principles of Social Reconstruction* (1916) was read by Sassoon, and probably by Owen (see Hibberd 1986: 132), and its strategy of demystifying war is one that is comparable to the approach of both poets in at least part of their work. Russell deliberately includes war within a discussion of other social issues such as education, marriage and religion, implying, in the tradition of nineteenth-century liberalism, that even a 'Great' war must be understood as part of the social and political life of nations rather than as some moral or metaphysical imperative. The chapter 'War as an Institution', from which the extracts are taken, argues provocatively that 'war is one of the permanent institutions of all free communities, just as Parliament is one of our permanent institutions'

(Russell 1916: 77). It is maintained as such, Russell suggests, through the desire of states to accrue wealth and power, and by the complicity of citizens motivated by personal desire for activity and development beyond the constraints of waged labour. This powerful alliance of political ambition and human impulse, Russell argues, makes war endemic in human society despite its terrible effects.

Russell's analysis of the manipulation of individuals by state organizations is strikingly similar to the views presented in Sassoon's satires on the evasion of moral responsibility by army, church and government (see, for example, 'The General', '"They"' and 'Fight to a Finish' in Sassoon 1983), and both the works of both writers can be seen as part of a long tradition of liberal scepticism about the nature and conduct of war. As I have suggested, some of the most eminent liberal theorists of the nineteenth-century contributed to this tradition, and it is important to see that the arguments expressed by Sassoon and Russell were not unique to the First World War. Indeed, the work of both men has its immediate reference points in an ideological debate that took place in the heart of the liberal establishment in the years leading up to the First World War (for a detailed study of liberalism and war see Howard 1978).

The period between 1900 and 1914, as I argued in Chapter 2, was a time of national uncertainty and this found direct political expression in a rift between liberal supporters and opponents of imperialism and rearmament. The former faction argued for the need to match German economic and military power and expansionist ambitions, while the latter gained impetus from the setbacks of the Boer War, and theoretical and popular support from Norman Angell's book *The Great Illusion* (originally published in 1909 as *Europe's Optical Illusion*) which argued that the capitalist 'has no country, and ... knows that arms and conquests and juggling with frontiers serve no ends of his and may very well defeat them' (cited in Howard 1978: 70).

The political arguments about nationalism, war and rearmament were also pursued in poetry. In 1913 Sir Alfred Noyes, who is normally represented in accounts of First World War writing as a purveyor of simplistic militarism and unqualified patriotism, published *The Wine Press*, a long narrative poem which reveals a very different political position. It bears an ironic dedication to 'those who believe that Peace is the corrupter of nations', and presents a passionate argument against the insincerity of political leaders who encourage war for nationalist principles. The poem demystifies nationalist wars through a sombre story of betrayal and death in the Balkans, and its message is summed up in the ironic question of a wise peasant to the naïve hero: 'Why don't you understand/What war is? For a port to export prunes,/For Christ, my boy, and for the Fatherland' (Noyes 1920: 245).

The poetry of *The Wine Press* may not be as powerful or direct as that of Sassoon's first collection *Counter-Attack*, but their politics are very similar. Both Sassoon and Noyes are sceptical of the motivation and purpose of war, and both describe the sufferings of individuals which result from the cynicism and misconduct of those in power. The example of Noyes, though, leads back to Edgell Rickword's argument about the political limitations of Sassoon's stance. Despite the faultless liberal credentials of *The Wine Press*, Noyes became in both world wars a die-hard patriot and military enthusiast, and a persistent author of exhort-atory odes and lyrics recalling England's military past and asserting the morality of her position. His is a mirror image of Sassoon's progress during the First World War from unthinking patriot to principled objector, and a model for his subsequent revocation of radicalism and return to 'Silent Service'. Both men's change of heart and change of language can be seen as part of the crisis of liberal values brought to a head by the First World War when the issue was not only that of imperialism versus anti-imperialism, but also concerned fundamental questions of British national and social identity.

The philosophy of classic liberalism argued that old social structures were, in the words of the liberal theorist L. T. Hobhouse writing in 1911, 'slowly but surely giving place to the new fabric of the civic State' (Hobhouse 1974: 9). Such a state would develop the liberal principles of individual liberty and responsibility, free trade, and internationalism, and would therefore remove the underlying causes of war as defined by Paine, Bentham and Mill. But liberalism also had a commitment to the principles of national autonomy and, since the French Revolution, it had gained much of its emotional power from the support of nationalist liberation struggles in Europe and beyond. The libertarian and anti-war commitments of liberalism were brought into sharp conflict with the political implications of support for the principle of national self-determination when Germany invaded Belgium, and Britain entered the First World War.

Nationalism had always been a thorny issue for liberals because of its tendency to elevate emotional allegiances over rational thought. The results of such a conflict can be seen in the case of Alfred Noyes. His analysis of war's origins in commercial rivalry and the competing interests of national élites, expressed in *The Wine Press* in 1913, was overridden by his patriotism only a year later. The political theory that was relevant to a remote Balkan state could not be applied to Britain and her involvement in commercial and imperial competition. Sassoon, on the other hand, moved from unthinking patriotism to an emphasis on the libertarian aspect of liberalism, and his war poetry is informed by an outrage against individual suffering in the interests of state power. The concern for the individual soldier in poems like 'Counter-Attack' and 'Suicide in the Trenches' is set beside a perception of the betrayal of the individual by the state and its representatives. In poems like 'The General', 'Fight to a Finish', 'Blighters' and 'Base Details', Sassoon pursues the same liberal argument as Noyes in *The Wine Press*: the failure of political and military élites to fulfil their duty to the individuals under their command leads to the senseless destruction of those individuals. Such poems are not strictly 'anti-war' poems at all; rather, they are political poems which criticize the betrayal of the individual by the state, and the state's dishonesty in the representation of its motives for war, both issues emphasized by Russell's essay discussed earlier.

Sassoon's gradual renunciation of radical politics after the war and his apparently incongruous adoption of a nationalist rhetoric during the Second World War are part of the limitations and contradictions of the liberalism of the early years of the century. The inability of liberal politics to reconcile conflicting views of state interests and individual freedoms during the unprecedented crisis of the First World War forced Sassoon to develop his radical position, and led Russell to flirt with socialist and other collectivist theories immediately after the war. But the ambivalent pull of nationalism, which led Alfred Noyes to celebrate the nationalist aggression that he had deplored a year earlier, led to a similar abandonment of political radicalism by Sassoon when the critical moment had passed. Russell himself commented on Sassoon that he 'sees war, not peace, from the point of view of the proletariat' (Russell 1968: 89). In other words, Sassoon was only able to develop a radical position under exceptional circumstances and, as it were, by instinct rather than by political analysis. Like Rickword, Russell points to the reactionary potential in a separation of the conditions of war and peace, and implies the need for a radical vision which could come to terms with the theoretical contradictions of liberalism.

Sassoon's protégé Wilfred Owen went further than his mentor in his engagement with these political complexities. Owen's work, like that of Sassoon, is usually read as an expression of humanitarian protest rather than of specifically political concerns. However, in his later poetry there is an ambitious attempt to consider the effect of war in terms of the liberal tradition outlined above. In developing such a critique, he breaks away from the ideology which, as Rickword suggests, finally held Sassoon within the very systems of thought and politics that his work seems to oppose. Whereas Sassoon's poetry criticizes the conduct of social systems, Owen's poetry demonstrates and analyses their utter collapse.

I have already discussed the recasting of national identity in Owen's 'Smile, Smile, Smile' in Chapter 2; in other poems he emphasizes not only the suffering of the soldiers, but also their hopeless isolation from society itself. In 'Exposure' (Owen 1983: 185–6) the soldiers are made social outcasts by their suffering, and are unable to communicate with the society on whose behalf they are supposed to be fighting ('Shutters and doors all closed; on us the doors are closed'). 'Insensibility' (Poetry Anthology, p. 128) is a dark rewriting of liberal principles of individual moral responsibility. It acknowledges only the negative values of survival – lack of compassion, lack of thought, lack of imagination and so on. The dystopia of war demands a new political vision seen through the 'blunt and lashless eyes' of the survivor. Such a vision affirms the failure of traditional systems of social and ethical values. The 'kind old sun' does not fulfil its pastoral duty to wake the dead soldier in 'Futility' (Poetry Anthology, p. 133); the balance of civic, sexual, and generational relationships breaks down constantly, as in 'The Send-Off', 'Disabled' and 'Arms and the Boy'. Pity, so often seen as the humanist centre of Owen's writing, is also a despairing political gesture, the only possibility of human understanding to set against the anti-humanist apocalypse described in 'Spring Offensive' (Poetry Anthology, p. 133). In that poem Owen suggests the end of a world of humanist values. Replacing the values that are represented by reciprocity and pity are ambivalent and amoral judgements of violence – 'superhuman inhumanities' and 'immemorial shames'. Such new 'values' are shown to be the only political and psychological inheritance of the survivors of the war (for further discussion of 'Spring Offensive' see Chapter 7).

'Strange Meeting' (Poetry Anthology, p. 130) is Owen's most ambitious political poem. It makes explicit the debate between the liberal philosophy of social development and an apocalyptic vision of war by presenting a dialogue between the naïve speaker and the dead enemy (in an earlier draft, a 'German conscript'). The poet is forced to abandon the optimism with which he greets the dead man ('"Strange friend," I said, "here is no cause to mourn"') and to recognize his own violent complicity in the ruin of such idealism. The enemy forces him to accept that the idealistic English 'war poet' is also the anonymous killer of other war poets and idealists. Any hope for improvement is denied by the dead man's elegy and by his knowledge that the individual will be unable to affect the destructive course of national history: 'None will break ranks, though nations trek from progress'. The 'trek' of nations would normally imply a movement forward, but in Owen's poem all movement is regressive; the nations move away from the liberal ideal of perfectibility. Like the sharers of secret knowledge in 'Smile, Smile, Smile', the secret nation of the dead in 'Strange Meeting' is powerless to intervene in the apocalyptic future. Their warnings, like the warnings of the poet in the Preface Owen drafted for his poems perhaps, are fated to be ignored (Owen 1983: 535–6).

The persistent syntactic ambiguity of the poem, though maybe in part an indication of its lack of revision, is also linked to the political renunciation of the dead soldier. The 'hope' of the poet exists in conjunction with his alter ego's despair, 'Whatever hope is yours/Was my life also', a contrast in tense that is intensified later in the lines, 'And of my weeping something had been left/Which must die now'. Presumably we must read the first line to mean 'something would have been left if it was not for the war that has killed me', but the grammar of the following line denies this. It contains an imperative, something *must* die now. This presupposes the existence of the very quality that the previous line had denied and so sharpens the acute sense of the loss of possibility and potential in the enemy's speech. Though he knows that the war will bring only a 'trek from progress', the knowledge is hard-won and barely accepted by the dead man. There is a similar ambiguity in the use of the verb 'would'. In 'I would go up and wash' it seems to mean 'I would like to' or 'I intend to', still admitting the possibility of the redemption: 'Then when much blood had clogged their chariot-wheels,/I would go up and wash them from sweet wells'. But two lines later such hopes are clearly in the past: 'I would have poured my spirit without stint', implying that the possibility is no longer there. The poignancy of 'Strange Meeting' lies in this still raw argument between idealism and the realization of its destruction in the war. Although the conflict is not formally resolved, the poem's gesture of individual compassion ('I am the enemy you killed, my friend', the enemy redefined as friend) is the wisdom of the dead rather than a philosphy for the living. Like 'Spring Offensive', 'Strange Meeting' offers no vision beyond the sense of the apocalyptic consequences of the First World War.

The influence of Owen's critique of liberal values is apparent in the work of his contemporary, Herbert Read, who survived the First World War and maintained an active political radicalism through to the Second (see Chapter 5). Read's 'To a Conscript of 1940' (Poetry Anthology, p. 171) is a recasting of 'Strange Meeting' in the context of the later war. The dialogue seems at first to be between the poet and the conscript of the title. As the poem progresses, however, the soldier is revealed as one of the First World War dead delivering a message to the conscripts of another war. Owen's prophesy of a future where 'men will go content with what we spoiled/Or, discontent, boil bloody, and be spilled' has been fulfilled, and the veteran records the grim politics of the inter-war years in which the rhetoric of wartime nationalism was betrayed by the unchanged reality of peacetime capitalism:

> The world was not renewed.
> There was hope in the homestead and anger in the streets
> But the old world was restored and we returned
> To the dreary field and workshop, and the immemorial feud
>
> Of rich and poor.

For Read, as for Rickword in the essay referred to above, the First World War merely perpetuated the destructive political and economic conditions that caused it. The post-war failure to change those conditions led to the later civil and military conflicts that marked the 1930s and culminated in the Second World War. Read echoes the rhythms of Owen's metaphor of mental suffering in 'Strange Meeting', 'Foreheads of men have bled where no wounds were', in his openly political statement of this failure: 'Power was retained where power had been misused'. This is men being 'content with what we spoiled', and for the Read of the Second World War, as for Owen's German conscript in the First, the only possible attitude in such circumstances is 'to fight without hope':

> if you can go
> Knowing that there is no reward, no certain use
> In all your sacrifice, then honour is reprieved.

A similar theme is developed in Read's 'Ode Written During the Battle of Dunkirk, May, 1940'. In this poem Read sees the post-1918 world as returning to the illusions of liberalism,

> Feeling that our little house-boat was safe
> until the last lock was reached.
> Another twenty years
> would see us home.

This can be understood in terms of the psychological need to 'forget/ sights the mind cannot accommodate', but the result of such forgetting is once again the apocalyptic defeat of the individual and of liberal idealism by the system of war that liberal capitalism was unable to reform:

> But we who have put our faith
> in the goodness of man
> and now see man's image debas'd
> lower than the wolf or the hog –
>
> Where can we turn for consolation?

In the poetry of Sassoon, Owen and Read the basic ideas of liberal philosophy – historical progress, civic responsibility, social and individual perfectibility – are all questioned. The poems that I have discussed engage in a debate with the main assumptions of the dominant political ideology of the pre-First World War period. Sassoon's poetry is an outraged statement against the way that civic and political responsibilities were unfulfilled during the war. Owen's poetry provides a more searching examination of the failure of the philosophy of progress and social betterment, and Herbert Read, following Owen, confirms the political pessimism of poems like 'Strange Meeting' from the standpoint of the Second World War.

The work of Herbert Read suggests another aspect of the politics of war poetry. From his earliest publications, Read maintained an active interest in social and political matters, but his reputation rests largely on the poem 'The End of a War'. In many ways this is an uncharacteristic piece, without the overt politics of other First World War poems like 'My Company' (extract in Poetry Anthology, p. 170) and 'The Execution of Cornelius Vane', and the Second World War poems discussed above. That 'The End of a War' is Read's best-known poem has little to do with its innate quality. His marginalization is largely a result of the perceived eccentricity of Read's cultural and political positions. In the next chapter I will consider Read's 'eccentricities' in order to suggest that they form part of a little-discussed but influential tradition of provincial political and social thought. This marginal tradition can be linked with other traditions represented by poets in the anthology, such as that of Rosenberg's Jewish background, and the Gaelic and Scots cultures of Sorley MacLean and Hamish Henderson.

5
British Cultures I: Provincial
Intellectuals and Jewish Radicals

So far I have examined the effect of war on two of the dominant ideologies of the first half of the century, Englishness and liberalism. I suggested that the wars brought about a more complex change in these ways of thinking than a straightforward movement from patriotism to disillusionment. The poetry of Owen, Sassoon, Gurney and Jones did not reject ideas of Englishness and liberal politics, but recast them to meet the changing circumstances of the time. In this chapter I will start from a different premise: that the dominance of an English perspective in and upon war poetry has obscured the variety of cultural and political perspectives in the texts themselves. My intention is to show that war poetry is defined by these apparently marginal cultures just as much as by the ideologies of Englishness. As the work of the Ilkeston poets suggests, there exist powerful cultural influences outside the norms of the standard war poetry anthologies.

There are, of course, many non-English or non-metropolitan traditions within British writing, and many of these cultures made a significant contribution to the literature of war. I will concentrate on two distinct areas, each represented by two different kinds of writing. In this chapter I will look at the influence of 'marginal' English intellectual traditions on the work of Herbert Read and Isaac Rosenberg. In Chapter 6 I will examine the war poetry of two non-English cultures: the Gaelic and Scots traditions in the work of Sorley MacLean and Hamish Henderson, and the effects of emigration on writers stationed in North Africa during the Second World War.

Herbert Read's provincial radicalism

If ideas of Englishness, as they developed at the turn of the century, were rooted in the images of Southern England, then the idea of an English intellectual tradition in the same period was rooted in London. London was the unchallenged centre of literary and artistic life and remained so even for the expatriate modernist writers like Pound and Eliot who made London their base during and after the First World War. However, beyond the border of the Thames Valley, there emerged in the years before the war strong intellectual traditions which came to exert a crucial influence both upon war poetry and modernist writing. The work of Herbert Read, a poet, political theorist and aesthetician is a testament to this non-metropolitan culture. Read was born in Yorkshire and was a product of the lively cultural life of Leeds. His poem 'My Company', based on his wartime experience, and two political essays, one from the First and one from the Second World War (all represented by extracts in the Anthologies, pp. 170, 223–6), suggest the character of these non-metropolitan traditions which owe little to the dominant ideologies of Englishness and liberalism discussed earlier.

'My Company' is, in one way, an example of a mode of writing that began in the First World War and reappeared in the Second. It is characterized by an officer attempting to express his feelings of emotional attachment to the men he commands. In Read's poem, and in other examples of this kind of writing, such as Owen's 'Greater Love' and, from the Second World War, Bernard Gutteridge's 'My Platoon' and F. T. Prince's 'Soldiers Bathing', the officer recognizes the social difference between himself and his men, even as he affirms his closeness to them. The very title 'My Company' is at once affectionate and expressive of the 'pride of leadership' that establishes the officer's distance from his men. The argument of the poem is that there is the possibility of breaking down this barrier and establishing a powerful human relationship within the constraints of military authority. Read's metaphor for this process is erotic, as it is in the other poems mentioned earlier:

> You became
> In many acts and quiet observances
> A body and a soul, entire.
>
> I cannot tell
> What time your life became mine ...

The officer falls in love with his men and at the end of the first section the poem looks forward to the end of the war as to the end of an affair: 'I know that I'll wander with a cry:/"O beautiful men, O men I loved,/O whither are you gone, my company?"'

Accounts of erotic bonding are common in war writing (see Fussell

1975: 270–309 and Chapter 7), but in Read's poem, unlike those by Owen, Gutteridge and Prince, this is also a political bonding. The politics of the poem are analogous to those expressed in Read's essay, 'Sorel, Marx, and the War', written at the same time as 'My Company' (extract in Prose Anthology, p. 170). In the essay he argues that two results of the war would be a growth in the self-assurance of middle-class officers and an increased sense of 'the value of organisation ... of brotherhood in arms' amongst the proletariat. These realignments of class are also celebrated in 'My Company' by the assertion of human solidarity in the company ('we've fought together/Compact, unanimous') and by the transformation of the poet through his contact with 'his' men. The poet is said to be 'absorbed' by the ordinary soldiers, but he is also personally liberated into an ecstatic 'giant attitude and godlike mood' in the final section (not included in this Anthology). This simultaneous absorption and self-assertion is at the heart of the ambiguous politics of the poem. In one sense, 'My Company' argues the same case as Edgell Rickword in his essay 'Poetry and Two Wars'. Read, like Sassoon in Rickword's interpretation, can speak out because he has been 'stimulated by his contact with the masses in uniform'. However, the result of this stimulation is not the 'indignant pity and keen satire' that Rickword defines as the political edge of Sassoon's wartime experience. The exultation described in the final stanza of Read's poem owes nothing to Marx and everything to the language and ideas of the German philosopher Nietzsche whose work exerted an enormous influence on the *New Age*, the journal in which the essay first appeared, and on its editor A. R. Orage. It is Nietzsche's anti-democratic individualism that informs the later parts of Read's poem.

In one of Nietzsche's fables of spiritual growth, summarized by Orage in his *Nietzsche in Outline and Aphorism* (1907), there is a description of a change of identity very similar to that in the final part of 'My Company':

> The time arrives sooner or later to every man
> of spirit, overburdened with conscious responsibility
> and charged with duty, to ask, Why should I bear this
> load? ... Gross dereliction of 'duty' and ecstatic
> repudiation of responsibility are implied in this sudden
> frenzy, this birth-throe of a new spirit.
>
> (Orage 1907: 153)

In Read's poem this becomes:

> I can assume
> A giant attitude and godlike mood,
> And then detachedly regard
> All riots, conflicts and collisions ...
>
> From my giant attitude,
> In godlike mood,
> I laugh till space is filled
> With hellish merriment.

Here the poet rises above the men in a state of ecstatic separation from the material reality of the war. The final stage of Nietzsche's fable has man going beyond the will to serve or will to command. 'All in him is instinctive ... his duty is to be', Orage writes (p. 157), and at the end of 'My Company' the officer also abandons his 'will to command' in order to meet a 'shared doom' with his men.

Read's war experience is expressed in the language and ideas of two opposing traditions. The politics of the Nietzschean poem are seemingly irreconcilable with those of the essay which is, as far as I know, a unique example of a Marxist analysis of the war published by a serving soldier. In spite of the insight into cross-class experiences revealed there, the essay's main argument is that the necessary conditions for revolution on a Marxist model are being defused by a state willing to mediate between capital and labour. The state in wartime, Read suggests, both takes responsibility for the management of capital and persuades the leaders of the working class (particularly the trade union movement) to co-operate in the war effort, rendering impotent the forces for potential revolutionary change. The status quo is thus preserved. It is a sober demystification of the politics of war, and a warning about the consequences for working-class politics of the development of state influence in wartime. 'My Company', on the other hand, uses the language of mysticism to describe the transcendence of social and class divisions between officer and men.

The contradiction in Read's expression of war experience is an important one, I believe. It suggests, once again, that war writing is both an intellectual and an experiential pursuit; the political analysis stands alongside an expression of intense experience with seemingly very different implications. But that combination is not the only reason for the contradictory intellectual commitments that are revealed in the poem and the essay. In using both Nietzsche *and* Marx to interpret his experience of the war, Read is drawing upon a significant, though neglected, line of provincial political and cultural radicalism. Its most influential representative was A. R. Orage, the author of the book on Nietzsche referred to earlier.

Orage, like Read, came from Yorkshire. In 1900 he founded the Leeds Art Club, a forum for the discussion of issues related to modern art which Read began to attend in 1913 (for a detailed account of the activities of the club see Steele 1990). Orage had left for London in 1905, but his influence on what one hostile critic has called 'lower-middle-class provincial intellectuals' (Hynes 1972: 40) was still strong. It was maintained through the journal the *New Age* which Orage edited from 1907 to 1922, and which had a wide circulation, particularly in the arts clubs and reading rooms of the industrial Midlands and North (D. H. Lawrence read it as a young man in Eastwood, for example). The *New Age* reflected the eclectic political and intellectual interests of Orage. At various times it espoused syndicalism (a militant trade unionism organized through local, non-centralized activities), the philosophy of Nietzsche, the economic theory of Social Credit and the mystical philosophies of the emigré Russians Ouspensky and Gurdjieff. Orage also operated a catholic editorial policy and published writers as diverse as Arnold Bennett, Ezra Pound, Hilaire Belloc and T. E. Hulme. If the *New Age* was, in Hynes's phrase, a 'farraginous chronicle' (Hynes 1972: 40), it nonetheless reflected the turbulent state of British intellectual and political life more accurately than any other journal of the period.

As I have argued in earlier chapters, the complexity of so much of the political thought that lies behind war poetry has tended to be disguised by a retrospective simplification of its politics to pro- or anti-war attitudes. The reality was far more complex. The intellectual experiments of Read and Orage took place not only in the context of a provincial opposition to the norms of Georgian metropolitanism, but also in response to developments in European thought. Read's points of reference – Nietzsche, Marx and Georges Sorel – are not English, yet the obsession with English identity and self-representation brought about by the war, and the anglocentric critical accounts of writers like Owen and Sassoon, obscure any link between war writing and non-English sources, save perhaps in Owen's case Henri Barbusse's novel *Le Feu*. An initial distance from the centrifugal power of English metropolitan culture allowed Orage and Read to experiment with ideas that were largely unavailable or unattractive to writers who came from the

English public school system or were absorbed in metropolitan literary journalism. However, the eclecticism, even quirkiness, of the intellectual allegiances of Read and Orage are not just signs of provincial eccentricity. A consideration of Read's work, both during and after the war, restores a sense of the full variety of the cultural debate in England at this time. I will illustrate this by brief reference to two of Read's interests: the ideas of Georges Sorel and the guild socialist movement.

Georges Sorel was a French syndicalist and Marxist theorist, but his major work, *Réflexions sur la Violence* (*Reflections on Violence*) (1908), also attracted writers with other political interests. It was translated into English by T. E. Hulme, the anti-democratic, anti-Marxist militarist who engaged in a wartime controversy with Bertrand Russell (Sorel 1916). Hulme was a regular contributor to the *New Age* and his introduction to the translation of *Réflexions sur la Violence* appeared in the magazine in October 1915, eight months before Read's essay. Hulme's interest in Sorel sprang from the latter's emphasis on the importance of violence and discipline within a revolutionary movement. For Hulme, this was an aesthetic, rather than a Marxist, argument. It became part of his own modernist concern with art as an energetic, disciplined activity, something which also determined his initially positive attitude to the war (Hulme's attraction to war as a version of modernist aesthetics is also apparent in some of the writings and painting of his friends and fellow modernists Wyndham Lewis and C. R. W. Nevinson, as well as members of the European avant-garde such as the Italian Futurist Emilio Marinetti).

While Read shared Hulme's modernist allegiances (he edited a posthumous selection of Hulme's work [Hulme 1924]), his use of Sorel's ideas is quite different. In 'Sorel, Marx, and the War' Sorel's 'mythology' of violent collective action allows Read to interpret his own experience of the war as part of a positive preparation for a post-war revolution. It also allows him to include the anti-democratic, anti-humanist ideas of Nietzsche within a theory of war without jeopardizing his own libertarian commitments. The growth of individual self-confidence in the middle-class and the disciplined violence inculcated into proletarian soldiers (both themes of 'My Company') are seen as contributing to a 'new realisation of heroic values', a coming together of the individual and the mass in the cause of social justice. In a late essay, Read himself identifies the sources of his political beliefs in the experience of the war:

> Fidelity is the word I need to describe the simple idea that was revealed to me in the First World War – the fidelity of one man to another, in circumstances of common danger, the fidelity of all men to one another and to the group as a whole.
>
> (Read 1968: 41)

This simple idea found political expression for Read in guild socialism and the anarchism of Peter Kropotkin.

Like the *New Age*, guild socialism was a product of provincial radicalism. A. J. Penty, with Orage, a co-founder of the Leeds Art Club, developed a programme for a social order rooted in a democracy of the workplace. Guild socialism followed nineteenth-century thinkers like Morris and Ruskin in their advocacy of a return to the values of craftsmanship in place of mass production, and small-scale guilds or communities of workers instead of impersonal, large-scale industrialization. Unlike Sorel's syndicalism, which was never influential in Britain outside the South Wales coalfields and Clydeside, guild socialism attracted a number of influential adherants in the years around the First World War. These included the historian G. D. H. Cole, the socialist theorist R. H. Tawney, George Lansbury, later to be the leader of the Labour Party, and Bertrand Russell, the philosopher and anti-war activist. Its appeal for Read and many other followers lay in its mixture of nostalgia for a rural ideal of craft-based industry and a radical critique of contemporary social conditions. In this it draws upon some of the politically ambivalent aspects of pre-First-World-War definitions of Englishness discussed in Chapter 2 (for a more detailed account of guild socialism see Glass 1966; Webb 1976).

The ideas of guild socialism and the related social theories of the anarchist Peter Kropotkin allowed Read to develop a political theory and poetic practice that could acknowledge the devastations of war and yet could use the communal experience of war as a model for reorganizing society. The emotional bonding of the military unit described in 'My Company' is the source for Read's political ideal which he also saw expressed in Kropotkin's book *Mutual Aid* (Read 1968: 41). In an introduction to Kropotkin's work written during the Second World War, Read celebrates a philosophy that is 'libertarian, federative, devolving the widest possible autonomy to each nation, each region, and each commune – indeed to each individual' (Kropotkin 1942: 11), a summary of the relationship of officer and men described in 'My Company'.

Such idealism did not belong to Read alone. It motivated several different attempts to set up artistic and political communities during the 1920s and the Second World War, including his friend Eric Gill's communities at Ditchling and Capel-y-ffin, where David Jones worked in the 1920s, and pacifist farming communes in the Second World War (see MacCarthy 1989; Middleton Murry 1952; Duncan 1944). Read's sense of the apocalyptic ending of political and industrial life, expressed in First World War poems such as 'The Happy Warrior' and 'The Execution of Cornelius Vane', and reaffirmed in the Second World War in 'To a Conscript of 1940' (see discussion in Chapter 4) and many polemical prose pieces, is offset by possibilities for the reconstruction of a new kind of society. The positive use of the experience and conditions of war that was a theme of 'Sorel, Marx, and the War' thus becomes an important part of Read's thought during the Second World War.

In 'To Hell with Culture', a pamphlet originally published in 1941 (see extract in Prose Anthology, pp. 225–6), Read celebrates the destruction brought by air raids:

> Let us celebrate the democratic revolution with the biggest holocaust in the history of the world. When Hitler has finished bombing our cities, let the demolition squads complete the good work. Then let us go out into the wide open spaces and build anew.

Read's post-apocalyptic vision is that of a guild-socialist society with 'traffic flowing freely through … leafy avenues' and 'factories and workshops where natural conditions of supply make their location most convenient'. After the Second World War, Read argued, the opportunity for social change that he had anticipated in his poetry and prose of the First World War was available once more. As in 'My Company' and 'Sorel, Marx, and the War' it is a vision informed by both the experience of war and the political experiments of the Leeds Arts Club and the *New Age*.

The work of Herbert Read suggests the persistence of marginal political and cultural traditions within the writing of the two wars. The contradictions and ambivalences of such traditions reflect the political uncertainties of the period and in this way form part of wider political debates that were traced in Chapter 4. There are similarly powerful traditions lying behind the work of another major poet of the First World War, Isaac Rosenberg. In the next section I will consider the influence of Jewish culture and politics on Rosenberg and on an older writer from the East End of London, Israel Zangwill.

Isaac Rosenberg, Israel Zangwill and Jewish culture

Two Jewish writers from London's East End provide further examples of the diversity of political and cultural traditions in British writing during the First World War. Israel Zangwill and Isaac Rosenberg came from different generations of Jewish immigrants, but their work reflects a common sense of the contradictory political demands placed upon a minority culture in the first great nationalist war.

Israel Zangwill became the leading Jewish writer in English of the late nineteenth and early twentieth centuries. His stories of East End life, such as *Children of the Ghetto* (1892), were popular with non-Jewish audiences and he became part of the London literary establishment of the time. His status was acknowledged by an invitation to the meeting of leading literary figures at Wellington House in 1914 to co-ordinate a government-led propaganda policy (see Wright 1978). However, Zangwill's political beliefs were very different to those of the others who attended the Wellington House conference. He was a Zionist, a socialist and a feminist, and he maintained his contacts with radical groups throughout the war. His Jewishness and his political sympathies necessarily complicated his response to the war (for Zangwill's biography see Leftwich 1957).

Zangwill's work represents a difficult alliance of marginal and mainstream cultures, and in much of his writing of the First World War there is a sense of strain in his support for the British cause. In the essay 'Jewish Factor in the War and Settlement' (1916) (extract in Prose Anthology, p. 235), Zangwill's Jewish internationalism immediately limits his support for the alliance of which Britain was a member. Russia, until 1917 an ally of Britain, was notoriously anti-Semitic and Zangwill expresses his sympathy with Russian Jews who saw the German army as liberators. He also criticizes the racism of the British army, noting the rejection of Jewish volunteers and the persecution of Jewish soldiers (Isaac Rosenberg's poem 'The Jew' [Poetry Anthology, p. 143] makes a similar point). Zangwill's awareness of the complexity of ethnic and political allegiances in wartime leads to a scepticism concerning the demands of nationalism. His essay 'The Ruined Romantics' (1916) (extracts in Prose Anthology, p. 236) is a devastating attack on the 'public bankruptcy' of romantic militarism, written before the Somme offensive of 1916, yet marked by a grim realism about the mechanical killing, and the disease and the filth that make up the experience of modern war.

Despite his criticisms of official policy and patriotic rhetoric, however, Zangwill also recognizes his responsibilities as an *English* writer. His assertion of a Jewish identity is always offset by a commitment to the structures and codes of English society. In 'The Ruined Romantics', for example, there is an uneasy assumption of English class hierarchies when he mimics the 'labourers in my village', and in the same essay he tells a story about his willingness to extemporize to soldiers about 'national righteousness, … duty, … glory, and how they must shame the Goths by chivalry to their women and children'. The tone of the anecdote is hard to judge. Zangwill seems not to criticize the content of his improvised talk, but rather to turn the irony towards his own Jewishness in the comparison of himself to 'Abraham of old, in the door of a tent'. Throughout his work, he is drawn to the tone and style of the Edwardian 'man of letters' who was so easily co-opted into national service at Wellington House (one of his books was called *An Englishman Looks at the World*). Yet the frequent approving references to the establishment humour of *Punch* magazine sit oddly with the undoubted radicalism of much of the content of his essays. Such contrasts of content and style are indicative of Zangwill's difficult position between a dominant and a marginal culture. He never resolved these conflicts, and his work, with all its contradictions, provides a precise context for the poetry of one of the major writers of the First World War, Isaac Rosenberg. Rosenberg, born thirty years after Zangwill, regarded him as an important medial figure between the East End ghetto and the literary establishment, and sent him his early work for comment (see Rosenberg 1979: 180). Although of a different generation of Jewish immigrants, Rosenberg can be seen to develop the contradictory politics of Zangwill's wartime writing into a forceful political analysis of the experience of Jewish soldiers in an English army.

Rosenberg's father was part of the great wave of Jewish immigration at the end of the nineteenth century. William Fishman has shown that many of the immigrants came from intellectually sophisticated communities in Eastern Europe to be confronted by difficult social and economic conditions and a largely unwelcoming Anglo-Jewish community (Fishman 1975). A radical intellectual and political culture rapidly coalesced, however, particularly in the East End of London. Barnard Rosenberg, Isaac's father, seems to have been at least sympathetic to the radical politics of the time. He fled from Russia to avoid military service, and, it seems, remained a pacifist – Isaac wrote to R. C. Trevelyan in 1916 that 'my people are Tolstoylians and object to my being in khaki' (Rosenberg 1979: 234). Although Rosenberg makes relatively few comments on this radical culture, the ideas which were current in the pre-First-World-War East End had a determining influence on his writing and enabled him to escape some of the political and cultural contradictions of Israel Zangwill's work.

In one of the best accounts of the political and artistic life of the area in which Rosenberg grew up, Rosenberg's friend and fellow-poet Joseph Leftwich emphasizes the influence of Rudolf Rocker's Workers' Friend Club on the young writers and artists of the East End (see Leftwich's 'Introduction' in Rocker 1956). Rocker was a German anarcho-syndicalist who became active in Jewish radical politics at the turn of the century (see Fishman 1975: 229–309). He edited Yiddish newspapers and, in 1906, opened the Workers' Friend Club in Jubilee Street where the Rosenberg family was living at the time. The club was based on libertarian principles of access to knowledge for all, and provided a similar intellectual centre to that of the Leeds Arts Club, discussed above. It was a forum for political discussion, with regular lectures by Rocker himself and by other leading anarchists such as Peter Kropotkin, whose influence on Herbert Read's post-First-World-War work has already been mentioned. There were also productions of plays and talks on literature and music.

Rocker's anarchist politics were influential in the years before the First World War because they drew on the resources of the Jewish community rather than attempting to impose the values of English culture. His emphasis on small collective organizations, religious tolerance, education and the use of Yiddish to unify immigrants from different countries acknowledged the cultural diversity and the aspirations of the community. The political and cultural energy which Rocker generated was relatively short-lived, however. Fishman dates the rise and fall of Jewish radicalism between 1880 and 1914. During the later part of that period, he argues, the same kind of cultural schism that marked Zangwill's work affected the Jewish community as a whole. Second-generation immigrants, like Rosenberg, spoke English rather than Yiddish, and their aspirations went beyond the East End (Rosenberg won a place at the Slade School of Art, for example). Finally, the First World War led to the political fragmentation of East End anarchism when Kropotkin argued in favour of the war and the pacifist Rocker was interned as an enemy alien. The powerful exertion of wartime nationalist forces on a group already moving away from older ways must also have had its effect.

Isaac Rosenberg was at the centre of the movement from a radical, deracinated culture, represented culturally by the Jubilee Street Club and politically by Rocker's anarcho-syndicalism, to a more anglicized version of Jewishness. While his father led the displaced life of an immigrant, moving from city to city in search of work, and maintained his Yiddish language and his radical Tolstoyan politics, his son's ambitions lay in gaining access to British culture and education beyond the informal lectures and discussions of Rocker's club. In the early poems and letters he is eager to present an *English* literary sensibility and there is no hint of an awareness of the lively Yiddish tradition of poetry that Rocker encouraged in his newspapers and to which his friend Joseph Leftwich contributed. His literary references are to Shelley, Keats, Donne and Rossetti, and the contemporaries for whom he expresses an admiration are those associated with Edward Marsh's Georgian school of English writing, such as Lascelles Abercrombie, Laurence Binyon and Gordon Bottomley. Yet there is an obvious anxiety about his own access to such a culture. In a letter to Zangwill, written around 1910, he writes only half disingenuously of his 'desperate attempts to murder and mutilate King's English beyond all shape of recognition' (Rosenberg 1979: 180). In a later letter he is defensive about his own place in English culture: 'You mustn't forget the circumstances I have been brought up in, the little education I have had. Nobody ever told me what to read, or ever put poetry in my way' (p. 181). This hardly accords with Leftwich's description of the cultural life of the East End, but it indicates Rosenberg's confused relationship with his past and with the English culture he was attempting to assimilate. The early poems also indicate a difficult cultural perspective. 'A Ballad of Whitechapel', dated 1910, is one of the few pieces by Rosenberg which describes his home area, yet that description itself suggests his alienation from the place:

> I watched the gleams
> Of jagged warm lights on shrunk faces pale.
> I heard mad laughter as one hears in dreams,
> Or Hell's harsh lurid tale.
>
> The traffic rolled
> A gliding chaos populous of din ....
>
> And my soul thought,
> 'What fearful land have my steps wandered to?
> God's love is everywhere, but here is naught
> Save love his anger slew'.

What is significant here is the position of the poet. In order to describe Whitechapel he removes himself from the place and pretends to be a visitor in the tradition of middle-class slum voyeurism. It is as though the young Rosenberg has no language to talk about the East End except that of the dominant English poetic mode.

The political consequences of Rosenberg's cultural confusion are evident at the outbreak of war. In a letter to Edward Marsh, a week after war was declared, he writes that he 'despise[s] war and hate[s] war' (p. 205), and in 1915, when he was considering joining the army for financial reasons, this hatred becomes a moral imperative in the manner of his father's 'Tolstoylian' views: 'it is against all my principles of justice ... I would be doing the most criminal thing a man can do' (p. 216). Later, he writes of the 'immorality of joining with no patriotic convictions' (p. 219). These principles and doubts, however, don't find a voice in the poetry that he wrote in response to the war. 'On Receiving News of the War' presents war as a force of purgation in much the same way as Rupert Brooke's idea of 'swimmers into cleanness leaping':

> O! ancient crimson curse!
> Corrode, consume.
> Give back this universe
> Its pristine bloom.

'The Dead Heroes' shows even more clearly how the poetic language available to Rosenberg implicates him in a politics that his stated views deny:

> Flame out, flame out, O Song!
> Star ring to star,
> Strong as our hurt is strong
> Our children are.
>
> Their blood is England's heart;
> By their dead hands
> It is their noble part
> That England stands.

Here Jewish identity and radical politics are suppressed in a poem which celebrates poetry and death in the service of England.

Rosenberg, like Zangwill and like his contemporary Read, had some contact with both the established and avant-garde culture of their day.

During his time at the Slade School of Art, he encountered a talented generation of young British artists, including Mark Gertler (also from the East End), Stanley Spencer and Dora Carrington. He also corresponded regularly with the influential publisher Edward Marsh who moved in the highest political circles as Parliamentary Private Secretary to Winston Churchill (see Chapter 1 for Marsh's relationship with Rupert Brooke). As with Read, the social conflict between background and access to new cultural ideas is reflected in his poetry, and Rosenberg's wartime work is as much a struggle for social and cultural self-definition as a record of military experience. His first major attempt to go beyond the rhetoric of 'On Receiving News of the War' and 'The Dead Heroes' and to find a language to meet the demands of his situation is the poetic drama *Moses*, published at his own expense in May 1916, a fortnight before he left for France.

Moses is not a straightforward rendering of the Biblical story. In the play, Moses is presented as a man isolated between two cultures, the Jewish and the Egyptian. He struggles to find a way to break free from their constraints to 'Some new idea unwalled/To human by-ways, an apocalyptic camp of utterest and ulterior dreaming'. He is a revolutionary who wishes to free not only himself but both cultures to which he owes allegiance; by liberating the Jews from slavery, he also liberates the Egyptian tyrants from their tyranny. For the first time in his poetry, Rosenberg finds a way of representing the conflicts that concern him: his feeling of alienation from the world of the ghetto *and* the world of a ruling élite; his ambivalent identification of the condition of the ghetto with that of an army which shares its 'mud and lice' but is also deeply anti-Semitic; and his problem of finding a language and form that might embrace Jewish and English cultures. The political argument of *Moses* is not clear cut (Moses murders the Egyptian overseer but is arrested at the end of the play), however the impulse is undoubtedly libertarian both in its politics and its aesthetics. 'Egypt was in the way,' says Moses, 'I'll strike it out/With my ways curious and unusual' is an emphatic statement of Rosenberg's sense of his development of a new style and subject-matter.

Writing *Moses* seems to have freed Rosenberg from some of the uncertainties that marked his earlier writing. In a letter to Gordon Bottomley, soon after its publication, he accepts Bottomley's praise with a sharp comment on his earlier vulnerability to the criticism of those with a perceived cultural superiority:

> People are always telling me my work is promising – incomprehensible,
> but promising, and all that sort of thing, my meekness subsides before their
> patronising knowingness.
>
> (Rosenberg 1979: 236)

There is a new confidence in tone and judgement which enables him to
go on in letters of the same period to make adverse judgements on the
work of Rupert Brooke, Edward Marsh's protégé. More significantly,
Moses allowed Rosenberg to go on to write his first major poem about the
war, 'Break of Day in the Trenches' (Poetry Anthology, p. 144).

In this poem the imagery of *Moses* is used to explore the position of the
Jewish soldier in the First World War. The rat, the roots of the poppy in
blood and dust, and the adjectives 'queer' and 'sardonic' are all imported
from the play to the poem, but in the meeting of the mythical world of
Moses and the everyday reality of dawn in the trenches, the voice of the
poem changes from agonized rhetoric to an assured and wry commentary:

> Droll rat, they would shoot you if they knew
> Your cosmopolitan sympathies.
> Now you have touched this English hand
> You will do the same to a German
> Soon, no doubt, if it be your pleasure
> To cross the sleeping green between.
> It seems you inwardly grin as you pass
> Strong eyes, fine limbs, haughty athletes,
> Less chanced than you for life

There is a delicate irony here that has nothing to do with the polemical
edge of Sassoon's and Owen's satires, yet is political nevertheless.
Rosenberg identifies himself as English and in opposition to the Germans, but the force of the poem is in his more problematic identification
with the ultimate marginal creature. The rat, the creature of squalor,
plague and death, is transformed into a boulevardier with sophisticated
'cosmopolitan sympathies'. Rosenberg also transforms himself from
soldier into a wry poseur wearing a flower behind his ear (an image
which should be compared with the jaunty self-portraits of Rosenberg).
In a world of national oppositions only the rat connects the two, and
Rosenberg's grim pleasure in its freedoms is both an acknowledgement
of his own predicament and an imaginative escape. The suggestion of
the common lot of all soldiers is the same as that in 'Strange Meeting',
but the tone of Rosenberg's poem is that of the sardonic outsider. The

'droll' rat survives against the odds, as does the poet, whose sense of imminent death is offset by the frivolous yet defiant gesture of preserving the poppy.

'Louse Hunting' (Poetry Anthology, p. 145) also uses the metaphor of vermin to make a political point. The soldiers who are delousing themselves are transformed into a mob which enacts a grotesque parody of the war. The killing of the lice becomes a monstrous ritual of the destruction of the small by the great:

> See gargantuan hooked fingers
> Pluck in supreme flesh
> To smutch supreme littleness.

Again, there is a measured irony in the poet's involvement in the grim mimicry of the soldiers' own destruction. In both 'Louse Hunting' and 'Break of Day' soldiers are counterposed to vermin, yet the tone and the poise of the voice in each rescue the soldiers from a despairing irony of mass degradation. Each affirms the poem's own ability to transform even the most sordid of situations by a witty sense of the soldiers' commonality.

'Dead Man's Dump' (Poetry Anthology, p. 146) is Rosenberg's most ambitious attempt to use his own conflicts of identity to explore the experience of war. In this poem there is none of the ironic control of 'Break of Day' or 'Louse Hunting'. The alliance with the rat in the former poem becomes a terrible vision of the rat's territory, the no-man's-land between the trenches. Like the speaker in Owen's 'Strange Meeting', the poet hovers between life and death. He is unable to believe in the possibility of his own death ('Our lucky limbs as on ichor fed,/Immortal seeming ever') and yet obsessively describes the vulnerability of the soldiers. The descriptions of the dead are appalled but remote; unlike Owen, Rosenberg admits no possibility of even a poetic dialogue:

> Burnt black by strange decay,
> Their sinister faces lie
> The lid over each eye,
> The grass and coloured clay
> More motion have than they,
> Joined to the great sunk silences.

The emphasis is on the utter difference of the living and the dead, with the poet acknowledging his own complicity in the destruction of the final stanza, as the dying man's hope of rescue by the limber is denied:

> So we crashed round the bend,
> We heard his weak scream,
> We heard his very last sound,
> And our wheels grazed his dead face.

The living pass over the dead and the only mark of compassion is that here the wheels 'graze' the dead man rather than crush him. As in 'Louse Hunting', the living can survive only by displacing their own mortality and alienating themselves from the destruction that surrounds them.

The poem suggests in its imagery possibilities of hope and meaning in the extreme experience of war, but they are invoked only to be denied. The soldier's hope of rescue in the final stanza is also a Messianic hope that is unrealized; the limber is described at the beginning of the poem as carrying the redemptive symbols of a crown of thorns and sceptre to 'stay the flood of brutish men/Upon our brothers dear.' But the second stanza breaks down the metaphor to a cruelly material reality. The thorns remain barbed wire, the sceptres remain stakes and the limber that might be the chariot of a returning Messiah crushes the dead rather than bringing them resurrection. In stanza 3 the pastoral order of a natural sympathy with the victims of war is denied in a way analogous to Owen's 'Spring Offensive'. Earth is said to have been 'fretting' for the decay of the dead; however, the possibility that fretting might mean 'concerned about' rather than 'eager for' disappears with the exclamation mark at the end of the next line: 'Now she has them at last!'. As in Owen's poem, the sympathetic connection between man and Nature is broken by the war, and the natural world is seen as complicit in the killing.

'Dead Man's Dump' is Rosenberg's most extreme statement of isolation. It represents the culmination of his attempts to understand the experience of death and affirm the commonality of suffering in the war, yet the understanding always falters as the poem lurches into terrible contrasts of the living and the dead. This statement of extreme alienation is linked directly to the themes of distance and difference in Rosenberg's earlier work. The struggle to bridge social and cultural gaps becomes a struggle for imaginative control of the experience of war. In 'Dead Man's Dump' the incomprehension of the Jewish soldier at the racist despising of his 'God-ancestralled essences' (see 'The Jew', Poetry Anthology, p. 143) becomes the experience of any dying soldier as his call for help is ignored.

War, for Rosenberg, as for Read and Rickword, is a vast extension of the social alienations of peace. 'Dead Man's Dump', 'Louse Hunting' and 'Break of Day in the Trenches' work through the same problematic cultural and personal predicament that Israel Zangwill's work describes in its simultaneous identification with, and divergence from, the politics of the British cause and the social system that underlies it. However, Rosenberg goes further than Zangwill in exposing the terrible consequences of the politics of such a disjunction. In a way that is more reminiscent of the community politics of Rudolf Rocker than the nationalisms of Wellington House, Rosenberg affirms the common predicament of all those who suffer and the need for a language and form (political as well as literary) to include them.

6
British Cultures II: Scottish Cultures and Poets in Exile

War and Scottish cultures

The First World War gave a powerful impetus for nationalist movements within the British Isles. The war was supposedly fought on the principle of self-determination for small nations, and this, combined with the uneasiness of English/British identity in the period, encouraged opposition to English dominance. The most notable example of this was in Ireland. The Easter Rising of 1916, in which a group of Irish nationalists attempted to seize power, took place three months before the Battle of the Somme. Such is the power of an anglocentric version of the two world wars, however, that the Rising is not usually considered part of the events of the First World War at all.

The Easter Rising had its effect on small pockets of English radicalism (see Weller 1985), but its strongest influence was felt in Scotland. There, John MacLean, a Communist trade union organizer, had led opposition to the war from the outset and to conscription from its introduction in 1916. MacLean was influenced by the example of James Connolly, a Scottish trade unionist who was executed in the 1916 rising, and by the Bolshevik revolution in Russia. During the war he fused the two influences to create a socialist Scottish nationalism (see MacLean 1978). Though the significance of MacLean's influence on Scottish politics has been the subject of debate in recent years (see Howell 1986; Harvie 1981; McLean 1983), there can be no doubt of his effect on the main figure of post-First-World-War Scottish writing, C. M. Grieve (Hugh MacDiarmid), and on two Scottish writers of the Second World War, Sorley MacLean and Hamish Henderson.

A recent anthology of Scottish writing of the First World War suggests that there was little or no difference to the stock responses of English wartime writing, and nothing, save John MacLean's journalism and the poetry of Charles Hamilton Sorley, to suggest a radical critique of the war (Royle 1990). Even the future communist and nationalist Grieve wrote admiringly of John Masefield and produced only one poem, 'A Salonikan Storm Song' which Royle terms 'faintly embarrassing' (p. 25). Scottish literary responses generally contained a mixture of patriotism with an accent of tartanry ('Hey, Jock, are ye glad ye 'listed') and a sentimental affection for an idealized Celtic homeland derived from the 'Kailyard' school of literary Scottishness. In the aftermath of the war, however, the cultural situation of Scotland changed. C. M. Grieve adopted the identity of Hugh MacDiarmid and published collections of Scots lyrics and the long poem *The Drunk Man Regards the Thistle* in the 1920s. MacDiarmid showed that it was possible to write poetry which dealt with political and social issues from a definedly Scottish perspective and in a Scots language. His poems released a distinctive method and tone which drew on older traditions of Scottish writing than the inventions of the nineteenth century. Although MacDiarmid himself wrote little directly about either war, the example of his poetry and his politics exerted a crucial influence on Scottish poets of the Second World War.

The poetry of Sorley MacLean illustrates both the direct influence of MacDiarmid and the way that Scots Gaelic traditions of poetry were able to reassert themselves in the context of a nationalist culture. There had been Gaelic poetry of the First World War (Royle's anthology [1990] includes a few examples), but in its content and outlook this was little different to the prevailing English verse of the time and reflected the decline in Gaelic culture in the late nineteenth and early twentieth centuries. MacLean's great achievement in the 1930s and 1940s was to develop a Gaelic poetry that moulded traditional forms and subjects to confront contemporary social and political issues. Inspired by *The Drunk Man*, MacLean wrote *The Cuillin*, one of the most ambitious poems in any British language in the 1930s, which he describes as 'a very long poem … on the human condition, radiating from the history of Skye and the West Highlands to Europe and what I knew of the rest of the world' (MacLean 1985: 12). The poem remained unfinished at the outbreak of the Second World War, but the vision behind it, of the relevance of Scottish Highland history to contemporary European experience, and the capacity of Gaelic poetry to develop the intellectual force that MacDiarmid gave Scots in *The Drunk Man*, informs the poetry that MacLean wrote later as a soldier in the Western Desert.

MacLean's historical and cultural context is very different to that of English writers of both wars. In his work heroic and elegiac traditions are not coloured by imperialist/militarist or English pastoral associations.

The historical point of change or apocalyptic moment, which for so much of post-1918 English culture was the First World War, is, for MacLean, the period of the Highland Clearances in the eighteenth and nineteenth centuries, when Gaelic society and language were nearly destroyed. It is interesting in this regard to compare MacLean's sense of national identity to that of David Jones. For Jones the idea of a British national identity had nearly disappeared, and in *In Parenthesis* he reinvents the idea of Britain using the fragments of a largely forgotten past (see discussion in Chapter 2). MacLean's Gaelic identity, on the other hand, is never in doubt, nor is the traditional means of asserting it. In 'Dol an Iar/Going Westwards' (Poetry Anthology, p. 174) he resolves a poem of self-questioning with the lines:

> I am of the big men of Braes,
> of the heroic Raasay MacLeods,
> of the sharp-sword Mathesons of Lochalsh;
> and the men of my name – who were braver
> when their ruinous pride was kindled?

Here the heroic traditions of caste identity are freshly available to a soldier in the Second World War without any of the jingoist or imperialist connotations such allegiances would evoke in an English context. In MacLean's work the Gaelic heroic tradition is in opposition to imperialism, and becomes a flexible instrument for the interpretation of contemporary political and personal experience. This is demonstrated in the poems 'Alasdair MacLeoid/Alasdair MacLeod' and 'Curaidhean/Heroes' (both in Poetry Anthology, pp. 176, 177).

Both poems are elegies, but neither uses the conventions of elegy that underlie the verse of Owen and other English war poets. Alasdair MacLeod is mourned as a traditional Gaelic hero, without any irony or the ambivalence that marks a poem like Keith Douglas's 'Sportsmen' (Poetry Anthology, p. 206; see also discussion in Chapter 7). 'Curaidhean/Heroes' seems at first to gesture to such English ironies in its comparison of a soldier of the Second World War and heroes of Scottish and European history. It sets Napoleon's Marshal Lannes and the conspicuously brave Gillies MacBain against 'A poor little chap with chubby cheeks/and knees grinding each other,/pimply unattractive face'. But the purpose of the poem is not to create irony, but to elevate and praise the gunner. The swiftness and brutality of the man's death is not disguised: 'he himself got, about the stomach,/that biff that put him to the ground,/mouth down in sand and gravel'. But the conclusion of the poem, like that of 'Going Westwards', is overtly heroic:

> I saw a great warrior of England,
> a poor manikin on whom no eye would rest;
> no Alasdair of Glen Garry;
> and he took a little weeping to my eyes.

The poem works by its inclusion of the English officer within the Scottish heroic tradition and by the consequent affirmation of military traditions of honour and literary traditions of elegy. Unlike many English war poets, whose emphasis is on historical discontinuity and the separation of the two world wars from past experience, MacLean's theme is the continuity of suffering and hence the continuity of the poet's responsibility to praise and mourn.

A different Scottish tradition, though one analagous to Sorley MacLean's work, is represented by Hamish Henderson. Henderson is a Highland Scot, though not Gaelic-speaking. His work of the Second World War demonstrates a much closer relationship to English traditions than that of MacLean (he acknowledges the influence of Wilfred Owen on his poem sequence about the desert war *Elegies for the Dead in Cyrenaica*, for example [Henderson 1992: 322]), but the Scottish context of the writing is vital to its success. This is suggested in the 1948 Foreword to the *Elegies*. Here Henderson links the survival of elegy and the heroic poem to the specific predicament of the Highland soldiers who are

> conscripts of a fast vanishing race, on whom the dreadful memory of the clearances rests, and for whom there is little left to sustain them in the high places of the field but the heroic tradition of *gaisge* (valour).
>
> (Henderson 1990: 60)

As in MacLean's work, this particularity of reference is not limiting, but releases a different kind of political poetry to that possible within an English context.

'Seven Good Germans' (Poetry Anthology, p. 190), the seventh of Henderson's elegies, is close in theme to MacLean's 'Death Valley', which is quoted in the epigraph to the second part of the *Elegies*. It is an affirmation of the essential alliance of the soldiers of the two armies, and as such confirms the message of Owen's 'Strange Meeting'. But the Scottish and Highland context of the whole poem allows a very different kind of poetry to coexist with this strain. In 'Interlude: Opening of an

Offensive' (Poetry Anthology, p. 188), Henderson includes a 'shrill war-song' to accompany the bombardment of the German positions:

> Meaning that many
> German Fascists will not be going home
> meaning that many
> will die, doomed in their false dream
> We'll mak siccar!
> Against the bashing cudgel
> against the contemptuous triumphs of the big battalions
> mak siccar against the monkish adepts
> of total war against the oppressed oppressors
> mak siccar against the leaching lies
> against the worked out systems of sick perversion

The Scots phrase 'mak siccar' is a reference to the same kind of heroic tradition that MacLean is using in 'Heroes' and other poems (see note to l.26 of 'Interlude' in Poetry Anthology, p. 189). Henderson uses the historical reference to a Scottish nationalist struggle to modulate the internationalist message by showing an awareness of the necessary political struggle that the war represents. The 'good Germans' become here 'German Fascists' who are to be destroyed as part of a wider war against 'the oppressed oppressors'. This then becomes another way of identifying the condition of dispossessed highlanders and German soldiers, beguiled by their own leaders. The Scots phrase enables Henderson to deflect the suggestion of an *English* nationalism in this assertion, whilst he is quite happy to use an English (or at least non-Scottish) demotic in the parts of the sequence such as 'Seven Good Germans' which concern reconciliation.

Both Henderson and MacLean are able to find a continuity in the political objectives of the war and their earlier commitment to the socialist causes of the 1930s. In neither poet is there any sign of the kind of disillusionment or realignment that afflicted writers such as Stephen Spender and George Orwell in England. For Henderson and MacLean the war was a continuation of a tradition of heroic political struggle that found its expression in the oppositional language and traditions of Scottish nationalism and in the old alliance with European, rather than English, cultures. In a poem of the 1930s 'Clann Ghill-Eain/The Clan MacLean', Sorley MacLean describes John MacLean, international socialist, Scottish nationalist, and Bolshevik consul in Glasgow, as 'the top and hem of our story', affirming the continuity of John MacLean's radicalism and connecting his struggle with the long history of Gaelic resistance to oppression. 'Going Westwards' is about the relationship of Gaelic and Scots traditions to contemporary European politics, and links quite naturally 'Rotterdam, the Clyde and Prague' (see R. J. Ross 1986).

Henderson's ballads and songs demonstrate another aspect of a distinctively Scottish culture, and also indicate the continuing influence of the politics of John MacLean. The songs can be uncompromisingly Scottish; the wartime 'Victory Hoe-Down' and '51st Highland Division's Farewell to Sicily' (both in Poetry Anthology, pp. 195, 197), and the later 'John MacLean March' and 'The Freedom Come-All-Ye', take their language and spirit from the early Scots lyrics of Hugh MacDiarmid. Their language is dense, often literary Scots and the settings are to pipe-tunes. Yet, despite these assertions of a vigorous national culture, Henderson is careful to introduce into almost all his songs elements that transcend a purely national reading or hearing. *Ballads of World War II (1950)*, Henderson's collection of Second World War songs, is an international anthology, reflecting the internationalist politics at the heart of the *Elegies*. The development of definedly Scottish traditions by Henderson and MacLean poses a further challenge to the anglocentric accounts of war writing.

Poets in exile: India and Egypt

The anglocentric attitude, evident in the criticism of both First and Second World War writing, disguises not only the influence of various non-English cultures within Britain, but also the effect of foreign cultures on British war writing. In the Second World War particularly, soldiers and civilians encountered a wide range of non-British cultures in circumstances far removed from those of peacetime. Such encounters varied from the arrival of European refugee writers in the London literary world of the Second World War to the direct experience of foreign places by young soldiers who had never before left Britain. In this section I will concentrate on a number of poems that came from the British wartime experience of the East, and that show the soldiers' development of new senses of cultural displacement and identity.

The canon of First World War writing concentrates almost exclusively on the experience of the Western Front and the now-archetypal world of trench warfare. However, one of the most influential of all war books,

T. E. Lawrence's *Seven Pillars of Wisdom* (1926), came from outside this theatre of war. Lawrence's account of his part in the Arab revolt against the Turks combined with his own mysterious persona during and after the war to exert an enormous influence right up to the Second World War. The *Seven Pillars* is an alternative war book. In contrast to the spate of disillusioned memoirs and poems that emerged in the 1920s (C. E. Montague's *Disenchantment* [1922] and Robert Graves's *Goodbye to All That* [1929], for example), Lawrence provocatively subtitles his book 'A Triumph', and his mode of writing is consistently epic in its rejection of irony and its celebration of the arts of war. He emphasizes the freedom and movement of the desert war, in contrast to the static, obsessive world of the Western Front, and argues for the possibility of maintaining heroic values in the twentieth century (for a discussion of Lawrence's version of the heroic see Chapter 7).

Lawrence, like his literary mentor Charles Doughty, saw his work as an attempt at national redefinition. In a passage that is crucial to much of the later war writing that came from the East, Lawrence explains the influence of Eastern culture on the book's analysis of his own cultural identity:

> The efforts for these years to live in the dress of Arabs, and to imitate their mental foundation, quitted me of my English self, and let me look at the West and its conventions with new eyes: they destroyed it all for me. At the same time I could not sincerely take on the Arab skin: it was an affectation only … Sometimes these selves would converse in the void; and then madness was very near, as I believe it would be near the man who could see things through the veils at once of two customs, two educations, two environments.
>
> (Lawrence 1939: 30)

The heroic myth of English leadership that Lawrence attempts to create in the *Seven Pillars* emerges from the conflict of identities and loyalties expressed here, and it is this that sets his work apart from cruder strategies of patriotic expression. Lawrence explores Englishness from an outsider's perspective, as well as from within. His influence can be traced in the writings of a number of Second World War poets who served in the East, including Alun Lewis (whose short story 'Dusty Hermitage' is about Lawrence), Keith Douglas, and a group of writers who contributed to the Cairo-based magazine *Personal Landscape*.

Alun Lewis's early war poems, published in *Raiders' Dawn* (1942), are based on First World War models, as was his 'war poet' image (see Chapter 1). 'All Day It Has Rained ...' (Poetry Anthology, p. 181) uses English rural landscapes to explore the effect of the war, and elegizes the death of Edward Thomas, the poet of rural England who was killed in the First World War. Written in the 'phoney war' period, it shows the extent to which writers were trapped within the language and concepts of First World War poetry. Lewis evokes the feelings of troops at rest, in the manner of Owen's 'Spring Offensive', but he cannot write about war itself beyond a vague fantasy of 'dropping bombs on Rome' and 'the quiet dead'. Edward Thomas remains a Romantic figure who 'broods long/On death and beauty' and is destroyed by the anti-pastoral forces of war. This kind of pastoralism changes in Lewis's second collection, *Ha! Ha! Among the Trumpets* (1945), written, for the most part, after his posting to India, in which Lewis deliberately courts that quitting of the English self that Lawrence defines (Lewis was, of course, Welsh, but his involvement with and use of non-English cultures is far less marked than in a writer like Hamish Henderson or David Jones).

Ha! Ha! Among the Trumpets is organized as a sequence in three sections, 'England', 'The Voyage' and 'India', and these mark a self-conscious exploration of the effects of displacement. In the 'India' section, Lewis returns to the themes of 'All Day It Has Rained ...' and 'To Edward Thomas' in the context of an Indian, rather than an English, landscape. 'The Journey' (Poetry Anthology, p. 182) is based on Lewis's experiences as a scout. Like the earlier poems, it is as much about the romantic imagination as about the war, but the meditation on 'the memory of Death/And the recurrent irritation of ourselves' doesn't lead to an elegy or a reference to the First World War. The structure and tone of the poem is more fluid, and the conclusions more ambivalent. In 'The Jungle' such ambivalence is linked directly to the cultural opposition of West and East described by T. E. Lawrence.

As in 'All Day It Has Rained ... ', Lewis describes a scene of soldiers at rest, but here the setting is an Indian jungle rather than an English training camp. Lewis presents the meditation of the British soldier attempting to make sense of the strange experience of a foreign place and the war that is being fought there:

> But we who dream beside this jungle pool
> Prefer the instinctive rightness of the poised
> Pied kingfisher deep darting for a fish

> To all the banal rectitude of states,
> The dew-bright diamonds on a viper's back
> To the slow poison of a meaning lost
> And the vituperations of the just.

The passage begins the poet's withdrawal from the reference points of 'All Day It Has Rained …', namely the pastoral and the conventions of First World War poetry. Instead of the English landscape there is a 'trackless wilderness' and a stagnant jungle pool where 'sleep exudes a sinister content'. The soldiers of 'The Jungle' are 'anonymous, unknown' in a seductive yet lethal environment, far removed from the everyday boredoms of the training camp or from the figure of Thomas, the Romantic soldier-poet.

The journey described in 'The Jungle', like that enacted in the three sections of the collection itself, is one away from the 'English' values of *Raiders' Dawn*. The poet becomes conscious of a 'black spot in the focus [which] grows and grows' and suggests a deepening alienation from the moral and political certainties of the West. The moral inflections of Owen's war poetry, which appear throughout *Raiders' Dawn*, are replaced by a distanced observation of the poet's own complicity in war:

> The killing arm uncurls, strokes the soft moss;
> The distant world is an obituary,
> We do not hear the tappings of its dread.
> The act sustains; there is no consequence.

In the new world of the East, the old politics of 'the humming cultures of the West' are redundant. As in the passage from T. E. Lawrence quoted earlier, the effect of the East is to force the writer to 'look at the West and its conventions with new eyes'. 'The Jungle' ends, not with moral certainties, but with a series of questions about the consequences of individual actions, which seem to refer to the end of 'Strange Meeting' and that poem's radical uncertainties of voice and politics:

> And if the mute pads on the sand should lift
> Annihilating paws and strike us down
> Then would some unimportant death resound
> With the imprisoned music of the soul?
> And we become the world we could not change?
> Or does the will's long struggle end
> With the last kindness of a foe or friend?

The passage is obscure, but the change in tone and outlook is clear enough. In the new world of the East and the Second World War there is no place for a war poetry of protest or moral judgement. If Owen and Thomas remain influences, Lewis is no longer drawing on them as emblematic 'war poets'. It is the dark questioning of 'Strange Meeting' and 'Spring Offensive' and Thomas's despairing attempts at interpretation that become relevant to the soldier in the 'trackless wilderness' of India.

A comparable movement away from the perceived conventions of First World War poetry is apparent in the writing that came from Egypt during the Second World War. The anomalous position of Egypt – officially neutral, but providing the base for the British army in North Africa – made it a meeting place for writers from various backgrounds. Hamish Henderson, Keith Douglas, and G. S. Fraser were in the army; Robin Fedden and Terence Tiller were teachers at the university in Cairo; Bernard Spencer worked for the British Council; and Lawrence Durrell and Olivia Manning fled to Egypt to escape the German occupation of Greece, along with the Greek poets George Seferis and Elie Papadimitriou. The special political circumstances of Egypt, and the availability of supplies which enabled a number of small-scale poetry magazines to flourish, allowed these writers to create a very different kind of wartime culture to that of London (see Bowen 1982–3; Fedden 1966; Durrell 1944; Manning 1944 and Fraser's 'Recent Verse: London and Cairo' [extract in Prose Anthology, p. 266]).

The differences between Western and Eastern cultures, rather than the events of the war, provide the basis for much of the writing from Egypt. As in Alun Lewis's work, the war is seen through the strange perspectives of personal and cultural exile. Robin Fedden develops the metaphor of exile in his introduction to *Personal Landscape: An Anthology of Exile* (1945), a selection of poetry from the wartime magazine (see extract from 'An Anatomy of Exile' in Prose Anthology, p. 268). Exiles, Fedden argues, are cut off from their sense of cultural continuity and are unable to make sense of the culture and history of which they are a part. The interpretative equipment of the English poet – based on pastoral models – is redundant in Egypt, and Fedden points out the lack of relevance of the English pastoral tradition (which underlies so much First World War poetry) to Egypt's climate, its 'flaccid' landscape and its lack of a sense of historical continuity.

Such cultural dislocations provoked a distinctive kind of poetry. G. S.

Fraser, in 'Recent Verse: London and Cairo' (1944) (extract in Prose Anthology, pp. 266–7) contrasts the 'romantic' poetry of a wartime London which saw itself threatened by catastrophe, with the 'neo-classic' poetry written in Egypt, which had absorbed the cultural outlook of the Eastern Mediterranean. 'Cairo's best poetry will be placid and patient, rather than urgent in its tone, sad rather than tragic, persuasive rather than minatory, moral rather than prophetic', he writes. Both Fraser and Fedden claim a distinctively un-English, un-metropolitan bias for the wartime writing of Egypt, a quality which can be exemplified by poems by Keith Douglas, Terence Tiller and Fraser himself.

Douglas was in the Middle East from August 1941 until November 1943 and fought at El Alamein in 1942 (see Douglas 1979a). He maintained an enthusiastic social life in the base towns and a tangential connection with the poetry magazines of Cairo (see Graham 1974: 128–228). His poem 'Cairo Jag' (Poetry Anthology, p. 205), presents a powerful sense of the place. It sets the seedy, sensual world of Cairo, the base town, against the 'new world' of the desert battlefield which is only a short drive away. Such an opposition between the battlefield and home or the reserve lines is one of the basic structures of First World War poetry where it also represents a distance between past and present, knowledge and inno- cence, industrialism and the pastoral. It underpins Owen's 'Futility', for example, and is also present in 'Spring Offensive' in which a 'ridge of grass' divides the place of fields and rest from the apocalyptic place of war. In 'Cairo Jag', however, this differentiation of place takes on another, more disturbing aspect.

The voice of the poem is immediately problematic. The choice between getting drunk or cutting 'a piece of cake', a slang phrase for obtaining a woman, is menacingly indiscreet, and the women con- templated by the poet are disturbed and disturbing figures; they adopt melodramatic postures or they are preoccupied with death. The city is not a place of security or established values to be set against the uncertainties of war, for in Egypt, Douglas suggests, the customary opposition between war and civilian life has dissolved: 'it is all one, all as you have heard'. The 'real' battlefield of the desert is physically close to the city, and the components of each scene are the same – dirt, trivial objects, the dead. Legless men, death's heads and somnambulists are first mentioned as part of the city rather than the battlefield, and Cairo becomes in Terence Tiller's words 'a no-man's-land of flesh and bone' (see 'Big City', Poetry Anthology, p. 211). Douglas also moves the natural imagery, which we would normally associate with a description of home or the reserve lines in First World War poetry, to the battlefield itself. In a terrible parody of pastoral imagery, the vegetation is iron, and the brambles (which, in Owen's pastoral 'clutched and clung ... like sorrowing arms' at the feet of advancing soldiers in 'Spring Offensive') are explicitly identified as barbed wire.

'Cairo Jag' suggests the radical difference in the outlook and tone of Douglas's poetry to that associated with Owen and Sassoon. In their work, outrage is expressed through irony or though a modulation of the poem's voice, as in 'Futility' where Owen moves from the curt order of the opening to the desperate question in the final lines. In 'Cairo Jag' the distanced, analytical voice does not change. The speaker can consider the brutal contrast of the headless man and his pathetic souvenirs with the same dispassionate attention that he gives to an evening out in Cairo. This disturbing disinterestedness is characteristic of much of Douglas's writing (for further discussion of the voice and tone of Douglas's work, see Chapter 7). 'Mersa' (Poetry Anthology, p. 204) is another war poem distanced from the ideologies of Englishness that are so much a part of First World War writing.

Douglas's description of the ruined town of Mersa makes use of a convention of war writing that was seen most clearly in Herbert Read's 'My Company': an officer's description of a group of soldiers at leisure (for another Second World War version of this, see Tiller's 'Lecturing to Troops', Poetry Anthology, p. 210). As Paul Fussell suggests, the scene of soldiers bathing was a particularly important aspect of this convention, as it allowed an acknowledgement of homoerotic feelings, as well as a celebration of the military community (Fussell 1975: 299–309). In Douglas's poem, the image is typically distorted. The description of the soldiers is sensual (they are said to be 'cherryskinned') but they come from the 'skeletal town' to bathe, a similar linking of erotic description and death to that in 'Cairo Jag'. Mersa was once a resort devoted to sexual pleasure, containing 'Cleopatra's hotel' and the guesthouse of the 'amorous modern prince' (a reference to King Farouk I of Egypt), but now the town is only a skeleton, its interior having been destroyed by the war. The soldiers are menaced by the 'immensely long road' which leads to battle and possible death. The poem ends with the officer neither exulting nor sharing with the men, as in the poems by Read and Tiller. He is alone looking at his own feet in the water. In one sense this is an ironic reduction of the scene of soldiers bathing to that of an officer paddling, but once again the tone is darkened by the poet's sense of his own mortality as the fish 'nip the flesh/imagining I am one of the dead.'

Like Alun Lewis in his Indian poems, Douglas uses foreign landscapes, whether those of Cairo, the desert battlefields or a coastal town, to question any settled sense of value. Deception and uncertainty are persistent themes, and there are no clear demarcations between illusion and reality. In 'Mersa' the town has a mask of normality disguising its ruin; in 'Cairo Jag' the city and battlefield seem interchangeable; 'Dead Men' (Poetry Anthology, p. 207) presents the poet as uncertainly placed between the sensual world of the city and the dead of the desert (for further discussion of 'Dead Men' and other poems by Douglas, see Chapter 7).

A similar concern with illusion and uncertainty can be traced in the poetry of G. S. Fraser and Terence Tiller. In their work the urban world of Cairo, the desert and the landscape of the Nile delta are portrayed as mysterious and disturbing environments in which the 'exile' finds a metaphor for the strangeness of the times: 'all that I am sure of is/The exile's way is history's', Fraser writes. In Tiller's 'Big City' (Poetry Anthology, p. 211) the deracination of the poet is again a symptom of a greater crisis. Like Douglas in 'Mersa' and Lewis in 'The Jungle', the poet descibes an alienation from the norms of civic life and human communication. There is only 'the blind magnet of a self' in the midst of the foreign city where, as in 'Cairo Jag', 'passion … estranges all'. The individual in wartime is involved in a terrible struggle to find reciprocity and value, and the strangeness of wartime Cairo, like that of the Indian jungle in Lewis's poetry, becomes at once a setting and a metaphor for this condition.

7
Gender

Women and war writing

War poetry has been more exclusively masculine in its composition and outlook than any other comparable kind of writing. Standard anthologies, such as Silkin's *Penguin Book of First World War Poetry* (1972), contain virtually no poetry by women, and it is only recently that any representative selections of women's poetry written during the two wars have become available (see Reilly 1981, 1984). In addition, some of the most celebrated poems of the First World War are characterized by overt misogyny. In Wilfred Owen's 'Disabled', for example, women are shown as 'giddy jilts' who once encouraged the legless veteran to volunteer and now 'touch him like some queer disease'. Sassoon's 'Glory of Women' is a bitter attack on women's refusal to accept the reality of war, Isaac Rosenberg's 'The Daughters of War', describes Valkyrie-like figures who 'force their males/From the doomed earth', and his 'Girl to Soldier on Leave' (Poetry Anthology, p. 149) has its female speaker express a disturbing admiration for male violence.

The hostility of the poets and the neglect of the anthologists are both the result of the great emphasis placed upon the 'experience' of war, both in the poetry and critical accounts of the subject (see Chapter 1). The argument runs that war poetry emerges from direct experience of fighting and, because such experience was unavailable to women in the First World War and hardly any more so in the Second, there can be no women's war poetry. 'Anti-war' poetry acknowledges male cults of extreme experience and rites of military passage just as much as patriotic celebrations of military glory (something discussed in the second section of this chapter). The poetry of Owen and Sassoon sustains its arguments by reference to the authenticity of the poets' vision, in opposition to the illusions of propaganda or civilian ignorance, and Sassoon's exemplary military career gave him the moral authority to make his protest in the later stages of the war. Women's writing, be it pro- or anti-war, cannot carry a similar authority of firsthand knowledge. Women were bound to write about the fighting war by imaginative projection or hearsay, and this leads to accusations of wilful or naïve ignorance in several First World War poems, including Owen's 'Apologia Pro Poemate Meo' (Poetry Anthology, p. 127) and 'Greater Love'. Even when the home front of the Second World War exposed women to the same dangers of violent death as men, war poets were still, in publishers' minds, soldiers on 'active service' (see discussion of Alun Lewis in Chapter 1).

The absence of female writers from most accounts of the writing of the two world wars disguises the revolutionary changes in the position of women in British society in wartime. The First World War represented, in Sandra Gilbert and Susan Gubar's words, 'the first rupture with a socio-economic history that had heretofore denied most women chances at first-class jobs – and first-class pay' (Gilbert and Gubar 1989: 276). It also brought about psychological changes. Eric Leed writes that

> Women ... experienced with the onset of war the collapse of those established, traditional distinctions between an 'economic' world of business and a private world of sentiment. This felt collapse permitted a range of personal contacts that had been impossible in their former social lives where hierarchies of status ruled.
>
> (Leed 1979: 45)

The testimonies of women in all areas of war work confirm the personal and social significance of these experiences (see Marwick 1977; Sheridan 1990), yet there is apparently no female equivalent of the male literature of war. In part, this is because of the nature of the change in the position of women; engineering, agriculture and transport did not provide women writers with the dramatic subject-matter of the Western Front. But it was also to do with the literary language available to women to write about their experiences.

The poems in Catherine Reilly's anthology of women's poetry of the First World War, *Scars Upon My Heart* (1981) suggest both formal limitations and uncertainty about the appropriate mode of writing to deal with female experience of the war. Two kinds of poetry predominate: doggerel verse and nineteenth-century lyricism. Jessie Pope uses the former to make grimly patriotic points ('Who's for the trench -/Are you, my laddie?' ['The Call']), but also to acknowledge the changing role of women in traditionally male civilian work ('Strong, sensible, and fit,/ They're out to show their grit' ['War Girls']). Unlike the Ilkeston poets discussed earlier, Pope doesn't have either the strong literary reference point of Kipling, nor the force of mundane war experience that makes a poem like 'The Red Road to Hooge' so effective (one of the few poems in *Scars Upon My Heart* to imitate Kipling, Sybil Bristowe's 'Over the Top', is very uneasy with the idiom).

Rose Macaulay and Vera Brittain are two writers who use the literary conventions of late-nineteenth-century Romanticism to talk about the devastating effects of war. They are obviously competent poets (and both were to write notable prose works about the war), but unlike Owen and Sassoon, whose early poetry has similar influences, they never challenge the language of representation. Whereas Owen uses and adapts the sensuous Keatsian rhetoric of his early poems to point up the extremity of his war experience, Brittain and Macaulay rely on heightened poeticisms alone. There is also an occasional uneasy acknowledgement of the second-hand nature of their observations. An excerpt from Macaulay's 'The Shadow' illustrates the point:

> The weak blood running down the street, oh, does it run
>   like fire, like wine?
> Are the spilt brains so keen, so fine, crushed limbs so
>   swift, dead dreams so sweet?
> There is a Plain where limbs and dreams and brains to set
>   the world a-fire
> Lie tossed in sodden heaps of mire ... Crash! Tonight's show
>   begins, it seems.
>
> (Reilly 1981: 68)

The disillusioned view of war's destruction, and the sensuous imagery are comparable to Owen's poetry, but the verse is betrayed by poeticisms (the 'oh', 'a-fire', and so on) without the countervailing realism and ambivalence of tone that Owen's best poetry achieves. Macaulay's use of army slang ('Tonight's show') is unconvincing after the bathetic 'Crash!' and before the qualifying 'it seems'. There were, of course, many male poets who used the same kind of language and were limited by the same constraints of poetic convention. However, as I suggested in Chapter 1, the canon of war poetry has been established on the premise of a development from a conventional poetic rhetoric to a radical revision of that language. Such a change did not happen in women's poetry of the war, and the kind of poetry reprinted in the Virago anthologies therefore remains peripheral to the major work of male poets (but see Khan 1988 for a more positive assessment). Two issues arise from this. The first concerns the reasons for the limitations on the kind of women's war poetry represented by *Scars Upon My Heart*; the second offers the possibility of defining another kind of women's war poetry, something I will explore by reference to the poetry of H.D..

The apparent failure of women's poetry to come to terms with the social and psychological changes in women's position during the wars was largely a result of the lack of a distinctively female political or public discourse. For most women writers, there was no ready alternative to the adoption of doggerel or conventional poeticisms. The intellectual constraints on women before the war had been severe and the changes brought about by war, dramatic though they were in the context of women's social struggles, were not sufficient to cause the critical questioning of the available poetic language (the case of women's fiction is different, as I suggest below). Nevertheless, a theoretical understanding of the ways in which women were intellectually and culturally restrained was developed by a number of feminist writers during the war. Mary Sargant Florence and C.K. Ogden, for instance, argue, in terms reminiscent of Edgell Rickword's later work, that the war perpetuated rather than precipitated a militarist society and its 'perpetual subjection' of women. *Militarism Versus Feminism* (1915) develops the view that male control of the language and content of education, history and religion creates a hidden militarist state – what they term 'the Man's House' – which both excludes and controls women in peace as well as war:

> [the Man's House] is forced more and more to interfere with the affairs of the family and in particular with the life and work of woman. To the authority of man inside the home is added the external authority of the Man's House as such – that house which women may not enter, since war and preparation for war which still determine its action in so many ways are the concern of man alone.
>
> (Florence *et al.* 1987: 113–14)

Ogden and Florence's argument is pertinent to the question of women's war poetry. For living under the influence of 'the Man's House', women writers have only the language and experience of male culture with which to interpret its actions and effects. It does not allow them the kind of social freedom or experience to develop other languages. The patriotic and sentimental discourses represented by the poems of Jessie Pope and Rose Macaulay were the only poetic languages readily available to women, whether in peace or war. Thus female experience, in war as in peace, could only be represented as a refraction of male experience.

The Sex Disqualification Act of 1919, which gave women access to certain professions, and the enfranchisement of women nine years later seemed to meet the main demands of the pre-war women's suffrage movement. However, as a new generation of feminists were to argue, such legislation had little effect on underlying social structures. Instead it produced new contradictions in the contrast between the apparent inclusion of women within the civic state and the continuation of the Man's House of militarist social organization. Virginia Woolf's *Three Guineas* (1938) (extract in Prose Anthology, p. 243) makes just this point. Woolf maintains the arguments outlined in *Militarism Versus Feminism*, assuming a fundamental connection between wartime and peacetime social control. However, what Woolf perceives as the failure of women's political agitation and its post-war appeasement, leads her to give a different response to the question at the heart of both works, 'How...are we to prevent war?'. For the First World War writers, the feminist's task is to climb 'up to the clearer air above the battlefield and [cry] aloud in her anguish to her sisters afar off: "These things must not be, they shall never be again!"' (Florence *et al.* 1987: 140). Through such appeals to women, they argue, it might be possible to influence men who perpetrate the wars. Woolf, writing from a perspective of disillusioned enfranchisement, rejects such action. The duty of 'the educated man's daughter' (that is, the woman who benefited most from the post-war legislation) in the event of another war is 'not to incite their brothers to fight or to dissuade them, but to maintain an attitude of complete indifference' (Woolf 1943: 194). For Woolf, the very position of pacifism implies a connection by opposition to a militarism that is utterly foreign to the instincts and understanding of women. Thus 'the daughters of educated men...should give their brothers neither the white feather of cowardice nor the red feather of courage, but no feather at all'.

Woolf argues for a feminist politics that works outside 'the Man's House' of militarism. The language and ideology of patriotism and heroism has no meaning for women:

> [I]f you insist upon fighting to protect me, or "our" country, let it be understood, soberly and rationally between us, that you are fighting to gratify a sex instinct which I cannot share; to procure benefits which I have not shared and probably will not share; but not to gratify my instincts, or

to protect either myself or my country. For, the outsider will say, 'in fact, as a woman, I have no country. As a woman I want no country. As a woman my country is the whole world.'

Woolf here makes central to her political argument the very thing that marginalizes women's war poetry in terms of the male canon – women's lack of direct experience of war. For Woolf, such a lack is to be seen alongside lack of experience of education, professional status and economic security as part of the general exclusion of women from civil society. In the face of such exclusions, Woolf projects a different political practice to that of protest. She affirms a separatist politics of disinterest in militarism in all its forms, and, in its place, a politics of feminist self-determination.

The vision of *Three Guineas* was, in many ways, unfulfilled in the succeeding years. During the Second World War women made munitions and nursed the wounded in just the way Woolf argued against. Their social advancement was as problematic as it had been twenty-five years before, with the admission into 'the Man's House' of well-paid work not extending beyond the end of the war. Despite its failure in political terms, however, Woolf's work, and that of Florence and Ogden before, does provide a theoretical position from which to interpret the uneasy achievement of women's poetry of the First World War. The kind of cultural constraints on women described by Woolf are clearly demonstrated in the language and approach of the poets in Reilly's anthology. At the same time, Woolf's arguments offer the possibility of a new approach to defining the nature of women's contribution to war poetry which is best illustrated by the work of H.D..

H.D. is not usually classed as a war poet. She appears in neither the male anthologies of First and Second World War writing, nor the Virago anthologies. The reason for this omission is that her poems are not 'about' war in the way we have come to expect. Although most of the poetry published in her *Collected Poems* (1925) was written during the First World War, there is no drastic change in subject matter or style from her pre-war work. The poetry remains fixed in Hellenic mythology and history and in the terse, allusive manner of the Imagist movement. H.D.'s personal life was deeply affected by the war, however. Her marriage to the poet Richard Aldington broke up after his enlistment; her relationship with D. H. Lawrence coincided with his persecution as the husband of an enemy alien; and her brother was killed in France in 1918 (for a detailed account of this period see Guest 1985). H.D.'s experience of the war was extreme, but, as for almost all women at this time, the extremity was domestic and personal, and so detached from the 'real war'.

The difference between H.D.'s poetry and that represented by *Scars Upon My Heart*, is that it refuses to deal with this detachment by fantasizing about male experience or using the conventions of male war poetry. Indeed, she doesn't write openly about the war at all, hence her omission from anthologies of war poetry. Her strategy is one of developing a language apart from the accepted public discourse of politics and (female) sentiment, and in this she can be compared with non-combatant writers like D. H. Lawrence and T. S. Eliot and the more celebrated female prose writers about the war. In novels like Woolf's *Jacob's Room* (1922) and *Mrs Dalloway* (1925) and Rebecca West's *Return of the Soldier* (1918) the war is never directly described, yet its devastations within an apparently remote social world of women are always apparent. H.D., like Woolf a stylistic innovator, continued the Imagist experiments with form and diction to develop a poetry which, in Gary Burnett's words, is 'constructive rather than destructive – set against the war rather than defined by it' (Burnett 1987–8: 61).

'After Troy' (Poetry Anthology, p. 165) is representative of H.D.'s wartime work. Like many of her poems, it has a classical setting. The speaker is apparently a Trojan soldier lamenting the destruction of his city and its army. This reference has nothing in common with the naïve heroic classicism which marked some male war poetry; H.D.'s poem is written from the viewpoint of defeat rather than victory, and, as it progresses, it becomes clear that the war described is not a war between nations, but one between values. The defeated Trojan forces are defined by their allegiance to Aphrodite, goddess of love. They are beaten by a more disciplined, cerebral army, 'better taught in skill,/subtler with wit of thought'. By identifying an opposition in values, H.D. transforms the Trojan war into one between a passionate and poetic female sensibility aligned with Aphrodite, and what she calls in a wartime review 'the great overwhelming mechanical daemon, the devil of machinery, of which we can hardly repeat too often, the war is the hideous offspring' (H.D. 1987–8b: 52). For H.D., the First World War is itself in conflict with the female principles of creativity and love. These are destroyed by a force defined by the male principles of mechanism and rationality. The Trojans' opponents feel 'no shiverings/of the white enchantress,/radiant Aphrodite's spell'; that is they feel no poetic, female inspiration. Thus their victory is a hollow one. Like Virginia Woolf in *Three Guineas*, H.D. affirms the need for a female response to the destructiveness of a militarist ideology which does not accept the language or assumptions of that ideology. Although the poem describes a defeat, the verse itself, in all its allusiveness and sensuousness, celebrates the survival of the values of the female principle, Aphrodite.

In the wartime review referred to above, H.D. writes of the need to 'redefine and reconstruct boundaries and barriers' in response to the war (H.D. 1987–8b: 53). Her poetry of this period attempts to create a new kind of language that deviates from the established oppositions and meanings of male war poetry. She tries to integrate her experiences of personal crisis with a vision that goes beyond the constraints of war and her war poetry is concerned with what she terms an 'inner region of defence' (H.D. 1987–8a: 73). But it is also a political language, as her poem 'The Tribute' demonstrates (extract in Poetry Anthology, p. 166).

First published in 1916, 'The Tribute' foreshadows the visions of social and cultural collapse in post-war works such as Ezra Pound's *Hugh Selwyn Mauberley* (1920) and T. S. Eliot's *The Waste Land* (1922). War is shown to devalue culture and society, leaving only 'the broken sherds/of the market-place'. Poetry itself is destroyed by the war when 'squalor has entered and taken our songs'. Yet, unlike so much of the male writing of the First World War, the poem works to an affirmative statement. Like 'After Troy', it celebrates aesthetic and personal values in a manner far removed from the customary language and subject of the First World War. The poem itself becomes an argument against the destructive values of the 'overwhelming mechanical daemon'. Its speakers deliver not elegy or protest, but a vision of continuity and hope in the face of military and economic destruction.

Beauty survives wars, and poetry, H.D. argues, must maintain a faith in a poetic language that acknowledges but also transcends the demon. This affirmative vision becomes even more intense in H.D.'s poetry of the Second World War.

H.D. remained in London during the Second World War and the landscapes of the Blitz are the starting point for *Trilogy*, three long poems written between 1942 and 1944. The extract from the first section of the trilogy, *The Walls Do Not Fall* (1944) (Poetry Anthology, p. 167) suggests the continuity of outlook between H.D.'s work in both wars. In the opening section the ruins of bombed London are equated with the ancient ruins of Luxor on the Nile. But this historical link is not a suggestion of epochal decline in the manner of Eliot's *The Waste Land*. H.D. emphasizes the way in which the destruction of the city is also an opening out of previously enclosed spaces, a vision which recalls Eliot's *Little Gidding*, also written during the Second World War. The city churches are no longer confined, exclusive buildings of worship, but structures which invite a new sense of discovery and freedom from limitation; 'enter,/there as here, there are no doors', she writes, inviting exploration in the same way as archaeologists enter previously unknown tombs in Egypt. The everyday experience of urban life is radically undermined by the extraordinary circumstances of war, and H.D. gives a vivid description of physical and mental disorientation, as the known world is transformed:

> over us, Apocryphal fire,
> under us, the earth sway, dip of a floor,
> slope of a pavement
>
> where men roll, drunk
> with a new bewilderment

But the time of destruction is also a time of discovery, when 'inspiration stalks us/through gloom' and the seemingly permanent urban landscape is changed. The 'sliced wall' reveals previously hidden interiors, and the literal breaking open of the city acts as a metaphor for the discovery of new mental or spiritual states.

In *The Walls Do Not Fall*, survival in the extreme circumstances of war, and the effects of the experience of large-scale violence and destruction become, for the first time, a subject for women's poetry. The section ends with the same question that is asked by the survivors in Owen's 'Spring Offensive': 'we passed the flame: we wonder/what saved us? what for?' For H.D., the question is one that demands a vision of the world that escapes and transforms the destruction of war. In the following sections of *The Walls Do Not Fall* and the other two books of *Trilogy* (*Tribute to the Angels* and *The Flowering of the Rod*) she develops a complex personal mythology in which Christian and pagan images interfuse to create an affirmative and redemptive vision of survival in wartime, a 'half-burnt-out apple-tree/blossoming' as she terms it in *Tribute to the Angels*. As in her First World War poetry, H.D. argues for the potential for liberation from the structures of the mechanical demon of war. Although she does not share the openly political interests of Virginia Woolf, and advocates a very different kind of feminism, her poems about war, written outside the constraints of a male language and form, provide the most convincing poetic evidence for the achievement of Woolf's vision of a separatist feminist response to militarism.

Masculinity

If the period 1914–45 was a time of change in the social and political positions of women, it marked no less of a challenge to ideas of masculinity. The feminist analyses of war, discussed in the previous section, tend to obscure this challenge in their assumption of an un-questioned alliance between militarist values and ideas of masculinity. Yet the male war poetry of both wars calls such a straightforward alliance into question. The complexity of the changes in representations of the masculine can be seen by an examination of the treatment of male sexuality in First World War poetry and ideas of heroism in the writing of the Second World War.

Owen's 'Apologia Pro Poemate Meo' (Poetry Anthology, p. 127), written in November/December 1917, is avowedly an argument for a redefinition of poetic purpose and language in response to the war, and a realignment of the poet-officer's social relations with his men. How-ever, its main emphasis is upon a redefinition of the nature and language of masculine relationships. Owen recasts the old militarist values of state religion, courage and male fellowship into a new vision of male sexuality. For the men of the First World War, 'love is not the binding of fair lips/ With the soft silk of eyes', but is 'wound with war's hard wire whose stakes are strong'. The erotic and aesthetic conventions of civilian heterosexual life and of love poetry are transposed to the overtly male world of the war. Women's ribbons become soldiers' wire, bandages and webbing; beauty is found in cursing; exultation (religious or sexual ecstasy) is seen in the filthy faces of ordinary soldiers.

In the 'Apologia' Owen celebrates the capacity of the soldiers to find new possibilities for self-fulfilment within the terrible and absurd world of the war. He also demonstrates how exclusive and tightly-knit the masculine communities have had to become in order to survive. The dismissive final stanzas, addressed to all civilians, but especially perhaps to women, state that '… except you share/With them in hell … / … You shall not hear their mirth'. The most powerful human emotions con-cerned with community, caring and intimacy are thus displaced from conventional heterosexual relationships to the intensely masculine relationships of the war and Owen's poetic method for communicating this displacement is by the use of a resolutely sensual, homoerotic discourse ('Greater Love', written a month before the 'Apologia', is an overtly misogynist statement of this theme).

Homoeroticism is a vital part of Owen's poetry but its importance has been generally ignored by critics, perhaps because it compromises his exemplary status as an anti-war poet. Jonathan Cutbill, in one of the few essays on Owen to address the significance of his sexuality, argues that Owen's homosexuality defined his experience of the war, and accuses critics and biographers of 'a failure of the heterosexual imagination' in their refusal to come to terms with its importance (Cutbill 1987: 24). There is undoubtedly some discomfort with this aspect of his work among many writers on war poetry. Even Paul Fussell, who focuses upon what he terms Owen's 'homoerotic sensuousness', sees it as largely idealized. He writes that Owen 'arrives by disciplined sublimation at a state of profound pity' for those men whose physical beauty he admires (Fussell 1975: 291). 'Disciplined sublimation', though, doesn't really describe the tone of angry sensuality in 'Apologia Pro Poemate Meo' and 'Greater Love' in which the attacks on the conventions of political, civic and social language are informed by a quite unsublimated homoeroticism.

The issue here is not just the sexuality of Owen or any other poet of the war. As in the work of women writers of the period, it concerns the language available to poets to write about extraordinary circumstances in which social and personal values are constantly challenged. Herbert Read and David Jones, poets whose outlook is not overtly homosexual in the manner of Owen, nevertheless use a homoerotic discourse to explore aspects of the social experience of war. Both poets transform the military organization of troops into communities of intense pleasure and intimacy, suggesting the new kinds of male relationships that emerged during the war. Read's 'My Company' remains the definitive statement of this transformation and the creation of a world in which, in David Jones's words 'Roland could find and, for a reasonable while, enjoy, his Oliver' (see extract from *In Parenthesis* in Poetry Anthology, p. 151); for a discussion of 'My Company' see Chapter 5. Several of Ivor Gurney's poems also concern the creation of a gentle, loving community within the extreme conditions of war. 'First Time In' (Poetry Anthology, p. 122) describes his experience of going to the front line for the first time and the way in which his arrival is made bearable by the generous welcome and the singing of the Welsh soldiers that Gurney's regiment was relieving: 'there the boys gave us kind welcome,' he writes, 'So that we looked out as from the edge of home'. All of these writers articulate a utopian discourse in opposition to the dystopia of the war, and their utopianism is expressed in the transformation of the destructive organization of the army into a loving community of men. While this is not necessarily homoerotic in expression or impulse, there is nevertheless a power redefinition of the heterosexual conventions of military heroism such as those parodied in Rosenberg's 'Girl to Soldier on Leave' (Poetry Anthology, p. 149) and Owen's 'Disabled'.

The questioning of masculine values and the affirmation of new kinds of male relationships by writers like Owen, Read and Gurney can be seen as part of a wider adjustment of social and political values. As well as reflecting intense personal experience, poems such as 'My Company' articulate a sexual politics which challenges the structures of militarism from within. They present not just personal relationships but new societies in which the disciplined organizations of the army, committed to restriction and destruction, become loving and intimate communities, whose complexity and values of generosity and passionate self-reliance are celebrated. The military ideology of heroism, obedience to authority and service to the nation is transformed into one of emotional reciprocity, love and physical celebration through an intensification of existing values of comradeship and loyalty within military units.

The redefinitions of masculinity in the poetry of writers like Gurney and Jones, however, are not straightforward in their utopian, anti-war politics. As I argued at the beginning of the section, the poems often express a bitter misogyny, and frequently maintain allegiances to some of the values of militarist ideology that such war poetry is normally thought to have rejected. Owen's work in particular shows the complexity of the revision of conventions of masculinity during the war. The final letters and poems of Owen contain accounts of fighting that have few 'anti-war' sentiments as such. They are more often celebrations of male resilience and the sharing of extreme experience. 'I can find no word to qualify my experiences except the word SHEER,' he writes to his mother in October 1918, '[it] passed the limits of my Abhorrence. I lost all my earthly faculties, and fought like an angel' (Owen 1973: 107). This is not protest, but an experiment in finding a new way of talking about an extraordinary experience. A similar avoidance of moral judgement or protest is apparent in some of Owen's later poems. 'Spring Offensive'

(Poetry Anthology, p. 133), written between July and September 1918, is quite unlike, say, the deliberately shocking and openly polemical 'Dulce et Decorum Est' of October 1916, although both describe the terrible consequences of battle. The later poem is not directed at an ignorant civilian public, but probes the experience of fighting and survival in terms which pass no political or moral judgement on the activity of war. Owen writes of the soldiers' 'superhuman inhumanities,/Long-famous glories, immemorial shames using the language of military heroism ('glory' and 'shame') not ironically, but in a new context. The poem presents a masculine psychology of the survivors of unimaginable violence, those who 'from existence' brink/Ventured but drave too swift to sink'. There is, he suggests, no existing language to talk about this; the soldiers don't speak at the end of this poem, just as the soldiers in 'Smile, Smile, Smile' remain silent, and the enemy's speech trails off into silence at the end of 'Strange Meeting'. In order to express their state of mind, which corresponds to his own in the letter quoted above, Owen creates a new discourse which is neither pro- nor anti- war, but which borrows the registers of military heroism and moral values, even as it denies their political or moral force.

Owen's increasing fascination with the processes of change, bonding and forgiveness within a male community, and his virtual abandonment of anti-war propaganda are examples of a complex reaction to war experience that goes beyond simple rejection of militarism. A similar complexity of response can be found in other writers. René Hague writes of David Jones's surprising enthusiasm for pursuing a military career at the end of the war:

> the months in the trenches and the bloody battle of [Mametz] Wood left him spiritually and psychologically unscarred and even invigorated: and for a short time at least ready for more soldiering. After demobilisation he wished at first – until dissuaded by his father – to join the British forces in Russia.
>
> (Jones 1980: 28)

In many of Ivor Gurney's post-war poems there is a kind of nostalgia for the environment and culture created from the war by his fellow-soldiers. Gurney never writes anti-war poems as such. 'While I write war tells me truth,' he says ('While I write', Poetry Anthology, p. 125), and in 'Swift and Slow' (Poetry Anthology, p. 124) he contrasts the 'slow death in the loved street and bookish room' with the swift death in Flanders where 'there were no tweedledees or handy-danders', almost with approval of the latter. Gurney, like Jones, never denies the brutality of the war, but his writing is also never unqualified in its disparagement of it; the 'strange hells within the minds war made' are 'not so humiliatingly afraid/As one would have expected,' he writes ('Strange Hells', Poetry Anthology, p. 122). A significant part of the work of Owen, Jones, Gurney and other First World War writers, then, is not concerned with any polemical 'anti-war' purpose but aims instead to develop new languages to talk about extreme male experience. This includes the capacity of men to create new communities within war, as well as to experience the break-up of old forms of heterosexual male identity.

The challenges to masculine identity during the First World War have tended to be seen as limited in their effects. In the same way that changes in the social position of women were revoked in post-war periods, it can be argued that the visions of male community, characteristic of First World War writing, were dependent upon the extraordinary and extreme circumstances of the Western Front. After the war they disappeared relatively quickly, or survived only on the margins of social and political life, as in Gurney's bitter nostalgia expressed in unpublished poems, or in Herbert Read's quirky anarchism. This sense of the transience of the redefinitions of masculinity leads Paul Fussell to make an absolute distinction between versions of masculinity in the poetry of the First and Second World Wars. 'Compared with the passionate writing in the Great War,' he writes, 'the convention in the Second is that love is strenuously heterosexual' (Fussell 1989: 109). *Wartime*, Fussell's account of Second World War culture, confirms this distinction in its own thoroughgoing heterosexual and androcentric version of the period. Yet the relative scarcity of Second World War homoerotic poetry should not be taken to suggest that an unproblematic version of masculinity reasserted itself after the extreme challenges of the First World War. The different social and military conditions of the Second World War did not encourage the same kind of interest in masculine communities; the later war was a much more mobile affair without the territorial concentration of the First. Nevertheless, there was a similar complexity of response regarding ideas of male identity. In the final part of this chapter I want to argue that the link between the questioning of conventions of masculinity and the questioning of social and political values typical of the First World War did persist. In the later war the focus of such questioning changed from male sexuality to ideals of male conduct, particularly heroism. Richard Hillary's autobiography *The Last Enemy*

(1942) and Arthur Koestler's 1943 essay on Hillary (extract in Prose Anthology, p. 257) provide useful starting points.

Hillary was an RAF pilot who was shot down during the Battle of Britain and sustained terrible burns. His face and hands were rebuilt using plastic surgery and he returned to flying, only to die in an accident in 1943 at the age of 23. *The Last Enemy* is an account of his early days in the RAF and his struggle to recover from his injuries. It is also, as Koestler's essay suggests, a consideration of the nature of modern heroism. Koestler uses Hillary as a prototype of a new kind of writer, 'men who live the dangerous life' and demonstrate 'a curious alfresco introspection and an even more curious trend of contemplation, even mysticism, born in the dead centre of the hurricane'. The idea of this new culture of masculinity, combining mysticism and action, philosophy and war, underpins Koestler's investigation of the 'myth' of Hillary. He argues that Hillary's personal 'heroism' cannot be linked to public moralities of patriotism or political commitment. Those once-controlling ideologies of masculinity disappeared in the First World War and in the Spanish Civil War, and Hillary's disturbing account of his physical mutilation and the painful experiments in plastic surgery that followed is an implicit rejection of another – the link between sexual attractiveness and war popularized in poetry by the portraits of Rupert Brooke during the First World War. Their disappearance, Koestler argues in the first part of the extract, leaves only the various contradictory explanations that Hillary gives for his conduct in *The Last Enemy*. These form an unsettling miscellany of individual, philosophical and cultural imperatives which suggest that the hero can no longer justify his heroic actions by reference to any tradition of masculine conduct. To act heroically in the circumstances of the Second World War is to act as 'desperate crusaders in search of a cross'.

Koestler's argument demonstrates his debt to a European intellectual tradition that was to exert a crucial influence on British writing only after the war, when French existentialist philosophy and fiction became more widely available. However, he also points to a British precursor to Hillary's role of 'crusaders in seach of a cross' in T. E. Lawrence (see Chapter 6). As Hillary's work makes clear, Lawrence provides a crucial link between First and Second World War versions of heroism and masculinity. In *Seven Pillars of Wisdom* (1925) Lawrence created a heroic myth from his part in the Arab Revolt, and the *Seven Pillars*, as I noted earlier, is the only major work to come from the First World War that could have been subtitled 'A Triumph'. But Lawrence is not straight-forward in his definition of the heroic, and simultaneously celebrates and questions traditional male values. While he maintains nineteenth-century masculine ideals of individual initiative in exploration and military action, he also demonstrates a psychological complexity and physical vulnerability that is out of keeping with the public image of Victorian and First World War heroes. Lawrence was no Sir Richard Burton, nor yet a Rupert Brooke, but a slightly-built intellectual whose passive endurance and sexual self-abasement became as significant in his influence on writers in the 1920s and 1930s as his violent activity. Although still attached to traditional forms of masculinity – the cult of leadership, the life of military organizations, political intrigue and so on – he demonstrated (and celebrated) extreme divergences in his public adoption of Arab dress, his ambivalent sexuality, and his maso-chistic insights into military discipline (most clearly expressed in *The Mint* (1955), his posthumously published memoir of life in the army and RAF).

Lawrence's work and persona suggested the creative possibilities of a troubled masculinity for writers in the 1930s and he is the model for the explorer/leader figures in W. H. Auden's poetry of the early 1930s (Osborne 1980: 91, 103, 140). In the Second World War he offered writers like Alun Lewis a means of escape from the problem of repeating the work of the First World War poets, for he deviated from the classic model of protest and pity. Lawrence's work acknowledged both the utopianism of the homoerotic celebration of male community and the contempt for ignorant authority that characterized Sassoon's writing, but it resisted any form of political protest and maintained a powerful mythology of heroic action and existential crisis – both concerns of writers like Hillary and Alun Lewis, and central to the work of Keith Douglas.

Douglas's presentation of his war experience can appear as a reversion to pre-First-World-War militarist values. *Alamein to Zem Zem* (1946), his account of his involvement in the El Alamein offensive, is an enthusiastic war book. It shows his fascination with technology and strategy and his interest in war as a male rite of passage. He sees the battle as 'an important test, which I was interested in passing' (Douglas 1979a: 15), and, through-out the memoir, his point of view is studiedly objective, displaying none of the horror and disillusionment that mark First World War memoirs. He presents himself either as an onlooker or an almost naïve participant in violence upon which he offers no judgement:

I observed these battles partly as an exhibition – that is to say that I went through them a little like a visitor from the country going to a great show, or like a child in a factory – a child sees the brightness and efficiency of steel machines and endless belts slapping round and round, without caring or knowing what it is all there for.

(Douglas 1979a: 15)

The calculatedly distanced voices of *Alamein to Zem Zem* and many of the poems seem almost a deliberate attempt to deny the classic positions of First World War writing. He rejects protest, satire or any attempt to use poetry to articulate or empathize with ordinary soldiers and cultivates instead a tough, analytical approach. Two poems, 'Vergissmeinnicht' and 'How to Kill' (Poetry Anthology, p. 208) illustrate the point.

In 'Vergissmeinnicht' the description of a dead German soldier in the desert and the photograph of his girlfriend nearby seems to recall the scene and emotion of Owen's poem. But Douglas's poem attempts no outrage and ends with a characteristically disturbing description of death, unrelieved by any statement of sympathy or interpretation:

> We see him almost with content,
> abased, and seeming to have paid
> and mocked at by his own equipment
> that's hard and good when he's decayed.
>
> But she would weep to see today
> how on his skin the swart flies move;
> the dust upon the paper eye
> and the burst stomach like a cave.

'How to Kill' recasts Sassoon's poem of protest 'How to Die', with an examination of the activity of killing and the psychology of the killer replacing Sassoon's concern with the victim. In the same poem, a line from C. H. Sorley's famous poem of the First World War 'When I See Millions of the Mouthless Dead' is echoed, but is significantly changed. Sorley's expression of appalled empathy with the numberless victims of the war, 'How easy it is to die', becomes the disturbing observation of a killer, 'How easy it is to make a ghost'. In the new circumstances of the Second World War Douglas's emphasis is upon the objective description of the process of killing and the sniper's anxious self-observation, rather than Sorley's hopeless meditation on the pointlessness of elegy (for a more detailed discussion of 'How to Kill', see below).

Douglas's rejection of the protest of First World War writing, however, does not imply an uncritical reversion to pre-war values of militarism, as his prose statement on poetry also makes clear (extract in Prose Anthology, p. 255). He is fascinated by forms of male power and in his poems he is variously an analyst of his own death ('Simplify me when I'm dead', Poetry Anthology, p. 203), a sniper and sorcerer ('How to Kill'), and a voyeur and predator ('Cairo Jag' and 'Dead Men' both in Poetry Anthology, pp. 205, 207). But without ever committing himself to a moral or political position, Douglas uses the poems to analyse these attitudes, the effects of war upon the men involved in it and the distortions of attitude and response that it causes. 'Sportsmen' and 'How to Kill' (both in Poetry Anthology, pp. 206, 208) demonstrate two different aspects of this investigation of masculinity.

In 'Sportsmen' Douglas evokes the values of a 'gentle/obscelescent breed of heroes'. These are aristocratic English officers whose codes of understatement and stoicism ('It's most unfair, they've shot my foot off') survive in an age of tank warfare. Such men are regarded ironically as unicorns – mythical heraldic emblems of Englishness – yet Douglas also suggests a sympathy with their extravagant postures of courage and languor in the face of mortal danger. They become emblems of chivalry and stupidity, and their deaths provoke a weeping that is an expression both of sincere grief and frustrated incomprehension of their attitudes. The values of the hunt and the cricket pitch haunt the poem as anachronistic yet powerful images of masculinity, and Douglas acknowledges his contradictory responses to their survival. The poet affirms, even celebrates, the survival of the heroic attitude, but the celebration is hedged with irony and doubt.

'How to Kill', as I have already suggested, is a disturbing study of wartime masculine psychology in which a sniper meditates on the process of killing. The child's ball of the first stanza becomes the 'gift designed to kill' without any change in the speaker's tone. The description of the act of killing is frighteningly remote, yet intimately fascinated with the results:

> The wires touch his face: I cry
> NOW. Death, like a familiar, hears
>
> and look has made a man of dust
> of a man of flesh.

In one sense this is a study of the delusions of masculine violence. At the point of pulling the trigger, the sniper moves imaginatively from the modern technology of gun-sights ('The wires') to the fantasy of himself as a Faustian necromancer who calls up familiars, performs sorcery and is damned. But the same fantastic language that appears to show the killer avoiding moral responsibility for his action also forces readers to consider their responses. The fascination of the careful preparation for the killing has been our fascination too, and the line 'How easy it is to make a ghost' is a bleak truism as much as an evasion. If the speaker of 'How to Kill' is a new, pitiless soldier-poet, without heroism or compassion, we are readers of war poetry left without the guidance of irony or outrage and forced to consider our own responses.

Throughout his war poetry, Douglas presses this question of an appropriate response. 'How to Kill' refers to, but ultimately rejects, the familiar positions of First World War protest poetry – the idea of the dead enemy being some mother's son, the pointlessness of the act of killing, the anonymous distance of modern technological warfare, and so on. There is no possibility of outrage or compassion in the blunt statement 'This sorcery/I do'. Neither is there any possibility of empathy between killer and killed, as in 'Strange Meeting'. Douglas poses the same dilemma as that which Koestler sees in Richard Hillary: the dilemma of a writer in a war that has gone beyond heroic ideologies of sacrifice and honour, but has also gone beyond the anti-heroic moralities of pity and protest. If Owen struggles to inform the debased existence of men in war with a new kind of heroism, Douglas is determined to affirm the need for a language that is without moral judgement, yet, in its very scepticism, is preserved from complicity with brutality or militarism.

This fine balance is evident in the final stanzas of 'Dead Men' (Poetry Anthology, p. 207), a poem which considers the response of the living soldier to the dead on the desert battlefield:

> Then leave the dead in the earth, an organism
> not capable of resurrection, like mines,
> less durable than the metal of a gun,
> a casual meal for a dog, nothing but the bone
> so soon. But tonight no lovers see the lines
> of the moon's face as the lines of cynicism.

And the wise man is the lover
who in his planetary love revolves
without the traction of reason or time's control
and the wild dog finding meat in a hole
is a philosopher. The prudent mind resolves
on the lover's or the dog's attitude for ever.

The poem seems almost casually hardened in its attitudes, yet the apparent celebration of forgetfulness or ignorance in response to the war is finally denied by the very self-consciousness of the poem's development. The need to escape from the realities of death into erotic fantasy or bestial realism is acknowledged as a soldier's truth, but the probing of the poem itself, with its search for the appropriate way of describing and thinking about the dead, can hardly be classed as 'prudent' – a pointedly understated adjective for the context. The mind that lacks prudence must surely take the risky attitude of the poem itself and question the consequences of the responses that are described.

Like Owen's later poetry and that of Isaac Rosenberg, the only First World War poet to whom Douglas explicitly refers, Douglas's work rejects political commitments or polemics. His poetry acknowledges the masculine values of militarism – the heroic/ridiculous understatement in 'Sportsmen', even the pathological satisfactions of 'How to Kill' – and these are never explicitly condemned. However, the poems detach such responses from the nationalist and militarist ideologies to which these versions of masculinity are customarily allied, and subject them to a sceptical analysis. The 'heroes' of 'Sportsmen' and the sniper of 'How to Kill' are exposed in all their own vulnerability to 'the mosquito death' and, as in 'Mersa' (see discussion in Chapter 6), the objective observation of the poet is always set against the threat of imminent destruction.

The work of Douglas, Hillary and Koestler does suggest a change in the literary representation of masculinity in the Second World War. The political idealism expressed through male community and the homo-erotic intensity of some of the First World War lyrics are notably absent in the later war. However, as I suggested earlier, such versions of masculinity are never straightforward. Their questioning of the conventions of militarist and heterosexual culture also reinforce aspects of that culture – particularly its misogyny – and the opposition to war that is so often said to be a feature of First World War writing, is rarely clear-cut in the later writings of Owen and the poetry of Gurney and Jones. If the poetry of Douglas and the autobiography of Hillary mark a return to heroic values of masculinity, it is by no means a simplistic return to heterosexuality and patriotism. Like T. E. Lawrence, Hillary and Douglas use the conventions of heroic and militarist masculinity to explore rather than to celebrate. Their work, along with that of Owen, Gurney and Jones, should be seen, with that of the women writers discussed in the previous section, as another aspect of the questioning of gender roles in wartime.

Part II

POETRY

Ivor Gurney
1890–1937

Gurney was born in Gloucester, and the city and its surrounding country remained constant reference points for his poetry throughout his life. In 1911 he won a scholarship to the Royal College of Music where Sir Charles Stanford was his tutor and during his time at the RCM he composed lyrical, small-scale works in the manner of the English school of the day. Gurney volunteered on the outbreak of war, but was only accepted in February 1915. His regiment (2nd/5th Gloucesters) were posted to the Laventie-Fauquissart sector of the Flanders front and the landscape and place-names of this area were to appear frequently alongside those of Gloucestershire in his poetry. Gurney was gassed during the Battle of Passchendaele in September 1917 and never returned to active service. He was discharged with 'deferred shell-shock' in October 1918.

Gurney wrote poetry and music throughout the war. His first collection of poems, *Severn and Somme* was published in October 1917 with a second, *War's Embers*, appearing in 1919. In that year he returned to the RCM, where he was taught by Ralph Vaughan Williams. Although he continued to write and compose prolifically, his mental health deteriorated and in 1922 he was committed to a hospital in Kent where he remained for the rest of his life. After 1926 his output slowed and he apparently wrote nothing after 1933. Although some selections of his poetry appeared in 1954 and 1973, a full range of Gurney's verse was unavailable until 1982.

Texts
P. J. Kavanagh's revised *Collected Poems* (Gurney 1984) is the standard edition. Edmund Blunden's edition of *Poems by Ivor Gurney* (Gurney 1954) has an interesting introduction. Gurney's letters have also been collected (Gurney 1991).

Biography
The standard biography, which also contains critical comment on the poetry and music, is Hurd 1978.

Criticism
The lack of a reliable edition of Gurney's poetry led to critical neglect, but there is a short chapter in Jon Silkin's *Out of Battle* (1972). Donald Davie and Geoffrey Hill have both written on Gurney (Davie 1989, Hill 1984).

Recordings

There are a number of recordings of Gurney's music. *War's Embers* (Hyperion CDA 66261/2) is a representative collection of Gurney's songs, while Chandos CHAN 8831 contains songs by Gurney and his contemporary Arthur Butterworth, an associate of Cecil Sharp who was also killed in the war. Gurney's settings of poems from A. E. Housman's *A Shropshire Lad* are included on Meridian CDE 84135, and his piano works are available on Gamut GAMCD 5/6.

Strange Service

Little did I dream, England, that you bore me
Under the Cotswold hills beside the water meadows,
To do you dreadful service, here, beyond your borders
And your enfolding seas.

5   I was a dreamer ever, and bound to your dear service,
Meditating deep, I thought on your secret beauty,
As through a child's face one may see the clear spirit
Miraculously shining.

Your hills not only hills, but friends of mine and kindly,
10   Your tiny knolls and orchards hidden beside the river
Muddy and strongly-flowing, with shy and tiny streamlets
Safe in its bosom.

Now these are memories only, and your skies and rushy sky-pools
Fragile mirrors easily broken by moving airs ...
15   In my deep heart for ever goes on your daily being,
And uses consecrate.

Think on me too, O Mother, who wrest my soul to serve you
In strange and fearful ways beyond your encircling waters;
None but you can know my heart, its tears and sacrifice;
20   None, but you, repay.

DATE: in *Severn and Somme* (1917) (Gurney 1984).
DISCUSSION: Chapter 2.

De Profundis

If only this fear would leave me I could dream of Crickley Hill
  And a hundred thousand thoughts of home would visit my
    heart in sleep;
But here the peace is shattered all day by the devil's will,
  And the guns bark night-long to spoil the velvet silence deep.

5   O who could think that once we drank in quiet inns and cool
  And saw brown oxen trooping the dry sands to slake
Their thirst at the river flowing, or plunged in a silver pool
  To shake the sleepy drowse off before well awake?

We are stale here, we are covered body and soul and mind
10   With mire of the trenches, close clinging and foul,
We have left our old inheritance, our Paradise behind,
  And clarity is lost to us and cleanness of soul.

O blow here, you dusk-airs and breaths of half-light,
  And comfort despairs of your darlings that long
15 Night and day for sound of your bells, or a sight
  Of your tree-bordered lanes, land of blossom and song.

Autumn will be here soon, but the road of coloured leaves
  Is not for us, the up and down highway where go
Earth's pilgrims to wonder where Malvern upheaves
20   That blue-emerald splendour under great clouds of snow.

Some day we'll fill in trenches, level the land and turn
  Once more joyful faces to the country where trees
Bear thickly for good drink, where strong sunsets burn
  Huge bonfires of glory – O God, send us peace!

25 Hard it is for men of moors or fens to endure
  Exile and hardship, or the northland grey-drear;
But we of the rich plain of sweet airs and pure,
  Oh! Death would take so much from us, how should we not
    fear?

DATE: in *War's Embers* (1919) (Gurney 1984).
TITLE: 'from the depths', the first line of Psalm CXXX.
L.1: 'Crickley Hill' – a hill near Gloucester.

Strange Hells

There are strange hells within the minds war made
Not so often, not so humiliatingly afraid
As one would have expected – the racket and fear guns made.
One hell the Gloucester soldiers they quite put out:
5   Their first bombardment, when in combined black shout

Of fury, guns aligned, they ducked lower their heads
And sang with diaphragms fixed beyond all dreads,
That tin and stretched-wire tinkle, that blither of tune:
'Après la guerre fini', till hell all had come down,
10   Twelve-inch, six-inch, and eighteen pounders hammering
      hell's thunders.

Where are they now, on state-doles, or showing shop-patterns
Or walking town to town sore in borrowed tatterns
Or begged. Some civic routine one never learns.
The heart burns – but has to keep out of face how heart burns.

DATE: 1919–22.
  L.9: 'Après la guerre fini' – soldiers' song (see Brophy and
     Partridge 1965: 33).

First Time In

After the dread tales and red yarns of the Line
Anything might have come to us; but the divine
Afterglow brought us up to a Welsh colony
Hiding in sandbag ditches, whispering consolatory
5   Soft foreign things. Then we were taken in
To low huts candle-lit, shaded close by slitten
Oilsheets, and there the boys gave us kind welcome,
So that we looked out as from the edge of home.
Sang us Welsh things, and changed all former notions
10   To human hopeful things. And the next day's guns
Nor any line-pangs ever quite could blot out
That strangely beautiful entry to war's rout;
Candles they gave us, precious and shared over-rations –

15 Ulysses found little more in his wanderings without doubt.
'David of the White Rock', the 'Slumber Song' so soft, and that
Beautiful tune to which roguish words by Welsh pit boys
Are sung – but never more beautiful than there under the
    guns' noise.

> DATE: from *Rewards of Wonder*, rejected by his publishers in
>   1919.
> L.14: 'Ulysses' – Roman name for Odysseus, the Greek soldier
>   whose journey home from the Trojan wars is the subject
>   of *The Odyssey*.
> L.15: 'David of the White Rock' and the 'Slumber Song' –
>   Welsh folk-songs.

The Silent One

Who died on the wires, and hung there, one of two –
Who for his hours of life had chattered through
Infinite lovely chatter of Bucks accent:
Yet faced unbroken wires; stepped over, and went
5 A noble fool, faithful to his stripes – and ended.
But I weak, hungry, and willing only for the chance
Of line – to fight in the line, lay down under unbroken
Wires, and saw the flashes and kept unshaken,
Till the politest voice – a finicking accent, said:
10 'Do you think you might crawl through there: there's a hole.'
Darkness, shot at: I smiled, as politely replied –
'I'm afraid not, Sir.' There was no hole no way to be seen
Nothing but chance of death, after tearing of clothes.
Kept flat, and watched the darkness, hearing bullets whizzing –
15 And thought of music – and swore deep heart's deep oaths
(Polite to God) and retreated and came on again,
Again retreated – and a second time faced the screen.

> DATE: 1919–22.

Swift and Slow

Death swooped suddenly on men in Flanders
There were no tweedledees or handy-danders
The skull was cleft, the life went out from it
And glory in a family tale was set.
5   But here, having escaped the steely showers
Endured through panged intolerable hours
The expensive and much determined doom,
Find slow death in the loved street and bookish room.
Liver and bowels congested to devil's pitch
10 For a pittance or sake of benefit, what matters which?
Life witch-like seen as Dürer saw, the detested witch.

DATE: 1919–22.
L.2: 'tweedledees' – light, improvised music; 'handy-danders' –
   children's game.
L.11: 'Dürer' – Albrecht Dürer (1471–1528), German painter and
   engraver.
DISCUSSION: Chapter 7.

The Mangel-Bury

It was after war: Edward Thomas had fallen at Arras –
I was walking by Gloucester musing on such things
As fill his verse with goodness; it was February; the long
   house
Straw-thatched of the mangels stretched two wide wings;
5   And looked as part of the earth heaped up by dead soldiers
In the most fitting place – along the hedge's yet-bare lines.
West spring breathed there early, that none foreign divines.
Across the flat country the rattling of the cart sounded;
Heavy of wood, jingling of iron; as he neared me I waited
10 For the chance perhaps of heaving at those great rounded
Ruddy or orange things – and right to be rolled and hefted
By a body like mine, soldier still, and clean from water.
Silent he assented; till the cart was drifted
High with those creatures, so right in size and matter.

15 We threw with our bodies swinging, blood in my ears
    singing;
His was the thick-set sort of farmer, but well-built –
Perhaps, long before, his blood's name ruled all,
Watched all things for his own. If my luck had so willed
Many questions of lordship I had heard him tell – old
20 Names, rumours. But my pain to more moving called
And him to some barn business far in the fifteen acre field.

> DATE: 1922–5.
> L.1: 'Edward Thomas' – poet and writer on rural England. He
>   was killed at Arras in 1917.
> DISCUSSION: Chapter 2.

While I Write

While I write war tells me truth; as for brave
None might challenge Gloucesters, save those dead who have
Paid prices for pre-eminence, perhaps have got their pay.
But the common goodness of those soldiers shown day after day,
5 And the sight of each-hour beauty brilliant or most grave,
Stays with me yet. While I am forbidden to write
Tale of the continual readiness for a bad bloodiness,
And steadiness against hell-fire; and strained eyes with
    humour bright.
War told me truth: I have Severn's right of maker,
10 As of Cotswold: war told me: I was elect, I was born fit
To praise the three hundred feet depth of every acre
Between Tewkesbury and Stroudway, Side and Wales Gate.

Who may be now trembling with a vast impatience
And anxieties and mixed hopes for a resurrection
15 Out of the mouldering soil – to be new form, have perfections
Of flowers and petal and blade, to die, to be born to clean action.

> DATE: 1922–5.
> L.2: 'Gloucesters' – Gurney's regiment.
> L.9: 'Severn' – the main river of Gloucestershire.
> L.12: 'Tewkesbury ... Stroudway, Side ... Wales Gate.' –
>   places in Gloucestershire.
> DISCUSSION: Chapter 7.

Wilfred Owen
1893–1918

Owen was born in Shropshire, the son of a railway superintendent. He was educated at Shrewsbury Technical School, and became a lay assistant to a parish priest in Oxfordshire before leaving to teach in Bordeaux in 1913. He joined the army in October 1915 and was commissioned as a second lieutenant in June 1916. In May 1917 he was diagnosed as 'shell-shocked' and was sent for treatment to Craiglockhart War Hospital in Edinburgh. There he met Siegfried Sassoon and became editor of the hospital magazine. Sassoon's influence was crucial to the development of Owen's poetry, and the two men corresponded regularly after Owen left Craiglockhart in October 1917. He returned to France in August 1918 and was awarded the MC in October for his part in a successful attack. He was killed in November 1918, a week before the Armistice.

Few of Owen's poems were published during his lifetime. The first edition of his poetry was prepared by Sassoon and Edith Sitwell in 1920, and Edmund Blunden edited a more comprehensive collection in 1931.

Texts

The standard edition of Owen's poetry was edited by Jon Stallworthy (Owen 1983) and a study edition of this is available (Owen 1990). Owen's letters have also been collected (Owen 1967). There are useful selections of his major poems interspersed with extracts from the letters edited by Dominic Hibberd (Owen 1973) and Jennifer Breen (Owen 1988).

Biography

The standard biography is Stallworthy 1974. The biography written by his brother, Harold Owen, is less reliable (Owen 1963–5). Dominic Hibberd's *Wilfred Owen: The Last Year 1917–18* (Hibberd 1992) is a detailed account of Owen's life and work in the period.

Criticism

There are two book-length studies (Welland 1960; Hibberd 1986). There are also useful sections in Silkin 1972, Fussell 1975 and Hibberd 1981. Philip Larkin's two essays on Owen are interesting assessments of Owen's role in English culture (in Larkin 1983). Jonathan Cutbill's 'The truth untold' is a polemical article on Owen as a poet of homosexual experience (Cutbill 1987).

Apologia Pro Poemate Meo

I, too, saw God through mud, –
    The mud that cracked on cheeks when wretches smiled.
    War brought more glory to their eyes than blood,
    And gave their laughs more glee than shakes a child.

5   Merry it was to laugh there –
    Where death becomes absurd and life absurder.
    For power was on us as we slashed bones bare
    Not to feel sickness or remorse of murder.

I, too, have dropped off Fear –
10   Behind the barrage, dead as my platoon,
    And sailed my spirit surging light and clear
    Past the entanglement where hopes lay strewn;

And witnessed exultation –
    Faces that used to curse me, scowl for scowl,
15   Shine and lift up with passion of oblation,
    Seraphic for an hour; though they were foul.

I have made fellowships –
    Untold of happy lovers in old song.
    For love is not the binding of fair lips
20   With the soft silk of eyes that look and long,

By Joy, whose ribbon slips, –
    But wound with war's hard wire whose stakes are strong;
    Bound with the bandage of the arm that drips;
    Knit in the webbing of the rifle-thong.

25   I have perceived much beauty
    In the hoarse oaths that kept our courage straight;
    Heard music in the silentness of duty;
    Found peace where shell-storms spouted reddest spate.

Nevertheless, except you share
30   With them in hell the sorrowful dark of hell,
    Whose world is but the trembling of a flare
    And heaven but as the highway for a shell,

You shall not hear their mirth:
　　You shall not come to think them well content
35　By any jest of mine. These men are worth
　　Your tears. You are not worth their merriment.

DATE: November–December 1917.
TITLE: 'a defence of my poem'.
DISCUSSION: Chapter 7.

Insensibility

1

Happy are men who yet before they are killed
Can let their veins run cold.
Whom no compassion fleers
Or makes their feet
5　Sore on the alleys cobbled with their brothers.
The front line withers.
But they are troops who fade, not flowers,
For poets' tearful fooling:
Men, gaps for filling:
10　Losses, who might have fought
Longer; but no one bothers.

2

And some cease feeling
Even themselves or for themselves.
Dullness best solves
15　The tease and doubt of shelling,
And Chance's strange arithmetic
Comes simpler than the reckoning of their shilling.
They keep no check on armies' decimation.

3

Happy are those who lose imagination:
20   They have enough to carry with ammunition.
Their spirit drags no pack.
Their old wounds, save with cold, can not more ache.
Having seen all things red,
Their eyes are rid
25   Of the hurt of the colour of blood for ever.
And terror's first constriction over,
Their hearts remain small-drawn.
Their senses in some scorching cautery of battle
Now long since ironed,
30   Can laugh among the dying, unconcerned.

4

Happy the soldier home, with not a notion
How somewhere, every dawn, some men attack,
And many sighs are drained.
Happy the lad whose mind was never trained:
35   His days are worth forgetting more than not.
He sings along the march
Which we march taciturn, because of dusk,
The long, forlorn, relentless trend
From larger day to huger night.

5

40   We wise, who with a thought besmirch
Blood over all our soul,
How should we see our task
But through his blunt and lashless eyes?
Alive, he is not vital overmuch;
45   Dying, not mortal overmuch;
Nor sad, nor proud,
Nor curious at all.
He cannot tell
Old men's placidity from his.

6

50 But cursed are dullards whom no cannon stuns,
That they should be as stones.
Wretched are they, and mean
With paucity that never was simplicity.
By choice they made themselves immune
55 To pity and whatever moans in man
Before the last sea and the hapless stars;
Whatever mourns when many leave these shores;
Whatever shares
The eternal reciprocity of tears.

DATE: October 1917–January 1918.

Strange Meeting

It seemed that out of battle I escaped
Down some profound dull tunnel, long since scooped
Through granites which titanic wars had groined.

Yet also there encumbered sleepers groaned,
5 Too fast in thought or death to be bestirred.
Then, as I probed them, one sprang up, and stared
With piteous recognition in fixed eyes,
Lifting distressful hands, as if to bless.
And by his smile, I knew that sullen hall, –
10 By his dead smile I knew we stood in Hell.

With a thousand pains that vision's face was grained;
Yet no blood reached there from the upper ground,
And no guns thumped, or down the flues made moan.
'Strange friend,' I said, 'here is no cause to mourn.'
15 'None,' said that other, 'save the undone years,
The hopelessness. Whatever hope is yours,
Was my life also; I went hunting wild
After the wildest beauty in the world,
Which lies not calm in eyes, or braided hair,
20 But mocks the steady running of the hour,
And if it grieves, grieves richlier than here.

For by my glee might many men have laughed,
And of my weeping something had been left,
Which must die now. I mean the truth untold,
25 The pity of war, the pity war distilled.
Now men will go content with what we spoiled,
Or, discontent, boil bloody, and be spilled.
They will be swift with swiftness of the tigress.
None will break ranks, though nations trek from progress
30 Courage was mine, and I had mystery,
Wisdom was mine, and I had mastery:
To miss the march of this retreating world
Into vain citadels that are not walled.
Then, when much blood had clogged their chariot-wheels,
35 I would go up and wash them from sweet wells,
Even with truths that lie too deep for taint.
I would have poured my spirit without stint
But not through wounds; not on the cess of war.
Foreheads of men have bled where no wounds were.

40 'I am the enemy you killed, my friend.
I knew you in this dark: for so you frowned
Yesterday through me as you jabbed and killed.
I parried; but my hands were loath and cold.
Let us sleep now....'

DATE: January–March 1918.
DISCUSSION: Chapter 4.

Smile, Smile, Smile

Head to limp head, the sunk-eyed wounded scanned
Yesterday's *Mail*; the casualties (typed small)
And (large) Vast Booty from our Latest Haul.
Also, they read of Cheap Homes, not yet planned.
5 'For', said the paper, 'when this war is done
The men's first instincts will be making homes.
Meanwhile their foremost need is aerodromes,
It being certain war has but begun.
Peace would do wrong to our undying dead, –
10 The sons we offered might regret they died
If we got nothing lasting in their stead.
We must be solidly indemnified.
Though all be worthy Victory which all bought,
We rulers sitting in this ancient spot
15 Would wrong our very selves if we forgot
The greatest glory will be theirs who fought,
Who kept this nation in integrity.'
Nation? – The half-limbed readers did not chafe
But smiled at one another curiously
20 Like secret men who know their secret safe.
(This is the thing they know and never speak,
That England one by one had fled to France,
Not many elsewhere now, save under France.)
Pictures of these broad smiles appear each week,
25 And people in whose voice real feeling rings
Say: How they smile! They're happy now, poor things.

DATE: September 1918.
TITLE: line from soldiers' song 'Pack Up Your Troubles'.
L.2: '*Mail*' – the *Daily Mail*, a notoriously jingoistic daily
   British newspaper.
L.5FF.: a reference to an article in the *Daily Mail* and a
   speech by the French Prime Minister Clemenceau.
   Owen referred to both in a letter to Sassoon written at
   the same time as the poem (Owen 1967: 578).
DISCUSSION: Chapter 2.

Futility

Move him into the sun –
Gently its touch awoke him once,
At home, whispering of fields half-sown.
Always it woke him, even in France,
5   Until this morning and this snow.
If anything might rouse him now
The kind old sun will know.

Think how it wakes the seeds –
Woke once the clays of a cold star.
10   Are limbs, so dear achieved, are sides
Full-nerved, still warm, too hard to stir?
Was it for this the clay grew tall?
– O what made fatuous sunbeams toil
To break earth's sleep at all?

DATE: May 1918.

Spring Offensive

Halted against the shade of a last hill
They fed, and eased of pack-loads, were at ease;
And leaning on the nearest chest or knees
Carelessly slept.
          But many there stood still
5   To face the stark blank sky beyond the ridge,
Knowing their feet had come to the end of the world.
Marvelling they stood, and watched the long grass swirled
By the May breeze, murmurous with wasp and midge;
And though the summer oozed into their veins
10   Like an injected drug for their bodies' pains,
Sharp on their souls hung the imminent ridge of grass,
Fearfully flashed the sky's mysterious glass.

Hour after hour they ponder the warm field
And the far valley behind, where buttercups
15 Had blessed with gold their slow boots coming up;
When even the little brambles would not yield
But clutched and clung to them like sorrowing arms.
They breathe like trees unstirred.

Till a cold gust thrills the little word
20 At which each body and its soul begird
And tighten them for battle. No alarms
Of bugles, no high flags, no clamorous haste, –
Only a lift and flare of eyes that faced
The sun, like a friend with whom their love is done.
25 O larger shone that smile against the sun, –
Mightier than his whose bounty these have spurned.

So, soon they topped the hill, and raced together
Over an open stretch of herb and heather
Exposed. And instantly the whole sky burned
30 With fury against them; earth set sudden cups
In thousands for their blood; and the green slope
Chasmed and deepened sheer to infinite space.

Of them who running on that last high place
Breasted the surf of bullets, or went up
35 On the hot blast and fury of hell's upsurge,
Or plunged and fell away past this world's verge,
Some say God caught them even before they fell.

But what say such as from existence' brink
Ventured but drave too swift to sink,
40 The few who rushed in the body to enter hell,
And there out-fiending all its fiends and flames
With superhuman inhumanities,
Long-famous glories, immemorial shames –
And crawling slowly back, have by degrees
45 Regained cool peaceful air in wonder –
Why speak not they of comrades that went under?

DATE: July–September 1918.
DISCUSSION: Chapter 7.

[134]

Poems from the Ilkeston Pioneer *and the* Ilkeston Advertiser

The following poems are taken from two local newspapers published in the East Midlands, but they are typical of such writing throughout Britain. In the First World War Ilkeston was a town based on coalmining, steel and hosiery, with a population of 31,000. The poems selected here are representative of those that appeared regularly throughout the war. They illustrate traditions of working-class writing in First World War England, drawing upon ballad traditions, the poetry of Rudyard Kipling, music-hall songs and an oral culture of soldiers' songs and rhymes.

There are no books which deal specifically with working-class poetry of the period. John Brophy and Eric Partridge's pioneering study of soldiers' songs and slang is informative (Brophy and Partridge 1965) and Fuller's more recent study of First World War popular culture is the best survey of this subject (Fuller 1990). For collections of soldiers' songs see Palmer 1990; Page 1975; Dallas 1972. Brian Murdoch's study of wartime song is the best account of popular and mass song production (Murdoch 1990).

This Is My Story

Pte Thomas Beardsley, Royal Field Artillery in Ypres – 'me and 5 pals made this up'. Sung to the tune of 'This Is My Story'.

1st Voice
This is my story, the Kaiser replied,
If England surrenders, the World would be mine.
I'll make one Empire, I'll rule the globe,
But not while this Bull-dog stands in my road.

Chorus
5   This is my story, this is my song,
Right section ranging, limbers drive on,
Gunners and Drivers are glad when they say –
Battery cease firing: they've all run away.

2nd Voice

When our guns start firing there isn't a doubt
10   The Germans that's left they know we're about;
They boast of Jack Johnsons and Krupps' big guns,
But our little country boasts of her sons.

3rd Voice

The boys that composed this they sit in the dark,
And they've only composed it just for a lark;
15   We've been to Mons, Marne, the Aisne and Ypres,
But roll on, old England, and we'll sit at our ease.

4th Voice

Driver Hinken was writing, said Morre 'Now we'll close',
While Gordon and Brenna blew smoke down their nose,
Said Swinburne to Beardsley, 'When I think of this lot
20   It very near drives us six off the dot'.

DATE: *Ilkeston Advertiser* 12 March 1915.
TITLE: reference to a well-known hymn.
L.6: 'limbers' – front parts of gun-carriages.
L.11: 'Jack Johnsons' – artillery shells; 'Krupps' – German arms manufacturer.
L.15: 'Mons, Marne, the Aisne and Ypres' – battles of the First World War.
DISCUSSION: Chapter 3.

My Little Wet Home in the Trench

Pte George Shipstone (10th Royal Hussars) – to be sung to the tune of 'My Little Grey Home in the West'.

My little wet home in the trench
The rainstorms continually drench.
There's a dead cow close by,
With its hoofs to the sky,
5   That gives off such a terrible stench!
Underneath, in place of a floor,
There's a heap of mud and wet straw,
And when Jack Johnsons creep
You'll find me asleep
10   In my little wet home in the trench.

DATE: *Ilkeston Advertiser* 9 April 1915.
TITLE: The poem is a parody of the popular song mentioned here.
L.8: 'Jack Johnsons' – artillery shells (named after a great American boxer).
DISCUSSION: Chapter 3.

Tribute to the 11th Division

Pte J. C. Johnson (9th Lancs Fuseliers)

It was on the 6th of August
  When they made that terrible clash,
And the Turks along the hillside
  Were trying our boats to smash.

5   The order came, 'Fix bayonets',
  As out of the boats they got;
Every man there was a hero
  Who was facing the Turkish shot.

Funnels of ships were smashed,
10   While the ocean in part was red:
But they fought their way through the water
  To the beach that was covered with dead.

Creeping at last up the hillside,
  While shot and shell fell around;
15   They made a last desperate effort,
  And charged over the Turkish ground.

The Turks at last gave it up,
  When they saw the bayonets play;
And turned their back on the British,
20   And retired from Suvla Bay.

And far away on the hillside,
  Lying beneath the clay,
Are some of the gallant lads who died
  Trying to win the day.

[137]

DATE: *Ilkeston Pioneer* 17 March 1916.
L.20: 'Suvla Bay' – on the west of the Dardanelles Peninsula. An Allied landing took place in August 1915. See the soldiers' song 'Suvla Bay' in Palmer 1990: 101.

On the Red Road to Hooge

Pte W. Lloyd (12th Sherwoods)

On parade get your spade,
Fall in the shovel and pick brigade;
There's a carrying fatigue for half a league,
Work to be done with a spade.
5   Through the dust and ruins of Ypres town,
The seventeen-inch guns still batter down,
Spurting death with its fiery breath
On the red, red road to Hooge.
Who is the one whose time has come?
10 Who won't return when the work is done?
Who will leave his bones on the blood-stained stone,
On the red, red road to Hooge?
Onward the Sherwoods, never a stop,
To the sand bag trench and over the top;
15 Stick 'em in, and share your lot,
On the red, red road to Hooge.
Hard to the sound of hand grenades
Which welcome us in death parades,
In the pit of gloom, in the weary woods,
20 Which canter down at Hooge.
Full many a soldier from the Rhine
Must sleep tonight in a bed of lime;
There are fertile graves for many a brave
On the red, red road to Hooge.

25 Hark to the start of the cannonade,
Sling your rifle, bring your spade,
And fade away before break of day
Or a hole you'll fill at Hooge.
Call the role and another name
30 Is sent to swell the roll of fame,
So we put a cross to mark the loss
Of a chum who fell at Hooge.
Not a deed for the paper man to write,
No glorious charge in the dreary night,
35 The 'Daily Mail' won't tell the tale
Of the night work at Hooge.
Look out, my boys, it's the sound of the gong,
The gas is on its way, around you it hangs,
On the red, red road to Hooge.
40 But the general knows of the praise we won,
Was pleased with the work the Sherwoods had done,
While amidst shot and shell, at the gates of hell,
On the red, red road to Hooge.

DATE: *Ilkeston Pioneer* 24 March 1916.
TITLE: 'Hooge' – former châtaeu east of Ypres.
L.5: 'Ypres' – town in Belgium. Gave its name to three great
offensives of the First World War.
L.13: 'Sherwoods' – Sherwood Foresters, a local regiment.
DISCUSSION: Chapter 3.

Send 'Em Along

Entraining the Wounded by the R.A.M.C. Pte C. Butters

Send 'em along in twenty-fives!
The halt, the maimed, the blind –
With blood-stained lips they're smoking fags,
Limping old sweats, with their clothes in rags,
5   Whose trouser legs are blood-stained bags,
And some of 'em can't sit down.

Send 'em along! There's room for five,
With straw in a big horse truck,
A chew of baccy – a broken pipe –
10   There's Bob and Jim, with Scottie and Mike
From the Emerald Isle and the land-o'-th'-tyke,
With honours of thick trench mud.

Send him along! he's a vacant look,
On his lips a far-off smile;
15   A few hours ago he was eager enough,
– Just how it's a case of 'quantum suff' –
In the scrap – well, he gave the Bosches snuff!
Now he's willing to rest awhile.

Send 'em along! Chum, how do you feel?
20   Chipp, I bet, though you smile!
Give us a light! Oh, hang this boot,
You ought to have seen the blighters scoot
When they felt our steel you could hear them hoot
Down the trenches for half a mile.

25   Send 'em along! ere the train rolls out,
There's only three steps to climb,
For the folk at home will want to hear
Of the big advance – Lord send us beer –
So we're hopping along while victory's cheer
30   Is rolling along the line.

Send 'em along in batches of ten!
But those who can never come,
Are lying out there on the battlefield,
For a nation's honour they've been a shield,
35 And to only Death have they had to yield –
Yes! a glorious name they've won.

DATE: *Ilkeston Advertiser*: 5 January 1917.
TITLE: 'R.A.M.C. – Royal Army Medical Corps.
DISCUSSION: Chapter 3.

Isaac Rosenberg
1890–1917

Rosenberg was brought up in a Jewish family in the East End of London (see Chapter 5). After two years as an apprentice engraver, he found sponsorship to attend the Slade School of Art in 1911 where he studied until 1913 and came into contact with the artists Mark Gertler and David Bomberg. He also met the publisher and civil servant Edward Marsh (with whom he corresponded regularly throughout his life) and the poet and philosopher T. E. Hulme. After nine months in South Africa recuperating from ill-health, he returned to England and enlisted (apparently out of financial need) in October 1915. His first major work, the play *Moses*, was privately printed in May 1916, shortly before Rosenberg was sent to France. In December 1916 his poem 'Break of Day in the Trenches' was printed in the leading American modernist journal *Poetry*. Rosenberg was killed in April 1918. The first selection of his poems was published in 1922.

Text

The standard text is Ian Parsons' edition of the collected works (Rosenberg 1979). This includes poetry, prose writings, letters and plates of Rosenberg's paintings.

Biography

There are three biographies (Cohen 1975; Liddiard 1975; Wilson 1975). Diane Collecott gives a good account of Rosenberg's East End (Collecott 1981), as does Joseph Leftwich in his introduction to the autobiography of Rudolf Rocker (Rocker 1956).

Criticism

There are long chapters on Rosenberg in Silkin 1972 and Graham 1984. Fussell 1975 includes an excellent analysis of 'Break of Day in the Trenches'.

The Jew

Moses, from whose loins I sprung,
Lit by a lamp in his blood
Ten immutable rules, a moon
For mutable lampless men.

5   The blonde, the bronze, the ruddy,
With the same heaving blood,
Keep tide to the moon of Moses,
Then why do they sneer at me?

DATE: *c.* 1916.
DISCUSSION: Chapter 5.

Break of Day in the Trenches

The darkness crumbles away.
It is the same old druid Time as ever,
Only a live thing leaps my hand,
A queer sardonic rat,
5 As I pull the parapet's poppy
To stick behind my ear.
Droll rat, they would shoot you if they knew
Your cosmopolitan sympathies.
Now you have touched this English hand
10 You will do the same to a German
Soon, no doubt, if it be your pleasure
To cross the sleeping green between.
It seems you inwardly grin as you pass
Strong eyes, fine limbs, haughty athletes,
15 Less chanced than you for life,
Bonds to the whims of murder,
Sprawled in the bowels of the earth,
The torn fields of France.
What do you see in our eyes
20 At the shrieking iron and flame
Hurled through still heavens?
What quaver—what heart aghast?
Poppies whose roots are in man's veins
Drop, and are ever dropping;

25 But mine in my ear is safe—
Just a little white with the dust.

DATE: June 1916.
L.5: 'parapet' – front of a trench.
DISCUSSION: Chapter 5.

Louse Hunting

Nudes—stark and glistening,
Yelling in lurid glee. Grinning faces
And raging limbs
Whirl over the floor one fire.
5   For a shirt verminously busy
Yon soldier tore from his throat, with oaths
Godhead might shrink at, but not the lice.
And soon the shirt was aflare
Over the candle he'd lit while we lay.

10   Then we all sprang up and stript
To hunt the verminous brood.
Soon like a demons' pantomime
The place was raging.
See the silhouettes agape,
15   See the gibbering shadows
Mixed with the battled arms on the wall.
See gargantuan hooked fingers
Pluck in supreme flesh
To smutch supreme littleness.
20   See the merry limbs in hot Highland fling
Because some wizard vermin
Charmed from the quiet this revel
When our ears were half lulled
By the dark music
25   Blown from Sleep's trumpet.

DATE: 1917.
DISCUSSION: Chapter 5.

Dead Man's Dump

The plunging limbers over the shattered track
Racketed with their rusty freight,
Stuck out like many crowns of thorns,
And the rusty stakes like sceptres old
5   To stay the flood of brutish men
Upon our brothers dear.

The wheels lurched over sprawled dead
But pained them not, though their bones crunched,
Their shut mouths made no moan,
10   They lie there huddled, friend and foeman,
Man born of man, and born of woman,
And shells go crying over them
From night till night and now.

Earth has waited for them
15   All the time of their growth
Fretting for their decay:
Now she has them at last!
In the strength of their strength
Suspended—stopped and held.

20   What fierce imaginings their dark souls lit
Earth! have they gone into you?
Somewhere they must have gone,
And flung on your hard back
Is their souls' sack,
25   Emptied of God-ancestralled essences.
Who hurled them out? Who hurled?

None saw their spirits' shadow shake the grass,
Or stood aside for the half used life to pass
Out of those doomed nostrils and the doomed mouth,
30   When the swift iron burning bee
Drained the wild honey of their youth.

What of us, who flung on the shrieking pyre,
Walk, our usual thoughts untouched,
Our lucky limbs as on ichor fed,
35   Immortal seeming ever?
Perhaps when the flames beat loud on us,
A fear may choke in our veins
And the startled blood may stop.

The air is loud with death,
40   The dark air spurts with fire
The explosions ceaseless are.
Timelessly now, some minutes past,
These dead strode time with vigorous life,
Till the shrapnel called 'an end!'
45   But not to all. In bleeding pangs
Some borne on stretchers dreamed of home,
Dear things, war-blotted from their hearts.

A man's brains splattered on
A stretcher-bearer's face;
50   His shook shoulders slipped their load,
But when they bent to look again
The drowning soul was sunk too deep
For human tenderness.

They left this dead with the older dead,
55   Stretched at the cross roads.
Burnt black by strange decay,
Their sinister faces lie
The lid over each eye,
The grass and coloured clay
60   More motion have than they,
Joined to the great sunk silences.

Here is one not long dead;
His dark hearing caught our far wheels,
And the choked soul stretched weak hands
65 To reach the living word the far wheels said,
The blood-dazed intelligence beating for light,
Crying through the suspense of the far torturing wheels
Swift for the end to break,
Or the wheels to break,
70 Cried as the tide of the world broke over his sight.

Will they come? Will they ever come?
Even as the mixed hoofs of the mules,
The quivering-bellied mules,
And the rushing wheels all mixed
75 With his tortured upturned sight,
So we crashed round the bend,
We heard his weak scream,
We heard his very last sound,
And our wheels grazed his dead face.

DATE: 1917.
L.1: 'limbers' – fronts of gun-carriages.
L.34: 'ichor' – in Greek mythology the blood of the gods; also
    watery discharge from wounds.
DISCUSSION: Chapter 5.

Girl to Soldier on Leave

I love you—Titan lover,
My own storm-days' Titan.
Greater than the son of Zeus,
I know who I would choose.

5   Titan—my splendid rebel—
The old Prometheus
Wanes like a ghost before your power—
His pangs were joys to yours.

Pallid days arid and wan
10   Tied your soul fast.
Babel cities' smoky tops
Pressed upon your growth

Weary gyves. What were you,
But a word in the brain's ways,
15   Or the Sleep of Circe's swine?
One gyve holds you yet.

It held you hiddenly on the Somme
Tied from my heart at home.
O must it loosen now? I wish
20   You were bound with the old old gyves.

Love! you love me—your eyes
Have looked through death at mine.
You have tempted a grave too much.
I let you—I repine.

DATE: 1917.
L.1: 'Titan' – in Greek mythology, the Titans were the rulers
of Heaven and Earth who were overthrown by Zeus (See
l.3).
L.6: 'Prometheus' – Greek demigod who made man from clay
and stole fire from Olympus. He was chained to a rock
by Zeus in punishment for his rebellion.
L.15: 'Circe's swine' – in the *Odyssey*, Circe is a witch who
entraps Odysseus and turns his followers into swine.
L.16: 'gyve' – shackle.

David Jones
1895–1974

Jones was born in Kent. His father's family was from Wales and, although Jones never spoke Welsh, he identified strongly with Welsh culture, and its traditions and legends are constant reference points in his work. Jones trained as an engraver before joining the army in 1915 where he served as a private in the Royal Welch Fuseliers. He fought in the Battle of the Somme in 1916 and this experience forms the basis for his long poem *In Parenthesis* (1937). After the war Jones became a Roman Catholic and worked with the sculptor and engraver Eric Gill in his craft communities. His major post-Second World War poem is *The Anathemata* (1952), and there are other shorter poems, or 'fragments' as he termed them, several of which return to the themes of *In Parenthesis*.

Texts
In Parenthesis (Jones 1937). 'The Book of Balaam's Ass', a poem analogous to *In Parenthesis* which Jones began in 1938, is in Jones 1974. The essay 'Art in relation to war', written during the Second World War, is also relevant (Jones 1978).

Recording
There is a recording of Jones reading extracts from *In Parenthesis* and other poems. The record has useful sleeve-notes by Jones (Argo RG 520).

Biography
There is no standard biography, but René Hague edited a collection of letters and autobiographical writings (Jones 1980). There is also an autobiographical essay in Jones 1973.

Criticism
Jones himself spoke highly of the chapter in Johnston 1964. Full-length studies include Blamires 1971, Ward 1983, and Hague 1975. There is a useful chapter in Silkin 1972 and a provocatively sceptical appraisal of *In Parenthesis* in Fussell 1975. For Jones's paintings, see Jones 1989; Gray 1989. Colin Hughes's monograph relates *In Parenthesis* to the chronology and locations of Jones's experience during the Somme offensive (Hughes 1979).

from Part 7 of In Parenthesis

EXTRACT I

The memory lets escape what is over and above—
as spilled bitterness, unmeasured, poured-out,
and again drenched down—demoniac-pouring:
who grins who pours to fill flood and super-flow insensately,
5   pint-pot—from milliard-quart measure.

In the Little Hours they sing the Song of Degrees
and of the coals that lie waste.
Soul pass through torrent
and the whole situation is intolerable.

10   He found him all gone to pieces and not pulling himself together nor making the best of things. When they found him his
friends came on him in the secluded fire-bay who miserably
wept for the pity of it all and for the things shortly to come to
pass and no hills to cover us.

15   You really can't behave like this in the face of the enemy and
you see Cousin Dicky doesn't cry nor any of this nonsense—
why, he ate his jam-puff when they came to take Tiger away
—and getting an awfully good job in the Indian Civil.

After a while he got his stuff reasonably assembled, and '45
20   Williams was awfully decent, and wipe every tear, and solidified eau-de-cologne was just the thing so that you couldn't
really tell, & doubled along back, with the beginnings of dawn
pale on the chalky deep protected way, where it led out to
the sunken road, and the rest of the platoon belly-hugged the
25   high embankment going up steep into thin mist at past four
o'clock of a fine summer morning.
In regions of air above the trajectory zone, the birds
chattering heard for all the drum-fire,
counter the malice of the engines.

30 But he made them a little lower than the angels and their
inventions are according to right reason even if you don't
approve the end to which they proceed; so that there was
rectitude even in this, which the mind perceived at this moment of weakest flesh and all the world shrunken to a point
35 of fear that has affinity I suppose, to that state of deprivation
predicate of souls forfeit of their final end, who nevertheless know a good thing when they see it.

But four o'clock is an impossible hour in any case.
  They shook out into a single line and each inclined his body
40 to the slope to wait.
And this is the manner of their waiting:
Those happy who had borne the yoke
who kept their peace
and these other in a like condemnation
45 to the place of a skull.

Immediately behind where Private 25201 Ball pressed his body
to the earth and the white chalk womb to mother him,
          Colonel Dell presumed to welcome
some other, come out of the brumous morning
50 at leisure and well-dressed and all at ease
as thriving on the nitrous air.
Well Dell!
  and into it they slide … of the admirable salads of Mrs.
Curtis-Smythe: they fall for her in Poona, and its worth one's
55 while—but the comrade close next you screamed so after the
last salvo that it was impossible to catch any more the burthen
of this white-man talk.

And the place of their waiting a long burrow,
in the chalk a cutting, and steep clift—
60 but all but too shallow against his violence.
Like in long-ship, where you flattened face to kelson for the
shock-breaking on brittle pavissed free-board, and the gunnel stove, and no care to jettison the dead.

No one to care for Aneirin Lewis spilled there
65 who worshipped his ancestors like a Chink
who sleeps in Arthur's lap
who saw Olwen-trefoils some moonlighted night
on precarious slats at Festubert,
on narrow foothold on le Plantin marsh—
70 more shaved he is to the bare bone than
Yspaddadan Penkawr.
    Properly organised chemists can let make more riving
power than ever Twrch Trwyth;
more blistered he is than painted Troy Towers
75 and unwholer, limb from limb, than any of them fallen at
Catraeth
or on the seaboard-down, by Salisbury,
and no maker to contrive his funerary song.
And the little Jew lies next him
80 cries out for Deborah his bride
and offers for stretcher-bearers
            gifts for their pains
and walnut suites in his delirium
            from Grays Inn Road.

85 But they already look at their watches and it is zero minus
seven minutes.

Seven minutes to go ... and seventy times seven times to
the minute
this drumming of the diaphragm.
90   From deeply inward thumping all through you beating
no peace to be still in
and no one is there not anyone to stop
can't anyone—someone turn off the tap
or won't any one before it snaps.

95 Racked out to another turn of the screw
the acceleration heightens;
the sensibility of these instruments to register,
fails;
needle dithers disorientate.

100   The responsive mercury plays laggard to such fevers– you
      simply can't take any more in.
      And the surfeit of fear steadies to dumb incognition, so that
      when they give the order to move upward to align with 'A',
      hugged already just under the lip of the acclivity inches below
105   where his traversing machine-guns perforate to powder
      white—
      white creature of chalk pounded
      and the world crumbled away
      and get ready to advance
110   you have not capacity for added fear only the limbs are leaden
      to negotiate the slope and rifles all out of balance, clumsied
      with long auxiliary steel
      seem five times the regulation weight—
      it bitches the aim as well;
115   and we ourselves as those small
      cherubs, who trail awkwardly the weapons of the God in
                                          Fine Art works.

      The returning sun climbed over the hill, to lessen the shad-
      ows of small and great things; and registered the minutes to
120   zero hour. Their saucer hats made dial for his passage: long
      thin line of them, virid domes of them,
      cut elliptical with light
      as cupola on Byzantine wall,
      stout turrets to take the shock
125   and helmets of salvation.
      Long side by side lie like friends lie
      on daisy-down on warm days
      cuddled close down kindly close with the mole
      in down and silky rodent,
130   and if you look more intimately all manner of small creatures,
      created-dear things creep about quite comfortably
      yet who travail until now
      beneath your tin-hat shade.
                  He bawls at ear-hole:
135   Two minutes to go.
                  Minutes to excuse me to make excuse.

[154]

Responde mihi?
       for surely I must needs try them
so many, much undone
140   and lose on roundabouts as well and vari-coloured polygram
to love and know
       and we have a little sister
whose breasts will be as towers
and the gilly-flowers will blow next month
145   below the pound
with Fred Karno billed for *The Holloway*.

He's getting it now more accurately and each salvo brackets
more narrowly and a couple right in, just as 'D' and 'C' are
forming for the second wave.

150   Wastebottom married a wife on his Draft-leave but the whin-
nying splinter razored diagonal and mess-tin fragments drove
inward and toxined underwear.
   He maintained correct alignment with the others, face
down, and you never would have guessed.

155   Perhaps they'll cancel it.
O blow fall out the officers cantcher, like a wet afternoon
or the King's Birthday.
   Or you read it again many times to see if it will come different:
160   you can't believe the Cup wont pass from
or they wont make a better show
in the Garden.
Won't someone forbid the banns
or God himself will stay their hands.
165   It just can't happen in our family
even though a thousand
and ten thousand at thy right hand.

Talacryn doesn't take it like Wastebottom, he leaps up & says
he's dead, a-slither down the pale face—his limbs a-girandole
170   at the bottom of the nullah,
but the mechanism slackens, unfed
and he is quite still

which leaves five paces between you and the next live one to
the left.

175　　Sidle over a bit toward where '45 Williams, and use all
your lungs:
　　　Get ready me china-plate—but he's got it before he can
hear you, but it's a cushy one and he relaxes to the morning
sun and smilingly, to wait for the bearers.

180　Some of yer was born wiv jam on it
clicked lucky and favoured
　　　　　　pluckt brand from burning
and my darling from unicorn horn with only a minute to go,
whose wet-nurse cocked a superstitious eye to see his happy
185　constellation through the panes.

But it isn't like that for the common run and you have no men-
suration gear to plot meandering fortune-graph nor know
whether she were the Dark or the Fair left to the grinding.

Last minute drums its taut millennium out
190　you can't swallow your spit
and Captain Marlowe yawns a lot
and seconds now our measuring-rods with no Duke Josue
nor conniving God
to stay the Divisonal Synchronisation.

195　So in the fullness of time
　　　　when pallid jurors bring the doomes
　　　　mooring cables swipe slack-end on
barnacled piles,
and the world falls apart at the last to siren screech and
200　screaming vertical steam in conformity with the Company's
Sailings and up to scheduled time.

As bridal arranged-paraphernalia gets tumbled—eventually
and the night empties of these relatives
if you wait long time enough
205　and yesterday puts on to-day.

At the end of the suspense
come the shod feet
hastily or laggard
or delayed—
210   but anyway, no fretting of watch on the wall nor their hys-
teria,
can hamper nor accelerate
exact kinetics of his advent
nor make less miserable his tale to tell
215   and even Mrs. Chandler's tom
will stiffen one Maye Mornynge
to the ninth death.

Tunicled functionaries signify and clear-voiced heralds cry
and leg it to a safe distance:
220   leave fairway for the Paladins, and Roland throws a kiss—
they've nabbed his batty for the moppers-up
            and Mr. Jenkins takes them over
and don't bunch on the left
for Christ's sake.

EXTRACT 2

And to Private Ball it came as if a rigid beam of great weight
flailed about his calves, caught from behind by ballista-baulk
let fly or aft-beam slewed to clout gunnel-walker
below below below.
5   When golden vanities make about,
                    you've got no legs to stand on.
    He thought it disproportionate in its violence considering
the fragility of us.
    The warm fluid percolates between his toes and his left boot
10   fills, as when you tread in a puddle—he crawled away in the
opposite direction.

It's difficult with the weight of the rifle.
Leave it—under the oak.
Leave it for a salvage-bloke
15   let it lie bruised for a monument
dispense the authenticated fragments to the faithful.

[157]

It's the thunder-besom for us
it's the bright bough borne
it's the tensioned yew for a Genoese jammed arbalest and a
20   scarlet square for a mounted *mareschal*, it's that county-mob
back to back. Majuba mountain and Mons Cherubim and
spreaded mats for Sydney Street East, and come to Bisley
for a Silver Dish. It's R.S.M. O'Grady says, it's the soldier's
best friend if you care for the working parts and let us be 'av-
25   ing those springs released smartly in Company billets on wet
forenoons and clickerty-click and one up the spout and you
men must really cultivate the habit of treating this weapon with
the very greatest care and there should be a healthy rivalry
among you—it should be a matter of very proper pride and
30   Marry it man! Marry it!
Cherish her, she's your very own.
    Coax it man coax it—it's delicately and ingeniously made
—it's an instrument of precision—it costs us tax-payers,
money—I want you men to remember that.
35   Fondle it like a granny—talk to it—consider it as you would
a friend—and when you ground these arms she's not a rooky's
gas-pipe for greenhorns to tarnish.
    You've known her hot and cold.
You would choose her from among many.
40   You know her by her bias, and by her exact error at 300, and
by the deep scar at the small, by the fair flaw in the grain,
above the lower sling-swivel—
but leave it under the oak.

Slung so, it swings its full weight. With you going blindly on
45   all paws, it slews its whole length, to hang at your bowed neck
like the Mariner's white oblation.
    You drag past the four bright stones at the turn of Wood
Support.

It is not to be broken on the brown stone under the gracious
50   tree.
    It is not to be hidden under your failing body.
    Slung so, it troubles your painful crawling like a fugitive's
irons.

The trees are very high in the wan signal-beam, for whose slow
55 gyration their wounded boughs seem as malignant limbs,
manœuvring for advantage.
  The trees of the wood beware each other
            and under each a man sitting;
their seemly faces as carved in a sardonyx stone; as undiademed
60   princes turn their gracious profiles in a hidden seal, so did
these appear, under the changing light.

For that waning you would believe this flaxen head had for its
broken pedestal these bent Silurian shoulders.

  For the pale flares extinction you don't know if under his
65   close lids, his eye-balls watch you. You would say by the turn
of steel at his wide brow he is not of our men where he leans
with his open fist in Dai's bosom against the White Stone.

Hung so about, you make between these your close escape.

The secret princes between the leaning trees have diadems
70 given them.
  Life the leveller hugs her impudent equality—she may proceed at once to less discriminating zones.

The Queen of the Woods has cut bright boughs of various
flowering.
75   These knew her influential eyes. Her awarding hands can
pluck for each their fragile prize.
  She speaks to them according to precedence. She knows
what's due to this elect society. She can choose twelve
gentle-men. She knows who is most lord between the high
80 trees and on the open down.
  Some she gives white berries
            some she gives brown
  Emil has a curious crown it's
            made of golden saxifrage.
85   Fatty wears sweet-briar,
he will reign with her for a thousand years.
  For Balder she reaches high to fetch his.
  Ulrich smiles for his myrtle wand.

That swine Lillywhite has daisies to his chain—you'd hard-
90 ly credit it.
    She plaits torques of equal splendour for Mr. Jenkins and
Billy Crower.
    Hansel and Gronwy share dog-violets for a palm, where
they lie in serious embrace beneath the twisted tripod.

95   Siôn gets St. John's Wort—that's fair enough.
    Dai Great-coat, she can't find him anywhere—she calls
both high and low, she had a very special one for him.
    Among this July noblesse she is mindful of December wood
—when the trees of the forest beat against each other because
100 of him.
    She carries to Aneirin-in-the-nullah a rowan sprig, for the
glory of Guenedota. You couldn't hear what she said to
him, because she was careful for the Discipline of the Wars.
At the gate of the wood you try a last adjustment, but slung
105 so, it's an impediment, it's of detriment to your hopes, you
had best be rid of it—the sagging webbing and all and what's
left of your two fifty—but it were wise to hold on to your
mask.

You're clumsy in your feebleness, you implicate your tin-hat
110 rim with the slack sling of it.
    Let it lie for the dews to rust it, or ought you to decently
cover the working parts.
    Its dark barrel, where you leave it under the oak, reflects
the solemn star that rises urgently from Cliff Trench.
115   It's a beautiful doll for us
it's the Last Reputable Arm.
    But leave it—under the oak.
leave it for a Cook's tourist to the Devastated Areas and crawl
as far as you can and wait for the bearers.

120 Mrs. Willy Hartington has learned to draw sheets and so has
Miss Melpomené; and on the south lawns,
men walk in red white and blue
under the cedars
and by every green tree
125 and beside comfortable waters.

But why don't the bastards come—
Bearers!—stret-cher bear-errs!
or do they divide the spoils at the Aid-Post.
    But how many men do you suppose could bear away a third
130 of us:
drag just a little further—he yet may counter-attack.

Lie still under the oak
next to the Jerry
and Sergeant Jerry Coke.
135   The feet of the reserves going up tread level with your fore-
head; and no word for you; they whisper one with another;
pass on, inward;
these latest succours:
green Kimmerii to bear up the war.

140 Oeth and Annoeth's hosts they were
who in that night grew
younger men
younger striplings.

    The geste says this and the man who was on the field ... and
145 who wrote the book ... the man who does not know this
has not understood anything

DATE: published in 1937, but begun in the late 1920s.

CONTEXT: The poem covers the progress of a unit from December 1915 to the Somme offensive in July 1916. Part 7 begins in the minutes before an attack and describes the assault on Mametz Wood, ending with the wounding of the poem's main 'character', John Ball. The time covered is from 4.15 a.m. on 10 July to around 2 a.m. on 11 July 1916.

EXTRACT 1

L.6: 'Little Hours ... Song of Degrees' – reference to Roman Catholic canonical hours. At 1 a.m., 3 a.m., 6 a.m. and 9 a.m. the psalms known as 'Songs of Degrees' are sung.

L.45: 'place of a skull' – a reference to Golgotha, the place of the execution of Christ.

L.49: 'brumous' – misty.

L.54: 'Poona' – hill-station in imperial India.

L.61: 'kelson' – the timber which holds the wooden floor to the keel of a ship.

L.62: 'pavissed' – 'shielded'.

L.66: 'Arthur's lap': Falstaff is said to be in 'Arthur's bosom', i.e. dead, in *Henry V.* The play is referred to throughout *In Parenthesis.*

L.67: 'Olwen-trefoils' – a reference to an ancient Welsh story. Flowers magically appeared wherever the heroine Olwen walked.

L.68–9: 'Festubert ... Le Plantin' – places on the Somme battlefield.

L.71: 'Yspaddadan Penkawr' – giant in Welsh legend.

L.73: 'Twrch Trwyth' – a destructive boar in Welsh legend.

L.76: 'Catraeth' – sixth-century battle between English and Welsh commemorated in the poem *Y Gododdin.* Jones makes constant reference to this poem.

L.77: 'Salisbury' – reference to the battle of Camlann in Malory's Arthurian epic *La Morte d'Arthur.*

L.84: 'Grays Inn Road' – road in East End of London.

L.120: 'saucer hats' – the distinctively shaped British Army helmets.

L.123: 'cupola' – dome.

L.137: 'Responde mihi' – 'answer me'.

L.146: 'Fred Karno ... *The Holloway*' – Karno was a famous music-hall comedian. The Holloway was a London music-hall.

L.147: 'He's getting it ...' – 'he' was the customary way of referring to the German troops.

L.156: 'fall out the officers' – bugle call signifying the break-off of operations.

L.162: 'the Garden' – reference to the betrayal of Christ in the Garden of Gethsemane.

L.169: 'a-girandole' – moving like a revolving firework.

L.170: 'nullah' – trench.

L.177: 'china-plate' – cockney rhyming slang for 'mate'.

L.178: 'cushy one' – a wound that is serious enough to remove a soldier from the battle but is not life-threatening.

L.196: 'doomes' – judgements.

L.220: 'Paladins ... Roland' – Charlemagne's knights of whom Roland was the most celebrated.

L.221: 'batty' – batman.

EXTRACT 2

L.2: 'ballista-baulk' – ancient military catapult.

L.3: 'gunnel' – upper edge of a ship's side.

L.5: 'golden vanities' – *Golden Vanity* is the name of a ship in a folk-song.

L.19: 'arbalest' – crossbow.

L.20: 'mareschal' – marshal.

L.21: 'Majuba Mountain ... Mons Cherubim' – Majuba Mountain was the place where British troops were defeated by the Boers in 1881; the Angels of Mons were supposed to have appeared to British troops during the Retreat from Mons in 1915 (the story was invented by the novelist Arthur Machen).

L.22: 'Sydney Street East ... Bisley' – street (actually Sidney Street) in East London. Site of a siege in 1911 in which troops were deployed to capture alleged revolutionaries; Bisley is the location of the main Army small-arms shooting range.

L.23: 'R.S.M.' – Regimental Sergeant Major. R.S.M. O'Grady is a mythical figure used in army exercises.

L.46: 'the Mariner's white oblation' – the albatross in Samuel Taylor Coleridge's poem 'The Ancient Mariner'.

L.59: 'sardonyx' – type of quartz. In the ancient French epic, the *Song of Roland*, Roland dies beside a stone of sardonyx and a white rock (see l.63 and Extract 1, l.214).

L.63: 'Silurian' – Welsh.

L.67: 'White Stone' – see note to l.59.

L.73: 'The Queen of the Woods' – a wood spirit.

L.91: 'torques' – necklaces associated with ancient Celtic cultures.

L.102: 'Guenedota' – the north-west parts of Wales.

L.118: 'Cook's tourist' – Thomas Cook was the first promoter of organized tourism.

L.139: 'Kimmerii' – a race fabled to live in perpetual darkness.

L.140: 'Oeth and Annoeth's hosts' – in Welsh legend, a mysterious body of troops.

L.144–6: 'The geste ...': a quotation from the *Song of Roland*.

DISCUSSION: Chapter 2.

H.D. (Hilda Doolittle)
1886–1961

Hilda Doolittle was born in Pennsylvania and moved to London in 1911. She became part of the literary circle of Ezra Pound, and it was Pound who promoted her early poetry under the label of Imagism. During the First World War she suffered various personal difficulties, including the break-up of her marriage with the poet Richard Aldington, and the death of her brother in the war. The mixture of political and personal crises is reflected in her poetry of the period. In the 1930s she underwent psychoanalysis with Freud, and it was at his prompting that she wrote the fictionalized account of the war years, *Bid Me To Live* (H.D. 1984a). She remained in London during the Second World War where she wrote *Trilogy*, a sequence of three long poems based in the London of the Blitz. It presents a vision of personal salvation developed through an idiosyncratic poetic mythology.

Texts
The standard edition is H.D. 1984b. Her autobiographical novel *Bid Me To Live* deals with the period of the First World War (H.D. 1984a). The *Agenda* special number on H.D. includes 'Responsibilities', an important essay/review of the First World War (H.D. 1987–8b).

Biography
There are two biographies, Guest 1985 and Robinson 1982.

Criticism
The only easily-available full-length critical study is DuPlessis 1986. Gary Burnett's essay is helpful on H.D.'s First World War work (Burnett 1987–8). Levenson 1984 and Benstock 1987 are both useful on the cultural context of H.D.'s early work.

After Troy

We flung against their gods,
invincible, clear hate;
we fought;
frantic, we flung the last
5   imperious, desperate shaft
and lost;
we knew the loss
before they ever guessed
fortune had tossed to them
10   her favour and her whim;
but how were we depressed?
we lost yet as we pressed
our spearsmen on their best,
we knew their line invincible
15   because there fell
on them no shiverings
of the white enchantress,
radiant Aphrodite's spell:

we hurled our shafts of passion,
20   noblest hate,
and knew their cause was blest,
and knew their gods were nobler,
better taught in skill,
subtler with wit of thought,
25   yet had it been God's will
that *they* not we should fall,
we know those fields had bled
with roses lesser red.

DATE: first published in 1924.
L.18: 'Aphrodite' – Greek goddess of love. She supported the
Trojan side in the Trojan War.
DISCUSSION: Chapter 7.

from Part 1 of The Tribute

I

Squalor spreads its hideous length
through the carts and the asses' feet,
squalor coils and reopens
and creeps under barrow
5   and heap of refuse
and the broken sherds
of the market-place—
it lengthens and coils
and uncoils and draws back
10   and recoils
through the crooked streets.

Squalor blights and makes hideous
our lives—it has smothered
the beat of our songs,
15   and our hearts are spread out,
flowers—opened but to receive
the wheel of the cart,
the hoof of the ox,
to be trod of the sheep.

20   Squalor spreads its hideous length
through the carts and the asses' feet—
squalor has entered and taken our songs
and we haggle and cheat,
praise fabrics worn threadbare,
25   ring false coin for silver,
offer refuse for meat.

DATE: 1916.
DISCUSSION: Chapter 7.

from Section 1 of The Walls Do Not Fall

[1]

An incident here and there,
and rails gone (for guns)
from your (and my) old town square:

mist and mist-grey, no colour,
5   still the Luxor bee, chick and hare
pursue unalterable purpose

in green, rose-red, lapis;
they continue to prophesy
from the stone papyrus:

10   there, as here, ruin opens
the tomb, the temple; enter,
there as here, there are no doors:

the shrine lies open to the sky,
the rain falls, here, there
15   sand drifts; eternity endures:

ruin everywhere, yet as the fallen roof
leaves the sealed room
open to the air,

so, through our desolation
20   thoughts stir, inspiration stalks us
through gloom:

unaware, Spirit announces the Presence;
shivering overtakes us,
as of old, Samuel:

25   trembling at a known street-corner,
we know not nor are known;
the Pythian pronounces—we pass on

to another cellar, to another sliced wall
where poor utensils show
30   like rare objects in a museum;

Pompeii has nothing to teach us,
we know crack of volcanic fissure,
slow flow of terrible lava,

pressure on heart, lungs, the brain
35   about to burst its brittle case
(what the skull can endure!):

over us, Apocryphal fire,
under us, the earth sway, dip of a floor,
slope of a pavement

40   where men roll, drunk
with a new bewilderment,
sorcery, bedevilment:

the bone-frame was made for
no such shock knit within terror,
45   yet the skeleton stood up to it:

the flesh? it was melted away,
the heart burnt out, dead ember,
tendons, muscles shattered, outer husk dismembered,

yet the frame held:
50   we passed the flame: we wonder
what saved us? what for?

DATE: 1942.
L.5: 'Luxor' – site of ancient complex of temples on the Nile.
DISCUSSION: Chapter 7.

Herbert Read
1893–1968

Read was born in Yorkshire, and the importance of his provincial background is discussed in Chapter 5. He was one of the few British First World War poets to show an awareness of modernist poetry and art (his sequence of imagist poems 'The Scene of War' carries an epigraph from H.D.). His commitment to the avant-garde continued after the war in his support of the art of the British sculptors Barbara Hepworth and Henry Moore, and his involvement with surrealism in the 1930s.

Read's poetry is an idiosyncratic mixture of Wordsworthian Romanticism and modernist experiment. His major work that came from his experience of the First World War, *The End of a War* (1930), is a metaphysical meditation on an atrocity, and is quite unlike any other war poem. Much of his later poetry is haunted by the war experience. In the Second World War he was influential as poetry reader for Routledge, and encouraged many young poets, including Sidney Keyes and Alex Comfort. He also lent support to various anarchist and pacifist causes during the 1930s and 1940s.

Read's poems on war are usually long, and there is only space for one full poem and one extract in the anthology. Besides *The End of a War*, Read's other major poems are 'Kneeshaw Goes to War' and 'The Scene of War' from the First World War, and 'Ode' and 'World Within a War' from the Second.

Texts
Collected Poems (Read 1992). Silkin's anthology includes the full text of *The End of a War* (Silkin 1979).

Biography
The standard biography is King 1990. Read's autobiographical writings on the First World War are collected in *The Contrary Experience: Autobiographies* (Read 1963).

Criticism
There is a good chapter on Read in Silkin 1972. George Woodcock's study of Read has a chapter on the war poems (Woodcock 1972) and Skelton's symposium has an essay on the poetry (Skelton 1970). There is an interesting collection of essays on Read published during the Second World War (Treece 1944).

from *My Company*

Foule! Ton âme entière est debout dans mon corps.   JULES ROMAINS

I

You became
In many acts and quiet observances
A body and a soul, entire.

I cannot tell
5   What time your life became mine:
Perhaps when one summer night
We halted on the roadside
In the starlight only,
And you sang your sad home-songs,
10   Dirges which I standing outside you
Coldly condemned.

Perhaps, one night, descending cold
When rum was mighty acceptable,
And my doling gave birth to sensual gratitude.

15   And then our fights: we've fought together
Compact, unanimous;
And I have felt the pride of leadership.

In many acts and quiet observances
You absorbed me:
20   Until one day I stood eminent
And I saw you gather'd round me,
Uplooking,
And about you a radiance that seemed to beat
With variant glow and to give
25   Grace to our unity.

But, God! I know that I'll stand
Someday in the loneliest wilderness,
Someday my heart will cry
For the soul that has been, but that now
30   Is scatter'd with the winds,
Deceased and devoid.

I know that I'll wander with a cry:
'O beautiful men, O men I loved,
O whither are you gone, my company?'

DATE: in *Naked Warriors* (1919) (Read 1992).
EPIGRAPH: 'Crowd! Your whole soul exists in my body'.
 Jules Romains (1885–1972) was a French novelist and poet.
DISCUSSION: Chapter 5.

To a Conscript of 1940

Qui n'a pas une fois désespéré de l'honneur, ne sera jamais un héros.
GEORGES BERNANOS

A soldier passed me in the freshly fallen snow
His footsteps muffled, his face unearthly grey;
And my heart gave a sudden leap
As I gazed on a ghost of five-and-twenty years ago.

5   I shouted Halt! and my voice had the old accustom'd ring
And he obeyed it as it was obeyed
In the shrouded days when I too was one
Of an army of young men marching

Into the unknown. He turned towards me and I said:
10 'I am one of those who went before you
Five-and-twenty years ago: one of the many who never returned,
Of the many who returned and yet were dead.

We went where you are going, into the rain and the mud;
We fought as you will fight
15 With death and darkness and despair;
We gave what you will give—our brains and our blood.

We think we gave in vain. The world was not renewed.
There was hope in the homestead and anger in the streets
But the old world was restored and we returned
20 To the dreary field and workshop, and the immemorial feud

Of rich and poor. Our victory was our defeat.
Power was retained where power had been misused
And youth was left to sweep away
The ashes that the fires had strewn beneath our feet.

25   But one thing we learned: there is no glory in the deed
Until the soldier wears a badge of tarnish'd braid;
There are heroes who have heard the rally and have seen
The glitter of a garland round their head.

Theirs is the hollow victory. They are deceived.
30   But you, my brother and my ghost, if you can go
Knowing that there is no reward, no certain use
In all your sacrifice, then honour is reprieved.

To fight without hope is to fight with grace,
The self reconstructed, the false heart repaired.'
35   Then I turned with a smile, and he answered my salute
As he stood against the fretted hedge, which was like white lace.

DATE: in *A World Within a War* (1944).

EPIGRAPH: 'He who has never despaired of honour, will never be a hero.' Georges Bernanos (1888–1948) was a French novelist.

DISCUSSION: Chapter 4.

Sorley MacLean
(Somhairle MacGill Eain)
1911—

MacLean was born on the island of Raasay, off the east coast of Skye. He came from a family of Gaelic singers and musicians, and their traditions had a formative influence on his later poetry. He went to university in Edinburgh, and there met Hugh MacDiarmid, whose Scots poetry also influenced MacLean's early work. During the 1930s MacLean developed a Gaelic poetry that was able to deal with contemporary political themes, as well as traditional subject-matter. 'An Cuilithionn' (only recently published in full) is one of the most ambitious political poems of the 1930s. He joined the army in 1940 and served in the Western Desert until he was badly wounded during the Battle of El Alamein in November 1942. After the war MacLean returned to teaching and became headmaster of Plockton Secondary School in Wester Ross. He has been active in the reform of Gaelic teaching in Scottish education.

Texts
From Wood to Ridge is a bilingual edition of MacLean's poetry containing his own translations from the Gaelic (MacLean 1989). A recording of MacLean reading his poetry in the Gaelic is available on the Claddagh label (*Barran Agus Asbhuain* CCA 3).

Biography
There is a essay-length biography and appraisal and an interview with MacLean in Ross and Hendry 1986, and an autobiographical essay, 'My relationship with the Muse', in MacLean 1985. A more recent interview is in *Chapman 66* (MacLean 1991).

Criticism
Ross and Hendry 1986 contains a number of useful essays on various aspects of MacLean's poetry. Donald Davie is one of the few English critics to have written on MacLean (Davie 1989).

Going Westwards

I go westwards in the Desert
with my shame on my shoulders,
that I was made a laughing-stock
since I was as my people were.

5   Love and the greater error,
deceiving honour spoiled me,
with a film of weakness on my vision,
squinting at mankind's extremity.

Far from me the Island
10   when the moon rises on Quattara,
far from me the Pine Headland
when the morning ruddiness is on the Desert.

Camus Alba is far from me
and so is the bondage of Europe,
15   far from me in the North-West
the most beautiful grey-blue eyes.

Far from me the Island
and every loved image in Scotland,
there is a foreign sand in History
20   spoiling the machines of the mind.

Far from me Belsen and Dachau,
Rotterdam, the Clyde and Prague,
and Dimitrov before a court
hitting fear with the thump of his laugh.

25   Guernica itself is very far
from the innocent corpses of the Nazis,
who are lying in the gravel
and in the khaki sand of the Desert.

There is no rancour in my heart
30   against the hardy soldiers of the Enemy,
but the kinship that there is among
men in prison on a tidal rock

waiting for the sea flowing
and making cold the warm stone;
35   and the coldness of life (is)
in the hot sun of the Desert.

But this is the struggle not to be avoided,
the sore extreme of human-kind,
and though I do not hate Rommel's army
40   the brain's eye is not squinting.

And be what was as it was,
I am of the big men of Braes,
of the heroic Raasay MacLeods,
of the sharp-sword Mathesons of Lochalsh;
45   and the men of my name – who were braver
when their ruinous pride was kindled?

DATE: 1941–3.

L.9: 'the Island' – Skye.

L.10: 'Quattara' – Quattara Depression, part of the Alamein battlefield.

L.11: 'Pine Headland' – on Raasay.

L.13: 'Camus Alba' – bay in Raasay.

L.23: 'Dimitrov' – Georgi Dimitrov (1882–1949), Bulgarian communist charged by the Nazis with setting fire to the Reichstag in 1933.

L.25: 'Guernica' – Spanish town destroyed by German planes during the Spanish Civil War.

L.39: 'Rommel's army' – the German troops in Africa were under the command of Field Marshal Rommel.

L.42: 'Braes' – on Skye.

DISCUSSION: Chapter 6.

Alasdair MacLeod

(A day or two before the 'Battle of Knightsbridge' in
May 1942, I heard that he was lost from the RAF.)

Between Tobruk and Bir Hacheim
though our army was being broken
my thoughts were often on you
lost in Germany
5   or in France, with no news of you,
spirited courageous one,
so kind and generous,
so daring and handsome.

The MacLeod Land never reared
10   a MacLeod or another
who excelled the young man
who was humorous and strong,
and doubly a kinsman
of my own people:
15   my worst loss of this battle
that your fair head is laid low.

DATE: 1941–3.
L.1: 'Tobruk and Bir Hacheim' – sites of battles in North
    Africa.
DISCUSSION: Chapter 6.

Heroes

I did not see Lannes at Ratisbon
nor MacLennan at Auldearn
nor Gillies MacBain at Culloden,
but I saw an Englishman in Egypt.

5   A poor litle chap with chubby cheeks
and knees grinding each other,
pimply unattractive face –
garment of the bravest spirit.

He was not a hit 'in the pub
10   in the time of the fists being closed,'
but a lion against the breast of battle,
in the morose wounding showers.

His hour came with the shells,
with the notched iron splinters,

15   in the smoke and flame,
in the shaking and terror of the battlefield.
Word came to him in the bullet shower
that he should be a hero briskly,
and he was that while he lasted
20   but it wasn't much time he got.

He kept his guns to the tanks,
bucking with tearing crashing screech,
until he himself got, about the stomach,
that biff that put him to the ground,
25   mouth down in sand and gravel,
without a chirp from his ugly high-pitched voice.

No cross or medal was put to his
chest or to his name or to his family;
there were not many of his troop alive,
30   and if there were their word would not be strong.
And at any rate, if a battle post stands
many are knocked down because of him,
not expecting fame, not wanting a medal
or any froth from the mouth of the field of slaughter.

[177]

35   I saw a great warrior of England,
a poor manikin on whom no eye would rest;
no Alasdair of Glen Garry;
and he took a little weeping to my eyes.

DATE: 1941–3.

L.1: 'Lannes' – Jean Lannes (1769–1809), French marshal and one of Napoleon's first lieutenants. He was killed at the Battle of Essling.

L.2: 'MacLennan at Auldearn' – at the Battle of Auldearn in 1645 MacLennan was the standard bearer for the Earl of Seaforth and refused his order to retreat. MacLennan was killed and his men decimated as a consequence.

L.3: 'Gillies MacBain at Culloden' – MacBain was second-in-command of the MacIntosh regiment at the battle of Culloden in 1745. His body was found with thirty-eight bayonet wounds.

L.9–10: 'in the pub ...' – a reference to a beating received by Alan MacDonald (the husband of Flora) as a consequence of debt. The quotation is from a Gaelic song about the incident.

L.37: 'Alasdair of Glen Garry' – a soldier famed for his courage at the Battles of Killiekrankie (1689) and Sheriffmuir (1715). There were a great number of elegies written about him after his death and MacLean quotes the opening of that by Julia MacDonald.

DISCUSSION: Chapter 6.

Death Valley

Some Nazi or other has said that the Fuehrer had restored in
German manhood the 'right and joy of dying in battle'.

> Sitting dead in 'Death Valley'
> below the Ruweisat Ridge
> a boy with his forelock down about his cheek
> and his face slate-grey;
>
> 5   I thought of the right and joy
> that he got from his Fuehrer,
> of falling in the field of slaughter
> to rise no more;
>
> of the pomp and the fame
> 10   that he had, not alone,
> though he was the most piteous to see
> in a valley gone to seed
>
> with flies about grey corpses
> on a dun sand
> 15   dirty yellow and full of the rubbish
> and fragments of battle.
>
> Was the boy of the band
> who abused the Jews
> and Communists, or of the greater
> 20   band of those
>
> led, from the beginning of generations,
> unwillingly to the trial
> and mad delirium of every war
> for the sake of rulers?
>
> 25   Whatever his desire or mishap,
> his innocence or malignity,
> he showed no pleasure in his death
> below the Ruweisat Ridge.

DATE: 1941–3.
L.2: 'Ruweisat Ridge' – a ridge of strategic importance
     in the Battle of El Alamein.

Alun Lewis
1915–44

Lewis was born near to Aberdare in the coalfields of South Wales, an area which forms the subject of several of his early poems. He was educated at University College, Aberystwyth and Manchester University and joined the army in 1940. His first collection, *Raiders' Dawn and Other Poems* was published in 1942 and a collection of short stories, *The Last Inspection*, followed in 1943. In the same year Lewis was sent to India with the South Wales Borderers and was killed, seemingly accidentally, in March 1944. His second collection of poetry, *Ha! Ha! Among the Trumpets: Poems in Transit*, which deals with his Indian experience, was published posthumously in 1945. A second collection of stories appeared in 1948.

Texts

There is at present no collected edition, but there is a good selection (Lewis 1981), and a miscellany of Lewis's writings contains some interesting poetry omitted from the *Selected Poems* and the two separate collections (Lewis 1982). Lewis's short stories, which form an interesting complement to the poetry, are available in a collected edition (Lewis 1990).

Biography

The standard biography is Pikoulis 1984. Lewis's wartime letters to his wife are collected in Lewis 1989.

Criticism

The most helpful collection of essays on Lewis is in a *Poetry Wales* special number (vol. 10, No.3, n.d.). Alun John's monograph is useful (John 1970), as is the chapter in Banerjee 1976. Two journal articles are also worth consulting (Mathias 1980; Pikoulis 1972).

All Day it Has Rained . . .

All day it has rained, and we on the edge of the moors
Have sprawled in our bell-tents, moody and dull as boors,
Groundsheets and blankets spread on the muddy ground
And from the first grey wakening we have found
5   No refuge from the skirmishing fine rain
And the wind that made the canvas heave and flap
And the taut wet guy-ropes ravel out and snap.
All day the rain has glided, wave and mist and dream,
Drenching the gorse and heather, a gossamer stream
10   Too light to stir the acorns that suddenly
Snatched from their cups by the wild south-westerly
Pattered against the tent and our upturned dreaming faces.
And we stretched out, unbuttoning our braces,
Smoking a Woodbine, darning dirty socks,
15   Reading the Sunday papers – I saw a fox
And mentioned it in the note I scribbled home; –
And we talked of girls, and dropping bombs on Rome,
And thought of the quiet dead and the loud celebrities
Exhorting us to slaughter, and the herded refugees;
20   – Yet thought softly, morosely of them, and as indifferently
As of ourselves or those whom we
For years have loved, and will again
Tomorrow maybe love; but now it is the rain
Possesses us entirely, the twilight and the rain.

25   And I can remember nothing dearer or more to my heart
Than the children I watched in the woods on Saturday
Shaking down burning chestnuts for the schoolyard's merry
     play,
Or the shaggy patient dog who followed me
By Sheet and Steep and up the wooded scree
30   To the Shoulder o'Mutton where Edward Thomas brooded
     long
On death and beauty – till a bullet stopped his song.

DATE: from *Raiders' Dawn and Other Poems* (1942).
L.29: 'Sheet and Steep' – places in Hampshire associated with poet Edward
    Thomas (1878–1917) (see notes on Ivor Gurney's 'The Mangel-Bury').
DISCUSSION: Chapters 1 and 6.

The Journey

We were the fore-runners of an army,
Going among strangers without sadness,
Danger being as natural as strangeness.

We had no other urge but to compel
5   Tomorrow in the image of today,
Which was motion and mileage and tinkering
When cylinders misfired and the gasket leaked.
Distance exhausted us each night;
I curled up in the darkness like a dog
10 And being a romantic stubbed my eyes
Upon the wheeling spokeshave of the stars.

Daylight had girls tawny as gazelles,
Beating their saris clean in pools and singing.
When we stopped they covered up their breasts;
15 Sometimes their gestures followed us for miles.

Then caravanserais of gipsies
With donkeys grey as mice and mincing camels
Laden with new-born lambs and trinkets,
Tentage and utensils and wicker baskets,
20 Following the ancient routes of the vast migrations
When history was the flight of a million birds
And poverty had splendid divagations.

Sometimes there were rivers that refused us,
Sweeping away the rafts, the oxen;
25 Some brown spates we breasted.
The jungle let us through with compass and machets.
And there were men like fauns, with drenched eyes,
Avoiding us, bearing arrows.

There was also the memory of Death
30 And the recurrent irritation of ourselves.
But the wind so wound its ways about us,
Beyond this living and this loving,
This calculation and provision, this fearing,

That neither of us heard the quiet voice calling us,
35 Remorse like rain softening and rotting the ground,
We felt no sorrow in the singing bird,
Forgot the sadness we had left behind.
For how could we guess, oh Life, oh suffering and patient
    Life,
With distance spun for ever in the mind,
40 We among the camels, the donkeys and the waterfalls,
How could we ever guess,
Not knowing how you pined?

DATE: from *Ha! Ha! Among the Trumpets: Poems in Transit* (1945).
CONTEXT: 'The Journey', like 'The Jungle', is taken from the
    'India' section of *Ha! Ha! Among the Trumpets*.
L.16: 'caravanserais' – literally a stopping place for a caravan
    of merchants or pilgrims; Lewis appears to use the word
    for the caravan itself.
DISCUSSION: Chapter 6.

The Jungle

I

In mole-blue indolence the sun
Plays idly on the stagnant pool
In whose grey bed black swollen leaf
Holds Autumn rotting like an unfrocked priest.
5 The crocodile slides from the ochre sand
And drives the great translucent fish
Under the boughs across the running gravel.
Windfalls of brittle mast crunch as we come
To quench more than our thirst—our selves—
10 Beneath this bamboo bridge, this mantled pool
Where sleep exudes a sinister content
As though all strength of mind and limb must pass
And all fidelities and doubts dissolve,
The weighted world a bubble in each head,
15 The warm pacts of the flesh betrayed
By the nonchalance of a laugh,
The green indifference of this sleep.

[183]

II

Wandering and fortuitous the paths
We followed to this rendezvous today
20 Out of the mines and offices and dives,
The sidestreets of anxiety and want,
Huge cities known and distant as the stars,
Wheeling beyond our destiny and hope.
We did not notice how the accent changed
25 As shadows ride from precipice to plain
Closing the parks and cordoning the roads,
Clouding the humming cultures of the West—
The weekly bribe we paid the man in black,
The day shift sinking from the sun,
30 The blinding arc of rivets blown through steel,
The patient queues, headlines and slogans flung
Across a frightened continent, the town
Sullen and out of work, the little home
Semi-detached, suburban, transient
35 As fever or the anger of the old,
The best ones on some specious pretext gone.

But we who dream beside this jungle pool
Prefer the instinctive rightness of the poised
Pied kingfisher deep darting for a fish
40 To all the banal rectitude of states,
The dew-bright diamonds on a viper's back
To the slow poison of a meaning lost
And the vituperations of the just.

III

The banyan's branching clerestories close
45 The noon's harsh splendour to a head of light.
The black spot in the focus grows and grows:
The vagueness of the child, the lover's deep
And inarticulate bewilderment,
The willingness to please that made a wound,
50 The kneeling darkness and the hungry prayer;
Cargoes of anguish in the holds of joy,

The smooth deceitful stranger in the heart,
The tangled wrack of motives drifting down
An oceanic tide of Wrong.
55 And though the state has enemies we know
The greater enmity within ourselves.

Some things we cleaned like knives in earth,
Kept from the dew and rust of Time
Instinctive truths and elemental love,
60 Knowing the force that brings the teal and quail
From Turkestan across the Himalayan snows
To Kashmir and the South alone can guide
That winging wildness home again.

Oh you who want us for ourselves,
65 Whose love can start the snow-rush in the woods
And melt the glacier in the dark coulisse,
Forgive this strange inconstancy of soul,
The face distorted in a jungle pool
That drowns its image in a mort of leaves.

IV

70 Grey monkeys gibber, ignorant and wise.
We are the ghosts, and they the denizens;
We are like them anonymous, unknown,
Avoiding what is human, near,
Skirting the villages, the paddy fields
75 Where boys sit timelessly to scare the crows
On bamboo platforms raised above their lives.

A trackless wilderness divides
Joy from its cause, the motive from the act:
The killing arm uncurls, strokes the soft moss;
80 The distant world is an obituary,
We do not hear the tappings of its dread.
The act sustains; there is no consequence.
Only aloneness, swinging slowly
Down the cold orbit of an older world
85 Than any they predicted in the schools,
Stirs the cold forest with a starry wind,

And sudden as the flashing of a sword
The dream exalts the bowed and golden head
And time is swept with a great turbulence,
90 The old temptation to remould the world.

The bamboos creak like an uneasy house;
The night is shrill with crickets, cold with space.
And if the mute pads on the sand should lift
Annihilating paws and strike us down
95 Then would some unimportant death resound
With the imprisoned music of the soul?
And we become the world we could not change?
Or does the will's long struggle end
With the last kindness of a foe or friend?

DATE: from *Ha! Ha! Among the Trumpets: Poems in Transit* (1945)
L.44: 'banyan' – Indian fig-tree; 'clerestories' – windowed
    walls above cathedral aisles.
L.61: 'Turkestan' – region of Central Asia.
L.62: 'Kashmir' – North-western province of India.
L.69: 'mort' – great quantity.
DISCUSSION: Chapter 6.

Hamish Henderson
1919–

Henderson was born in Blairgowrie, Scotland and fought with the 51st Highland Division in Africa and Italy during the Second World War. His experiences in the desert form the basis of his verse sequence *Elegies for the Dead in Cyrenaica* (1948). He also wrote and collected songs on the war which were published in *Ballads of World War II* (1950). After the war, Henderson worked for the School of Scottish Studies at Edinburgh University. He was instrumental in finding and recording Scottish traditional singers and himself wrote songs which became standards of the folk-song revival of the 1950s and 1960s. Henderson also translated the work of the Italian communist Antonio Gramsci.

Texts
The *Elegies* are the only readily available text by Henderson (Henderson 1991). The *Ballads* is extremely scarce and, although Henderson's songs have been reprinted in various folk-song journals, these too are hard to come by. There is a collection of prose writings (Henderson 1992) and the Scottish literary magazine *Chapman* published a special number on Henderson (*Chapman* 42 Winter 1985) which contains previously unpublished poetry and prose.

Recordings
There are two recordings of Henderson reading and singing his work (*Freedom Come All Ye* Claddagh CCA 7; *Pipes, Goatskin and Bones* Grampian Television GPN 30011). Perhaps the best recorded versions of Henderson's songs are those by the Scottish singer Dick Gaughan. 'The 51st Highland Division's Farewell to Sicily' is on *Kist o' Gold* (Leader LER 2103); 'The John MacLean March' is on *No More Forever* (Leader LERCD 2072); and 'The Freedom Come-All-Ye' is on Five Hand Reel's *Earl o' Moray* (RCA PK 25150).

Biography
Henderson 1992 contains various autobiographical material, including an informative interview.

Criticism
Edwin Morgan's essay on the *Elegies* is in Morgan 1990 and Raymond Ross has written on Henderson's politics (Ross 1985). The best essay on Henderson's songs

is hard to trace (Mitchell 1966), but there is another essay on this subject in the *Chapman* special number (McNaughton 1985). Henderson's own account of the poetry of the Middle East is in Henderson 1992.

from 'Interlude: Opening of an Offensive', *Elegies for the Dead in Cyrenaica*

the Jocks

They move forward into no man's land, a vibrant sounding
    board.
           As they advance
the guns push further murderous music.
5   Is this all they will hear, this raucous apocalypse?
The spheres knocking in the night of Heaven?
The drummeling of overwhelming niagara?
No! For I can hear it! Or is it? ... tell
me that I can hear it! Now—listen!

10   Yes, hill and shieling
sea-loch and island, hear it, the yell
of your war-pipes, scaling sound's mountains
guns thunder drowning in their soaring swell!
—The barrage gulfs them: they're gulfed in the clumbering
15   guns,
gulfed in the gloom, gloom. Dumb in the blunderbuss black—
lost—gone in the anonymous cataract of noise.
Now again! The shrill war-song: it flaunts
aggression to the sullen desert. It mounts. Its scream
20   tops the valkyrie, tops the colossal
           artillery.

Meaning that many
German Fascists will not be going home
meaning that many
25 will die, doomed in their false dream
We'll mak siccar!
Against the bashing cudgel
Against the contemptuous triumphs of the big battalions
mak siccar against the monkish adepts
30 of total war against the oppressed oppressors
mak siccar against the leaching lies
against the worked out systems of sick perversion
mak siccar
              against the executioner
35 against the tyrannous myth and the real terror
mak siccar

TITLE: Cyrenaica is the northern part of Libya.
DATE: 1943–7.
L.10: 'shieling' – pasture (Scots).
L.26: 'mak siccar!' – 'make sure' (Scots). Henderson's own note
      explains its derivation in medieval Scottish history:
      'After Bruce had stabbed the Red Comyn in Dumfries
      Kirk he was found outside the building by Lindsay and
      Kirkpatrick. Lindsay asked if Comyn were dead. Bruce
      replied he didn't know. '"Aweel," said Kirkpatrick, "I'll
      make siccar."' (Henderson 1991: 54).
DISCUSSION: Chapter 6.

'Seventh Elegy: Seven Good Germans',
Elegies for the Dead in Cyrenaica

The track running between Mekili and Tmimi was at one time a kind of
no-man's-land. British patrolling was energetic, and there were numerous brushes with German and Italian elements. El Eleba lies about half-
way along this track.

> Of the swaddies
> who came to the desert with Rommel
> there were few who had heard (or would hear) of El Eleba.
> They recce'd,
> 5   or acted as medical orderlies
> or patched up their tanks in the camouflaged workshops
> and never gave a thought to a place like El Eleba.
>
> To get there, you drive into the blue, take a bearing
> and head for damn-all. Then you're there. And where are you?
>
> 10   —Still, of some few who did cross our path at El Eleba
> there are seven who bide under their standing crosses.
>
> The first a Lieutenant.
>   When the medicos passed him
> for overseas service, he had jotted in a note-book
> 15   *to the day and the hour   keep me steadfast   there is only the*
> *decision and the will*
>   *the rest has no importance*
>
> The second a Corporal.
>   He had been in the Legion
> 20   and had got one more chance to redeem his lost honour.
> What he said was
> *Listen here, I'm fed up with your griping—*
> *If you want extra rations, go get 'em from Tommy!*
> *You're green, that's your trouble. Dodge the column, pass the*
> 25   *buck*
> *and scrounge all you can—that's our law in the Legion.*

You know Tommy's got 'em. . . . He's got mineral waters,
and beer, and fresh fruit in that white crinkly paper
and God knows what all! Well, what's holding you back?
30 *Are you windy or what?*
Christ, you 'old Afrikaners'!
If you're wanting the eats, go and get 'em from Tommy!
The third had been a farm-hand in the March of Silesia
and had come to the desert as fresh fodder for machine guns.
35 His dates are inscribed on the files, and on the cross piece.

The fourth was a lance-jack.
He had trust in Adolf
while working as a chemist in the suburb of Spandau.
His loves were his 'cello, and the woman who had borne him
40 two daughters and a son. He had faith in the Endsieg.
THAT THE NEW REICH MAY LIVE prayed the flyleaf of his Bible.

The fifth a mechanic.
All the honour and glory,
the siege of Tobruk and the conquest of Cairo
45 meant as much to that Boche as the Synod of Whitby.
Being wise to all this, he had one single headache,
which was, how to get back to his sweetheart (called Ilse).
—He had said
Can't the Tommy wake up and get weaving?
50 *If he tried, he could put our whole Corps in the bag.*
May God damn this Libya and both of its palm-trees!

The sixth was a Pole
—or to you, a Volksdeutscher—
who had put off his nation to serve in the Wehrmacht.
55 He siegheiled, and talked of "the dirty Polacken",
and said what he'd do if let loose among Russkis.
His mates thought that, though "just a polnischer
Schweinhund",
he was not a bad bloke.
60 On the morning concerned
he was driving a truck with mail, petrol and rations.
The M.P. on duty shouted five words of warning.

He nodded
>> laughed
65 >>> revved
>>>> and drove straight for El Eleba
not having quite got the chap's Styrian lingo.

The seventh a young swaddy.
>> Riding cramped in a lorry
70 to death along the road which winds eastward to Halfaya
he had written three verses in appeal against his sentence
which soften for an hour the anger of Lenin.

>> Seven poor bastards
>> dead in African deadland
75 >> (tawny tousled hair under the issue blanket)
>> *wie einst Lili*
dead in African deadland

>>>> *einst Lili Marlene*

L.19: 'the Legion' – the Foreign Legion.
L.33: 'Silesia' – region now in south-west Poland occupied by
      German troops in 1939.
L.38: 'Spandau' – on the outskirts of Berlin.
L.40: 'Endsieg' – 'final victory' (German).
L.53: 'Volksdeutscher' – an ethnic German.
L.67: 'Styrian' – from the Austrian province of Styria.
L.76: 'wie einst Lili' – 'Lili did once': from the song 'Lili
      Marlene', adopted by both armies in the desert war.
DISCUSSION: Chapter 6.

'Tenth Elegy: The Frontier',
Elegies for the Dead in Cyrenaica

One must die because one knows them, die
of their smile's ineffable blossom, die
of their light hands

But dust blowing round them
5   has stopped up their ears
                o for ever
not sleeping but dead

The airliner's passengers,
crossing without effort the confines
10   of wired-off Libya, remember
little, regret less. If they idly
inspect from their windows the ennui
of limestone desert
           —and beneath them
15   their skimming shadow—
           they'll be certain
they've seen it, they've seen all

(Seen all, maybe, including
the lunar qattaras, the wadis like family trees,
20   the frontier passes with their toyshop spirals—
seen nothing, and seen all

And the scene yields them? Nothing)

Yet that coast-line
could yield much: there were recces and sorties
25   drumfire and sieges. The outposts
lay here: there ran the supply route.
Forgotten.
        By that bend of Halfaya
the convoys used to stick, raw meat for the Jabos.

30   And here, the bay's horseshoe:
how nobly it clanged through laconic communiqués!

Still, how should this interest the airborne travellers,
being less real to them than the Trojan defence-works
and touching them as little as the Achaean strategies?
35 Useless to deny. The memorial's obsequious
falsehoods are irrelevant. It has little to arrest them,
survivors by accident
        that dried blood in the sangars.

So I turn aside in the benighted deadland
40 to perform a duty, noting an outlying
grave, or restoring a fallen cross-piece.
Remembrancer.
       And shall sing them who amnestied
escaped from the tumult to stumble across sand-dunes
45 *and darken their waves in the sea, the deliverer.*

Run, stumble and fall in their instant of agony
past burnt-out brennpunkt, along hangdog dannert.
Here gutted, or stuck through the throat like Buonconte,
or charred to grey ash, they are caught in one corral.
50 We fly from their scorn, but they close all the passes:
their sleep's our unrest, we lie bound in their inferno—
this alliance must be vaunted and affirmed, lest they condemn
                        us!

Lean seedlings of lament spring like swordsmen around us;
the coronach scales white arêtes. Bitter keening
55 of women goes up by the solitary column.
Denounce and condemn! Either build for the living
love, patience and power to absolve these tormented,
or else choke in the folds of their black-edged vendetta!
Run, stumble and fall in our desert of failure,
60 impaled, unappeased. And inhabit that desert
of canyon and dream—till we carry to the living
blood, fire and red flambeaux of death's proletariat.
Take iron in your arms! At last, spanning this history's
apollyon chasm, proclaim them the reconciled.

L.19: 'qattaras … wadis' – depressions and ravines.
L.34: 'Achaean' – Greek.
L.38: 'sangars' – small trenches dug into the desert.

L.47: 'brennpunkt' – literally 'burning point' (German) – the
  focal point of fire; 'dannert' – wire.
L.48: 'Buonconte' – in Dante's *Divine Comedy*.
L.54: 'coronach' – Gaelic funeral song; 'arêtes' – steep
  mountain ridges.

Victory Hoe-Down

6th (Banffshire) battalion of the Gordon Highlanders celebrating the
German surrender in Italy, dancing a reel to the tune of 'Kate Dalrymple'.

<pre>
                      Hey for the tall
                horned shadows on the wall
      and the beer-cans bouncing in the crazy Corso.
                      Hey for a hoor
  5   for a meenit or an 'oor
      and a tanner for a taigle wi' her sonsy torso.
                      Banffies hustle
                  through the randy reel-rawl
      lowpin like a mawkin see oor dames fae hell go.
 10   Bang
                  through the steer
                  they advance
                  tae the rear
      and the ankles jiggin' like a fiddler's elbow.

 15   Slash o' a dirk
            bleeds the guts o' the mirk
      wi' the glentin cramassies, the greens and the yellows.
                  Wind cracks the cheeks
                  o' the dudelsack's breeks
 20   like twa damn poltergeists at wark wi' the bellows.
                  Tae hell wi' your oboes
                  and your douce violas –
      your flutes and your cellos and your concertinas
                  Oor pipes
 25   and oor reeds
                  they supply
                  a' oor needs
      o' oor dear wee silly little signorinas.
</pre>

Slap in the pan
30   fae a billy tae a dan –
o we'll pound aul' Musso tae a well-tanned tyke's hide.
We'll beery soon
yon melancholy loon
and we'll ding doon Kesselring tae dee in the dykeside.
35   Plums we'll pree 'em
wi' the *partigiani*
they bluid-red billyboys, the rantin'-rory.
Ye mean

crood o' bams
40   gie's anither
twal drams
and we'll reel auld Hornie and his gang tae glory.

L.6: 'sonsy' – plump, comfortable.
L.8: 'reel-rawl' – a disorder.
L.9: 'lowpin like a mawkin' – leaping like a hare; 'dames fae hell' – translation of a German phrase for the kilted Scottish troops.
L.11: 'steer' – commotion.
L.17: 'cramassies' – crimsons.
L.19: 'dudelsack' – bagpipes; 'breeks' – trousers.
L.30: 'billy' – boy; 'dan' – older person.
L.31: 'Musso' – Mussolini, the Italian dictator.
L.33: 'loon' – rascal.
L.34: 'Kesselring' – German Field Marshal.
L.35: 'pree' – taste.
L.36: 'partigiani' – Italian partisans.
L.42: 'auld Hornie' – the Devil.
DISCUSSION: Chapter 3.

The 51st Highland Division's Farewell to Sicily

The pipe is dozie, the pipie is fey;
He wull-nae come roon for his vino the day.
The sky ow'r Messina is unco and grey,
And a' the bricht chaulmers are eerie.

5   Then fare weel, ye banks o' Sicily,
Fare ye weel ye valley and shaw.
There's nae Jock will mourn the kyles o' ye,
Puir bliddy swaddies are weary.

Fare weel ye banks o' Sicily,
10   Fare ye weel ye valley and shaw.
There's nae hame can smoor the wiles o' ye,
Puir bliddy swaddies are weary.

Then doon the stair and line the water-side,
Wait your turn, the ferry's awa',
15   Then doon the stair and line the water-side,
A' the bricht chaulmers are eerie.

The drummie is polisht, the drummie is braw –
He canna be seen for his webbin' ava.
He's beezed himsel' up for a photy an a'
20   Tae leave wi' his Lola his dearie.

Sae fare weel, ye dives o' Sicily,
Fare ye weel, ye shieling and ha';
We'll a' mind shebeens and bothies
Where kind signorinas were cheerie.

25   Fare weel, ye banks o' Sicily,
Fare ye weel, ye shieling and ha';
We'll a' mind shebeens and bothies
Where Jock made a date wi' his dearie.

Then tune the pipes and drub the tenor drum,
30   Leave your kit this side o' the wa';
Then tune the pipes an' drub the tenor drum.
A' the bricht chaulmers are eerie.

DATE: 1945.

CONTEXT: the words are set to the pipe tune 'Farewell to the Creeks'.

L.1: 'pipie' – pipe-major; 'fey' – odd.

L.2: 'vino' – wine.

L.3: Messina – port in Sicily; 'unco' – uncanny.

L.4: 'a' the bricht chaulmers are eerie' – all the the bright rooms are strange.

L.6: 'shaw' – woodland.

L.7: 'kyles' – straits.

L.8: 'swaddies' – squaddies, private soldiers.

L.11: 'smoor' – cover over.

L.17: 'drummie' – drum major.

L.18: 'ava' – at all.

L.19: 'beezed ... up' – smartened up.

L.22: 'shieling' – shepherd's hut.

L.27: 'shebeens' – unofficial drinking houses; 'bothies' – farm workers' quarters.

DISCUSSION: Chapters 3 and 6.

Ballad of Anzio

When the M.G.s stop their chatter
And the cannons stop their roar
And you're back in dear old Blighty
In your favourite pub once more;
5 When the small talk is all over
And the war tales start to flow,
You can stop the lot by telling
Of the fight at Anzio.

Let them bum about the desert,
10 Let them talk about Dunkirk,
Let them brag about the jungles
Where the Japanese did lurk.
Let them boast about their campaign
And their medals till they're red:
15 You can put the lot to silence
When you mention – the beachhead.

You can talk of Anzio Archie
And the Factory, where the Huns
Used to ask us out to breakfast
20   As they rubbed against our guns.
You can talk of night patrolling
They know nothing of at home
And can tell them that you learned it
On the beachhead – south of Rome.

25   You can tell them how the Heinies
Tried to break us with attacks,
Using tanks, bombs and flamethrowers
And how we flung them back.
You can tell them how we took it
30   And how we dished it out as well
How we thought it was a picnic
And Tedeschi thought it hell.

And when the tale is finished
And going time is near
35   Just fill your pipes again, lads,
And finish up your beer.
Then order up another pint
And drink before you go
To the boys who fought beside you
40   On the beach at Anzio.

DATE: in *Ballads of World War II* (1950).
TITLE: Anzio is a coastal town south of Rome where Allied
    forces staged the invasion of Italy in January 1944.
L.1: 'M.G.'s – machine-guns.
L.3: 'Blighty' – home.
L.10: 'Dunkirk' – port in Belgium and scene of the retreat of
    the British Expeditionary Force in May 1940.
L.25: 'Heinies' – Germans.
L.32: 'Tedeschi' – Italians.
DISCUSSION: Chapter 3.

The Blubbing Buchmanite

When Moscow sends the call at night
"Workers of the world unite!"
The lads begin to wonder when
The human race will act like men.

5   And Tam (from Greenock) tells us why
The bosses send us out to die.
He says: "We Scots have gone to seed-
A revolution's what we need!"

But Micah Grant (from Shotts) starts in
10   To tell us how to deal with Sin-
He calls on us to turn again,
And then resumes this old refrain:

    "A revolution in the mind
        will be more couthie, will be more kind
15   A revolution in the brain
        will not annoy the boss again."

"At times," he says, "the workers feel
They've had a pretty rotten deal;
But if they search their inmost hearts
20   They'll find that's due to Satan's arts.

"I see what few have understood-
God tries the worker for his good;
Each lustful keek at Katie Brown
Will dock his wages half a crown!

25   "So don't provoke the Mighty God
Too sore, or you will feel the rod.
The Lord destroys the fool who fights
For earthly things like workers' rights."

    "A revolution in the mind
30   will be more couthie, will be more kind.
    A revolution in the brain
        will not annoy the boss again."

But Tam gets back his breath and cries:
'You creeping Jesus, damn your eyes!
35 It's canting cunts like you who sap
The worker's spirit. Shut your trap!

"A revolution in the soul
Will leave the bosses' profits whole.
A revolution in the heart
40 Won't help the workers' cause a fart.

"We cannot have too blinking few
God-awful bums the like of you!
If just once more you try to wreck
The workers' fight I'll wring your neck."

DATE: in *Ballads of World War II* (1950).
TITLE: a Buchmanite is a member of the Moral Rearmament
movement formed by Frank Buchman, an American
evangelist.
L.5: 'Greenock' – shipbuilding and engineering town on the
Clyde, north-west of Glasgow.
L.9: 'Shotts' – town east of Glasgow.
L.30: 'couthie' – pleasant, with overtones of woozy sentiment-
ality.
DISCUSSION: Chapter 3.

Keith Douglas
1920—44

Douglas was born in Tunbridge Wells and was educated at Christ's Hospital and Oxford University. He was an enthusiastic member of the Officer Training Corps and showed none of the political scepticism about war that marked the older generation of 1930s poets. In a proposed biographical note for an early collection of poems, Douglas wrote that he was 'interested in clothes, drawing and painting (my own and other people's), horses ... music, ballet, stage design'. He listed his recreations as 'tap-dancing, rugger, water-polo, [and] competitive swimming' (Douglas 1985: 83). He joined the army in 1940 and served in the Western Desert as a tank commander (see his prose account *Alamein to Zem Zem*). He was killed in France during the invasion of Europe.

Texts
The *Complete Poems* is the standard text (Douglas 1979b). Other material is contained in a miscellany of Douglas's letters and uncollected prose (Douglas 1985).

Biography
The standard biography is Graham 1974. *Alamein to Zem Zem* is Douglas's autobiographical account of the desert war (Douglas 1979a).

Criticism
The only full-length study of Douglas is Scammell 1988. Graham 1974 includes useful commentaries on the poems and there is a chapter on Douglas in Longley 1986. Hill 1964–5 is an essay by a later poet much influenced by Douglas. Douglas's own essay on war poetry, 'Poets in this war', is in Douglas 1985 (117–20).

Simplify me when I'm dead

Remember me when I am dead
and simplify me when I'm dead.

As the processes of earth
strip off the colour and the skin
5   take the brown hair and blue eye

and leave me simpler than at birth,
when hairless I came howling in
as the moon came in the cold sky.

Of my skeleton perhaps
10   so stripped, a learned man will say
'He was of such a type and intelligence,' no more.

Thus when in a year collapse
particular memories, you may
deduce, from the long pain I bore

15   the opinions I held, who was my foe
and what I left, even my appearance
but incidents will be no guide.

Time's wrong-way telescope will show
a minute man ten years hence
20   and by distance simplified.

Through that lens see if I seem
substance or nothing: of the world
deserving mention or charitable oblivion

not by momentary spleen
25   or love into decision hurled,
leisurely arrive at an opinion.

Remember me when I am dead
and simplify me when I'm dead.

DATE: 1941.

Mersa

This blue halfcircle of sea
moving transparently
on sand as pale as salt
was Cleopatra's hotel:

5   here is a guesthouse built
and broken utterly, since.
An amorous modern prince
lived in this scoured shell.

Now from the skeletal town
10   the cherryskinned soldiers stroll down
to undress to idle on the white beach.
Up there, the immensely long road goes by

to Tripoli: the wind and dust reach
the secrets of the whole
15   poor town whose masks would still
deceive a passer-by;

faces with sightless doors
for eyes, with cracks like tears
oozing at corners. A dead tank alone
20   leans where the gossips stood.

I see my feet like stones
underwater. The logical little fish
converge and nip the flesh
imagining I am one of the dead.

DATE: 1942.
TITLE: Mersa – Egyptian coastal town, west of El Alamein.
L.7: 'An amorous modern prince' – Prince, later King, Farouk
    who was well-known for his extravagant lifestyle.
L.13: 'Tripoli' – capital city of Libya.
DISCUSSION: Chapter 6.

Cairo Jag

Shall I get drunk or cut myself a piece of cake,
a pasty Syrian with a few words of English
or the Turk who says she is a princess—she dances
apparently by levitation? Or Marcelle, Parisienne
5   always preoccupied with her dull dead lover:
she has all the photographs and his letters
tied in a bundle and stamped *Décedé* in mauve ink.
All this takes place in a stink of jasmin.

But there are the streets dedicated to sleep
10   stenches and the sour smells, the sour cries
do not disturb their application to slumber
all day, scattered on the pavement like rags
afflicted with fatalism and hashish. The women
offering their children brown-paper breasts
15   dry and twisted, elongated like the skull,
Holbein's signature. But this stained white town
is something in accordance with mundane conventions—
Marcelle drops her Gallic airs and tragedy
suddenly shrieks in Arabic about the fare
20   with the cabman, links herself so
with the somnambulists and legless beggars:
it is all one, all as you have heard.

But by a day's travelling you reach a new world
the vegetation is of iron
25   dead tanks, gun barrels split like celery
the metal brambles have no flowers or berries
and there are all sorts of manure, you can imagine
the dead themselves, their boots, clothes and possessions
clinging to the ground, a man with no head
30   has a packet of chocolate and a souvenir of Tripoli.

DATE: 1943.
TITLE: 'Jag' – spree.
L.7: 'Décedé' – dead.
L.16: 'Holbein's signature' – Hans Holbein (1497–1543),
    German painter. His 'signature' was a skull.

L.30: 'Tripoli' – capital city of Libya.
DISCUSSION: Chapter 6.

Sportsmen

'I think I am becoming a God.'

The noble horse with courage in his eye,
clean in the bone, looks up at a shellburst:
away fly the images of the shires
but he puts the pipe back in his mouth.

5   Peter was unfortunately killed by an 88;
it took his leg off; he died in the ambulance.
When I saw him crawling, he said:
It's most unfair, they've shot my foot off.

How then can I live among this gentle
10   obsolescent breed of heroes, and not weep?
Unicorns, almost. For they are fading into two legends
in which their stupidity and chivalry are celebrated;
the fool and the hero will be immortals.

These plains were a cricket pitch
15   and in the hills the tremendous drop fences
brought down some of the runners, who
under these stones and earth lounge still
in famous attitudes of unconcern. Listen
against the bullet cries the simple horn.

DATE: 1943.
EPIGRAPH: the reputed last words of the Roman emperor
Caligula.
L.5: 'an 88' – type of shell.
L.15: 'drop fences' – types of fence in horse-riding where the
area of landing is below the level of the area of take-off.
DISCUSSION: Chapter 7.

Dead Men

Tonight the moon inveigles them
to love: they infer from her gaze
her tacit encouragement.
Tonight the white dresses and the jasmin scent
5   in the streets. I in another place
see the white dresses glimmer like moths. Come

to the west, out of that trance, my heart—
here the same hours have illumined
sleepers who are condemned or reprieved
10   and those whom their ambitions have deceived;
the dead men, whom the wind
powders till they are like dolls: they tonight

rest in the sanitary earth perhaps
or where they died, no one has found them
15   or in their shallow graves the wild dog
discovered and exhumed a face or a leg
for food: the human virtue round them
is a vapour tasteless to a dog's chops.

All that is good of them, the dog consumes.
20   You would not know, now the mind's flame is gone,
more than the dog knows: you would forget
but that you see your own mind burning yet
and till you stifle in the ground will go on
burning the economical coal of your dreams.

25   Then leave the dead in the earth, an organism
not capable of resurrection, like mines,
less durable than the metal of a gun,
a casual meal for a dog, nothing but the bone
so soon. But tonight no lovers see the lines
30   of the moon's face as the lines of cynicism.

And the wise man is the lover
who in his planetary love revolves
without the traction of reason or time's control
and the wild dog finding meat in a hole

35   is a philosopher. The prudent mind resolves
       on the lover's or the dog's attitude for ever.

DATE: 1943.
DISCUSSION: Chapter 7.

How to Kill

Under the parabola of a ball,
a child turning into a man,
I looked into the air too long.
The ball fell in my hand, it sang
5   in the closed fist: *Open Open*
Behold a gift designed to kill.

Now in my dial of glass appears
the soldier who is going to die.
He smiles, and moves about in ways
10   his mother knows, habits of his.
The wires touch his face: I cry
NOW. Death, like a familiar, hears

and look, has made a man of dust
of a man of flesh. This sorcery
15   I do. Being damned, I am amused
to see the centre of love diffused
and the waves of love travel into vacancy.
How easy it is to make a ghost.

The weightless mosquito touches
20   her tiny shadow on the stone,
and with how like, how infinite
a lightness, a man and shadow meet.
They fuse. A shadow is a man
when the mosquito death approaches.

DATE: 1943.
L.12: 'familiar' – demon or spirit attending a magician.
DISCUSSION: Chapter 7.

Cairo Poets:
Terence Tiller (1916–85) and
G. S. Fraser (1915–80)

G. S. Fraser
1915–80

Fraser was born in Scotland. He volunteered for the Army and, on being posted to Cairo, worked mainly in Army journalism. He was initially connected with the New Apocalyptic group of poets who favoured a florid style and drew upon surrealist and mystical sources. Fraser's own poetry, however, is much more in the controlled, urbane manner of Louis MacNeice and Bernard Spencer (Fraser's work appeared in Spencer's magazine *Personal Landscape*). After the war Fraser became a literary journalist and an academic.

Texts
Fraser's *Collected Poems* (Fraser 1981).

Biography
Fraser's autobiography gives an interesting insight into the literary world of the 1940s and 1950s (Fraser 1983).

Criticism
Tolley 1985 has a short section on Fraser. For Fraser's own views on the poetry of the wartime Middle East see 'Recent Verse: London and Cairo' (Prose Anthology p. 266).

Terence Tiller
1916–85

After studying at Cambridge University, Tiller went to Egypt in 1939 and taught English and history at Fuad I University. He contributed to the magazine *Personal Landscape*, and published two volumes of wartime poetry.

Texts
There is no collected poems. Tiller's wartime work appears in *The Inward Animal* (1943) and *Unarm, Eros* (1947).

Criticism
There is a short section on Tiller's work in Tolley 1985.

Lecturing to Troops

TERENCE TILLER

They sit like shrubs among the cans and desert
      thistles
     in the tree's broken shade and the sea-glare:
strange violent men, with dirty unfamiliar muscles,
sweating down the brown breast, wanting girls and
      beer.

5   The branches shake down sand along a crawling air,
        and drinks are miles towards the sun
        and Molly and Polly and Pam are gone.

Waiting for my announcement, I feel neat and shy,
      foreign before their curious helplessness,

10   innocence bought by action, like the sea's amnesty:
all my clean cleverness is tiny, is a loss;
and it is useless to be friendly and precise
      —thin as a hornet in a dome
      against the cries of death and home.

15   How can they be so tolerant—they who have lost
      the kiss of tolerance—and patient to endure
calm unnecessity? They have walked horror's coast,
loosened the flesh in flame, slept with naked war:
while I come taut and scatheless with a virgin air,

20   diffident as a looking-glass,
      with the fat lexicon of peace.

The strangeness holds them: a new planet's uniform,
      grasped like the frilly pin-ups in their tent
—something without the urgency of hate and harm,

25   something forgotten.
         But that is not what I meant:
I should have been the miles that made them
      innocent,
and something natural as the sun
      from the beginning to everyone

30   though Harry and Larry and Len are gone.
          Coastal Battery, Tripolitania

DATE: in *Unarm, Eros* (1947).

Big City

TERENCE TILLER

Crossing of strangers among lights
while cold and secret through the streets
we run on homeward wheels, and learn
a no-man's-land of flesh and bone.
5   Homeless the rolling blood that cries
of love and Love in hidden ways
where kisses like a bird fly back
and bring no bounty to their Ark,
since all about the city stands
10   night, like a monument for friends
whose lives in hills of darkness share
the serious motions of desire,
passion that estranges all
but the involuntary shell
15   and clings to nothing in the gulf
but the blind magnet of a self.
Our sense has only sense for light
and the flames are separate
while among them aimless words
20   have no home to move towards.
Once on a murmuring afternoon
speech was a dancer in the sun,
while cold as whips under the grass
the secret plants crawled up to us
25   who now are in their pulsing dark
while the dancer stamps us back
—a flower and a root that strives
towards it. And a god who grieves.

Cairo

DATE: in *Unarm, Eros* (1947).

Egypt

G. S. FRASER

Who knows the lights at last, who knows the cities
And the unloving hands upon the thighs
Would yet return to seek his home-town pretties
For the shy finger-tips and sidelong eyes.

5   Who knows the world, the flesh, the compromises
Would go back to the theory in the book:
Who knows the place the poster advertises
Back to the poster for another look.

But nets the fellah spreads beside the river
10   Where the green waters criss-cross in the sun
End certain migratory hopes for ever:
In that white light, all shadows are undone.

The desert slays. But safe from Allah's justice
Where the broad river of His Mercy lies,
15.   Where ground for labour, or where scope for lust is,
The crooked and tall and cunning cities rise.

The green Nile irrigates a barren region,
All the coarse palms are ankle-deep in sand:
No love roots deep, though easy loves are legion:
20   The heart's as hot and hungry as the hand.

In airless evenings, at the café table,
The soldier sips his thick sweet coffee up:
The dry grounds, like the moral to my fable,
Are bitter at the bottom of the cup.

DATE: in *The Traveller Has Regrets* (1948) (Fraser 1981).
L.9: 'fellah' – Egyptian peasant.

From *Exile's Letter*

G. S. FRASER

Exiled too long, my dear, I build
The dream by which the story's killed,
For if, in days of pride and glory,
The dream illuminates the story,
5   In days when things are what they seem
The story merely feeds the dream.
Exiled from you, what should I see?
A white hand on a wavering knee,
A sentence from a letter that
10   Is sly, and elegant, and pat,
A vista from a window where
The paths are brown, the trees are bare
(The dove-grey skies of evening laid
Across the olive shrub-choked glade)
15   And your white hand by wavering knee
Still offering buns, still pouring tea …
Tea done, what miry ways we walked
And what pedantic stuff we talked
(Abstruse, portentous, and oblique:
20   So shy and lettered lovers speak
And paused upon the stony brink
Too nicely feel, too vaguely think,
Peck, fumble, offer cigarettes,
Dive deep, and drown with choked regrets)
25   While waiting for the rumbling bus,
By continents dividing us:
But each sharp image I recall
Seems not to link with you at all,
A blank oppression clamps my mind,
30   At one sour sentence staring, blind,
The tritest thought that twists love's faith:
How time and distance *are* like death!

For ... sift, select, refine the past,
As if each letter were the last,
35 Yet when another letter comes
On a less vivid ear it drums
And more at random one must talk
To make the speaking phantoms walk,
These ghosts whom time and distance chase
40 Across a similar poise or face
As Jean, who turns her lion's head
Across a Cairo street, misread,
Or Tom whom in an hour of dearth
I sought in living ghosts in Perth:
45 Many the narrow shoulders had,
The noble air, though slightly mad,
Many the bush of burning hair,
But the whole picture was not there:
And so for fragments some will please,
50 The eye to coax, the voice to tease,
The new chase out the old at last:
The present love digests the past.
The curse! that exiles settle down
At home in the barbarian town
55 And learn the local dialect too
(Like Pontic Ovid or Scotch you)
And never truly more at home
Than when they sigh, 'Remember Rome!'
Could I return to London's streets,
60 Or weather Scotland's winter sleets,
Another past would rise to slay:
Nostalgia in a Greek café,
The camel-dust of Cairo's night,
And the last stub I'd left to light –
65 Regrets for our regrets we'll prove,
And can it be the same with love? –
That he and she are both content
With what they *hope* the other meant,
With what a memory refines
70 When with a confidant one dines

And, swearing this liqueur the last,
Smacking the lips, declaims—'The Past!'

But if the Past could present stand
With the raw nail-marks in Its hand
75 We'd wish It in the night outside
And fear to feel Its murdered side ...

And you would say our whole age is
Exiled from the realities
And man, by nature exiled, must
80 Traverse the flaring streets of lust
To the dull barracks of the mind
If man is obdurately blind.
But all that I am sure of is
The exile's way is history's:
85 The old are exiled from the young,
I from the songs my body sung
When basking by the summer shore
I thought and dreamt and wished no more
Except to lie a summer long
90 With all the summer for my song:
I'm exiled from the studious boy
With books and gardens for his toy
Whose attic-window in its cup
Tilted the wine-dark evening up.

95 So exiled from ourselves we live
And yet can learn to forgive
The past that promised us so much
And ends, alas, my dear, in such,
Such chatter in an exile's town:
100 Such towers so tall, so tumbledown,
Such shabby places as we find
To sleep in and pull down the blind
And think, 'At last I am alone,
With no more failures to atone!'
105 A state – all exiles know it well –
Some call content; some, sloth; some, hell ...

DATE: in *The Traveller Has Regrets* (1948) (Fraser 1981).

[215]

L.44: 'Perth' – town in Scotland.

L.56: 'Pontic Ovid' – The Roman poet Ovid was exiled to the Black Sea (Pontic) port of Tomi in AD 8. There he wrote the poems of exile, *Tristia* and *Epistolae ex Ponto*.

Part III

PROSE

Bertrand Russell
1872–1970

from *Principles of Social Reconstruction* (1916)

Russell was a prominent philosopher and mathematician before the First World War, but after 1914 his radical liberalism led him to pursue a vigorous anti-war campaign. He was a leading figure on the No Conscription Fellowship and editor of its magazine. He was deprived of his fellowship at Trinity College, Cambridge as a result of his activities, and, in 1918, was imprisoned for 'insulting an ally'.

Russell published a great deal of polemical material during the war, including a book version of a series of public lectures, *Principles of Social Reconstruction* (1916). In these lectures, Russell analyses war as a social phenomenon alongside other social institutions such as the law and marriage. The extract is from the chapter 'War as an Institution' in which Russell suggests the complicity of state ambition and individual desires in the maintenance of the institution of war.

DISCUSSION: Chapter 4.
SOURCE: Russell 1916: 77–8, 88–90.

from Principles of Social Reconstruction
(*1916*)

War is a conflict between two groups, each of which attempts to kill and maim as many as possible of the other group in order to achieve some object which it desires. The object is generally either power or wealth. It is a pleasure to exercise authority over other
5   men, and it is a pleasure to live on the produce of other men's labour. The victor in war can enjoy more of these delights than the vanquished. But war, like all other natural activities, is not so much prompted by the end which it has in view as by an impulse to the activity itself. Very often men desire an end, not on its own
10   account, but because their nature demands the actions which will

lead to the end. And so it is in this case: the ends to be achieved by war appear in prospect far more important than they will appear when they are realized, because war itself is a fulfilment of one side of our nature. If men's actions sprang from desires for what would in fact bring happiness, the purely rational arguments against war would have long ago put an end to it. What makes war difficult to suppress is that it springs from an impulse, rather than from a calculation of the advantages to be derived from war.[...]

Besides the conscious and deliberate forces leading to war, there are inarticulate feelings of common men, which, in most civilized countries, are always ready to burst into war fever at the bidding of statesmen. If peace is to be secure, the readiness to catch war fever must be somehow diminished. Whoever wishes to succeed in this must first understand what war fever is and why it arises.

The men who have an important influence in the world, whether for good or evil, are dominated as a rule by a threefold desire: they desire, first, an activity which calls fully into play the faculties in which they feel that they excel; secondly, the sense of successfully overcoming resistance; thirdly, the respect of others on account of their success. The third of these desires is sometimes absent: some men who have been great have been without the "last infirmity," and have been content with their own sense of success, or merely with the joy of difficult effort. But as a rule all three are present. Some men's talents are specialized, so that their choice of activities is circumscribed by the nature of their faculties; other men have, in youth, such a wide range of possible aptitudes that their choice is chiefly determined by the varying degrees of respect which public opinion gives to different kinds of success.

The same desires, usually in a less marked degree, exist in men who have no exceptional talents. But such men cannot achieve anything very difficult by their individual efforts; for them, as units, it is impossible to acquire the sense of greatness or the triumph of strong resistance overcome. Their separate lives are unadventurous and dull. In the morning they go to the office or the plough, in the evening they return, tired and silent, to the sober monotony of wife and children. Believing that security is the supreme good, they have insured against sickness and death, and have found an employment where they have little fear of dismissal and no hope of any great rise. But security, once achieved, brings a Nemesis of

50 *ennui.* Adventure, imagination, risk, also have their claims; but how can these claims be satisfied by the ordinary wage-earner? Even if it were possible to satisfy them, the claims of wife and children have priority and must not be neglected. To this victim of order and good organization the realization comes, in some moment of

55 sudden crisis, that he belongs to a nation, that his nation may take risks, may engage in difficult enterprises, enjoy the hot passion of doubtful combat, stimulate adventure and imagination by military expeditions to Mount Sinai and the Garden of Eden. What his nation does, in some sense, he does; what his nation suffers, he

60 suffers. The long years of private caution are avenged by a wild plunge into public madness. All the horrid duties of thrift and order and care which he has learnt to fulfil in private are thought not to apply to public affairs: it is patriotic and noble to be reckless for the nation, though it would be wicked to be reckless for oneself.

65 The old primitive passions, which civilization has denied, surge up all the stronger for repression. In a moment imagination and instinct travel back through the centuries, and the wild man of the woods emerges from the mental prison in which he has been confined. This is the deeper part of the psychology of the war fever.

Herbert Read
1893–1968

(i) from 'Sorel, Marx, and the War' (1916)
(ii) from 'To Hell with Culture' (1941)

For an account of Read's life, see Poetry Anthology p. 169.

The first extract is from an essay published in *The New Age* in June 1916 which demonstrates Read's interest in Marxist theory and the Nietzschean version of Marxism propounded by the French theorist Georges Sorel. Read uses Sorel's ideas on proletarian revolution developed in *Réflexions sur la Violence* (1908) (see Sorel 1916) to interpret the political effects of the war. In the opening paragraphs of the essay (not reproduced here) Read summarizes Marx's theory of capitalist accumulation, in which capitalists develop an increasingly intensive method of ownership and production at the same time as a proletariat becomes increasingly disciplined and united. When the two processes come into conflict, Marx argues, capitalism is itself 'expropriated' by a revolutionary proletariat.

The second extract shows Read's vision of a post-Second-World-War world founded on guild socialist principles of small-scale industrial organization and urban planning. Read demonstrates a similar optimism about post-war recovery and political revaluation to that in Stephen Spender's *Citizens in War – and After* (see Prose Anthology, p. 261).

DISCUSSION: Chapter 5.
SOURCES: (i) Read 1916: 128–9.
(ii) Read 1943: 65–6.

(i) from 'Sorel, Marx, and the War' (1916)

There is one vital comment to make on this hypothesis viewed in the light of more recent social development. Marx imagined capital developing along trust lines and the trust amalgamating into monopoly. We to-day see another possible development—the
5   concentration of the forces and power of capital in the State. But this does not vitiate the theory.

But what *would* vitiate it is the deployment in any manner whatsoever of either of these processes. This Sorel has realised. He, therefore, exposes the danger of capitalist degeneracy, social amelioration, co-operative movements, etc. They all tend to unite factors which should be kept implacably opposed. They are the symptoms of social rot.

To cure this social rot, Sorel advocates two remedies. He firstly endeavours to show the value of a psychological factor in socialistic activities. This is the inculcation into the minds of the working classes of the "myth" of a general strike, or, as it might be called, a collective will to revolution. Into this advocacy he interweaves a plea for the supreme value of heroic virtue—the idea that the war of Capital and Labour is a world-struggle of tragic significance.

His second remedy for our social decadence is proletarian violence. "Two accidents alone would be able to stop this [decadent] movement: a great foreign war, which might renew lost energies, and which in any case would doubtless bring into power men with the will to govern; or a great extension of proletarian violence, which would make the revolutionary reality evident to the middle class, and would disgust them with the humanitarian platitudes with which Jaurès lulls them to sleep" (Sorel, "Reflections on Violence," trans. by T. E. Hulme, p. 82). Sorel, in a note, dismisses the hypothesis of a great war as "very far fetched," and then goes on to deal with proletarian violence, which is, of course, the main theme of the book.

It is for us to consider in what degree the present war will do the work expected by Sorel to be done by a general extension of proletarian violence.

Examined from this standpoint, the war is having, and will continue to have, the following consequences:

I.—*The consolidation of the capitalist position.* This seems to arise out of three results of the war:-

A.—The war, immediately at any rate, will enrich capital. The high tension of industry, the decrease of foreign competition, reduplicate loans—all these tend to consolidate and enrich the employers.

B.—War legislation has effected and will effect the union of State and Capital in many industries; it is rigidly defining and separating Capital and Labour (e.g., the Munitions Act); and to these we may add the relative increase in the power of Capital

45 resulting from the restriction of Trade Union activities.

C.—Also worth considering are the psychological effects of command. The overwhelming majority of the officers of the New Army are drawn from the middle class: and the training they receive in the command of men must, it seems, inspire

50 them with a self-assurance greater than they possessed in their pre-war days.

II.—On the other hand the war will, I think, effect *the definition of the proletariat.*

And from three causes, corresponding very closely to those

55 given as consolidating the capitalist position:-

A.—The inevitable labour disorganisation following in the war will result in the poverty and misery of the working classes. This in its turn will give rise to an intense search for relief and betterment, only to be found in revolution.

60 B.—As implied above, war legislation is clearly differentiating the proletariat.

C.—If war has trained the capitalist in command, it also, on the other hand, has taught the proletariat the value of organisation, of *esprit de corps,* of brotherhood in arms. The mob of the

65 past will be an army in the future.

Then, too, there must inevitably during the war have been a cultivation of a warlike spirit within us all. There has passed over us like a wave a grand revival of the sentiment of glory—a new realisation of heroic values. At any rate, it seems safe to assume

70 that those who have fought for something so impersonal as the rights of this war will not hesitate to strive for their own personal rights of justice. The proletariat of the future will be inspired with something nobler, if more nebulous, than the fantastical Utopias of a Fabian.

75 Hence it seems the war will result in an intensification of class feelings, a rigid demarcation of class interests. The world will be full of vanity and bitterness. But the outlook is not one of despair. Remember that the premises of Marx's hypothesis will be on the way to fulfilment, and the fatalistic revolution well in sight.

80 Remember, too, that the more highly organised capitalist industry becomes, the more economically virile will be the industrial society which the guilds inherit.

(ii) from 'To Hell with Culture' *(1941)*

A culture begins with simple things—with the way the potter moulds the clay on his wheel, the way a weaver threads his yarns, the way the builder builds his house. Greek culture did not begin with the Parthenon: it began with a whitewashed hut on a hillside.
5 Culture has always developed as an infinitely slow but sure refinement and elaboration of simple things—refinement and elaboration of speech, refinement and elaboration of shapes, refinement and elaboration of proportions, with the original purity persisting right through. A democratic culture will begin in a
10 *similar* way. We shall not revert to the peasant's hut or the potter's wheel. We shall begin with the elements of modern industry— electric power, metal alloys, cement, the tractor and the aeroplane. We shall consider these things as the raw materials of a civilization and we shall work out their appropriate use and appropriate forms,
15 without reference to the lath and plaster of the past.

To-day we are bound hand and food to the past. Because property is a sacred thing and land values a source of untold wealth, our houses must be crowded together and our streets must follow their ancient illogical meanderings. Because houses must be built
20 at the lowest possible cost to allow the highest possible profit, they are denied the art and science of the architect. Because everything we buy for use must be sold for profit, and because there must always be this profitable margin between cost and price, our pots and our pans, our furniture and our clothes, have the same shoddy
25 consistency, the same competitive cheapness. The whole of our capitalist culture is one immense veneer: a surface refinement hiding the cheapness and shoddiness at the heart of things.

To hell with such a culture! To the rubbish-heap and furnace with it all! Let us celebrate the democratic revolution with the
30 biggest holocaust in the history of the world. When Hitler has finished bombing our cities, let the demolition squads complete the good work. Then let us go out into the wide open spaces and build anew.

Let us build cities that are not too big, but spacious, with traffic
35 flowing freely through their leafy avenues, with children playing safely in their green and flowery parks, with people living happily

in bright efficient houses. Let us place our factories and workshops where natural conditions of supply make their location most convenient—the necessary electric power can be laid on any-

40 where. Let us balance agriculture and industry, town and country —let us do all these sensible and elementary things and *then* let us talk about our culture.

Robert Graves
1895–1985

(i) from 'Secondary Elaboration' (1925)
(ii) from 'The Poets of World War II' (1942)

Graves was a poet and novelist, and author of one of the most celebrated accounts of First World War experience, *Goodbye to All That* (1929). He enlisted on the outbreak of war and was badly wounded in 1916. Although he recovered physically, he was mentally scarred by his war experiences, and the first extract concerns this psychological disturbance. He knew both Wilfred Owen and Siegfried Sassoon, and was instrumental in arranging Sassoon's committal to Craiglockhart hospital instead of to a court martial (see Graves 1988 and Seymour Smith 1982). Graves published two collections of poems during the war, *Over the Brazier* (1916) and *Fairies and Fuseliers* (1917) (reprinted in Graves 1988). After the war, he became a student at Oxford University, before leaving Britain to live in Majorca.

The first extract is from the essay 'Secondary Elaboration'. This was first published in *Poetic Unreason* (1925), a book based on Graves' post-war research at Oxford into imaginative sources of poetry. The essay is haunted by Graves's recent war experiences, and begins with extensive quotations from the work of W. H. R. Rivers, the psychiatrist who treated Sassoon at Craiglockhart hospital. Graves develops Rivers' ideas about the correspondence between the creative processes forming dreams and those forming poetry. 'Secondary elaboration' is a term borrowed from Freud and refers to the 'artistic' manipulation of an original psychological experience to create dreams or fantasies.

The second piece is a slightly amended version of an essay on First and Second World War poetry which first appeared in 1942. It stands with Edgell Rickword's 'Poetry of Two Wars' (Prose Anthology, p. 247) as the acutest contemporary analysis of war poetry. Graves's suggestions as to why there could be no poets of the Second World War are typically provocative. Graves was closely involved with the production of Alun Lewis's second collection of poetry, *Ha! Ha! Among the Trumpets* (1945), making the selection after Lewis's death and writing the Foreword.

DISCUSSION: Chapter 1.
SOURCES: (i) Graves 1925: 104–9.
    (ii) Graves 1949: 310–11, 312.

(i) *from* 'Secondary Elaboration' *(1925)*

As an example of structural repair I will give the history of another poem called *The Bedpost*. The first version represents the form the poem took after three drafts or so, which unfortunately for the demonstration I have not kept, in the summer of 1918. I must
5   apologize for giving the intimate history of the poem, but it is important for the argument. After having been three times in France and wounded, I came home suffering from "shell shock." In January, 1918, I married and was certified as temporarily unfit to return to my battalion. But the spring of that year was so disastrous
10   for our armies that it looked as though after all I would be bound to go back, whether fit or not, before the year was out. Meanwhile my thoughts were much concerned with the prospect of a family, and for the first time I realized fully the stupidity of getting killed instead of living happily ever after with my wife and the child that
15   we were expecting. The poem appeared in the following form:

BETSY

Sleepy Betsy from her pillow
    Sees the shadow tall
Of her mother's wooden bedpost
20   Flung upon the wall.

Now this grave and kindly warrior
    With his small round head
Tells her stories of old battles
    As she lies in bed.

25   How the Emperor and the Farmer
    Fighting knee to knee,
Broke their swords but whirled the scabbards
    Till they gained the sea.

How the sons of Ehud Vigo
30   Whom the ogre slew,
Caught and skinned their father's murderer
    Old Cro-bar-cru.
How two brothers Will and Abel
    Fought the giant Gog,

35 Threw him into Stony Cataract
    In the land of Og.

    How a girl called Ann Clarissa
    Fell in love with Will,
    And went with him to the Witches' Larder
40   Over Hoo Hill.

    How Gog's wife encountered Abel
    Whom she hated most,
    Stole away his arms and armour,
    Turned him to a post.

45 But Betsy likes the bloodier stories,
    Clang and clash of fight;
    And Abel wanes with the spent candle
    "Good-night; Good-night."

Here the conflict is, as I have said, between the hope of love and
50 peace, as symbolized by the child we were expecting, lying in bed
and telling itself stories, and the fear of continued war as bound up
in the stories themselves. In the same way as the child, in its
Amazonian age, preferred to hear about the horrible stories of war
and bloodshed, so the world, and myself, too, if the call should
55 come again, preferred to keep on at this ridiculous game of fighting.
Cro-bar-Cru and Gog were childish nightmares. Cro-bar-Cru
represents a phrase from a poem about a wicked landlord evicting
a hapless widow from a cottage with the help of his Crowbar Crew.
I thought as a child that Cro-bar-Cru was a giant. Gog, the
60 Guildhall giant, was mixed in my mind with the warlike Og, who
had the iron bedstead nine cubits long—note the bedstead association. In this poem one part of me, the Jekyll, had intended to write
a nursery poem for the child who was going to be born, and was
refusing to think about anything else. The other, the Hyde, most
65 interested in the preservation of life and love, was dominating the
Jekyll with a commentary on the folly of war.

Early in 1921 I suddenly picked up the poem, with which I was
now dissatisfied because my poet-friends had been objecting to my
preoccupation with "nursery sentimentalities," and re-wrote it.
70 This was at a time when it seemed that war was endless, Russia,

Ireland, the Near East, were all embroiled, and the immediate cause was reading a paragraph in the paper about new poison gases promised for the next war, and a rumour that a large house, quite close to where I was living, was to be converted into an ex-
75 perimental laboratory for making these. Since 1918 I had been deeply interested in Freudian psycho-analysis as being a possible corrective for my shell-shock, which had just returned, and I was thinking of putting myself under treatment. The poem then wrote itself as follows:

80 THE BEDPOST

Sleepy Betsy from her pillow
　　Sees the post and ball
Of her sister's wooden bedstead
　　Shadowed on the wall.

85 Now this grave young warrior standing
　　With uncovered head,
Tells her stories of old battle,
　　As she lies in bed.

How the Emperor and the Farmer
90 　　Fighting knee to knee,
Broke their swords but whirled their scabbards
　　Till they gained the sea.

How the ruler of that shore
　　Foully broke his oath;
95 Gave them beds in his sea-cavern,
　　Then stabbed them both.

How the daughters of the Emperor,
　　Diving boldly through,
Caught and killed their father's murderer,
100 　　Old Cro-bar-cru.

How the Farmer's sturdy sons
　　Fought the giant Gog,
Threw him into Stony Cataract
　　In the land of Og.

105   Will and Abel were their names,
          Though they went by others;
      He could tell ten thousand stories
          Of these lusty brothers.

      How the Emperor's eldest daughter
110   Fell in love with Will,
      And went with him to the Court of Venus
          Over Hoo Hill.

      How Gog's wife encountered Abel,
          Whom she hated most,
115   Stole away his arms and helmet,
          Turned him to a post.

      As a post he shall be rooted
          For yet many years,
      Until a maiden shall release him
120   With a fall of tears.

      But Betsy likes the bloodier stories,
          Clang and clash of fight;
      And Abel wanes with the spent candle,
          "Sweetheart, good night!"

125   If the two versions are compared it will be seen that a Freudian
      argument has suddenly changed the whole complexion of the piece
      while apparently preserving its original conflict. I would like to
      make it quite clear that I am no longer in sympathy with the
      sentiments or psychological tenets embodied in this poem; the
130 mechanism is all that is intended to appear.
      The argument is now as follows:
      A child lies in bed and repeats stories told to her by an elder
      sister. In these stories there are two princesses identified by the
      sister with herself and Betsy, and two heroes who are their
135 imaginary lovers. But Betsy in her own case rejects the sentimental
      lover given her and prefers to let him platonically tell her merely
      about battles, murders, and sudden death. The shadow of the
      bedpost is a sexual symbol which the child is not yet physically
      prepared to recognize, but when a certain time comes, Abel will
140 be released from the spell. In the same way the world, in spite of

the symbol of the Cross, originally a sex symbol and then the symbol of Christ's love and refusal to fight, prefers to go on fighting, actually making the cross a military decoration and standard.

145 The prototype of Betsy had been born shortly after the Armistice, and at the moment of writing this second version I was very anxious on her behalf owing to a belief that her nervous system had been undermined, unknown to my wife and myself, by the neurotic condition of her nurse, who had also suffered greatly in the war; what future nervous disturbances might result to the 150 little girl we did not dare to think. It will be seen that my love of the child and my own nervous condition, aggravated by threats of renewed war, were associated with the thought of psycho-analysis as a possible relief for both; and yet there was a resistance in my mind against being psycho-analysed. The poem is scattered thick 155 with very bold and definite sex-symbolism. It was printed in the blameless *London Mercury,* and applications have arrived for its inclusion in nursery anthologies: which shows how inscrutable are the ways of Apollo. It will be seen that the conflict between my friends and myself (of which I spoke) was being reconciled in this 160 piece, my nursery sentimentality balanced with its very opposite, the cynical Freudian view of childhood.

(ii) from 'The Poets of World War II' (1949)

This historical account is almost sufficient in itself to answer the question, 'Why has this war produced no war poets?' In the first place it will be realized that the passing of the Conscription Act, a few months before World War II, made volunteer pride irrelevant 5 and war poetry superfluous as a stimulus to recruiting. Next, the British Army has not yet been engaged on a grand scale with the enemy and, despite official reassurances, is not likely to be for some time. On the whole the soldier has lived a far safer life than the munition maker whom in World War I he despised as a 'shirker'; 10 he cannot even feel that his rendezvous with death is more certain than that of his Aunt Fanny, the firewatcher. As for the beauty of the English countryside, he has seen far too much of it through a tent-flap during his dreary exile from home.

Finally, the army of World War II is not the amateur, desperate,
15 happy-go-lucky, ragtime, lousy army of World War I. Its senior
officers and N.C.O.s are practically all professionals; even its
newest battalions are anything but ragtime; and it is being increasingly mechanized. Most of it is bored stiff with inactivity, and
any sort of eccentric behaviour in officer or man is more sternly
20 discountenanced than ever before in its history. (The right to
eccentricity is only earned in battle.) The sort of soldier who in
World War I would naturally have become a 'war poet' now feels
a khaki-blanco mist rise between him and the world of his
imagination. If the mist clears for a moment and he begins to
25 write a poem it will probably be about his sense of difference from
fellow-soldiers [...].

But it is extremely unlikely that he will feel any qualms about
the justice of the British cause or about the necessity of the war's
continuance; so that, even if he has experienced the terrors of an
30 air raid, he will not feel obliged to write horrifically about it, to
draw attention to the evils of war. Poems about the horrors of the
trenches were originally written to stir the ignorant and com-
placent people at home to a realization of what a 'fight to the finish'
involved. [...]

35 By the time that the rest of the British Army was at last engaged
in grand-scale fighting the poets serving in it were too highly
trained and conscientious as soldiers, and found the war too well-
staged and exciting, to write defeatist war poems on the model of
the 1917–18 sort; but what other sort was there to write? Even if they
40 felt ambitious 'to be war poets,' the tortuous modernistic fashions
in which they had been writing before their conscription were
unsuited to the higher journalism which war poetry essentially is;
and they disdained writing in the simpler styles which had served
the poets of World War I. Deliberate heroism was so far outmoded
45 as to seem vulgar or quaint. Besides, they saw no need to compete
with the trained war-correspondent, who lived rough, brought his
report back from the place of greatest danger and told the whole
truth—even if part of the truth was afterwards censored.

Israel Zangwill
1864–1926

(i) from 'Jewish Factor in the War and Settlement' (1916)
(ii) from 'The Ruined Romantics' (1916)

Zangwill was the leading British Jewish writer of his time. His novels and short stories, such as *Children of the Ghetto* (1892), were very popular and he was friendly with established Edwardian literary figures such as Hilaire Belloc and G. K. Chesterton. He was invited to contribute to government propaganda in 1914 and was instrumental in the creation of a Jewish regiment in the British forces (see Leftwich 1957). However, his political allegiances were not straightforwardly patriotic. Zangwill was a committed Zionist and maintained links throughout the war with socialist and feminist groups.

The two extracts are taken from essays in the collection *The War for the World* (1916). 'Jewish Factor in the War and Settlement' shows clearly the qualifications in Zangwill's support for the war caused by his Jewishness. 'The Ruined Romantics' is an early attack on romantic militarism which draws attention to the horrors of industrial warfare. It also demonstrates, in its style and references as much as its content, Zangwill's ambivalent response to English culture. The radical politics are balanced by a self-consciously English gentlemanly style and a taste for the establishment humour of the weekly magazine *Punch*.

DISCUSSION: Chapter 5.
SOURCE: (i) Zangwill 1916: 330–2.
  (ii) Zangwill 1916: 89–90, 93–4.

(i) from 'Jewish Factor in the War and Settlement' (1916)

A critic in a French magazine, reviewing some Ghetto stories, remarked that reading them was like seeing the bay on whose shore he lived from the opposite curve, so that all his familiar landmarks were reversed or revealed under a new aspect. Thus, his own

5 people, so serenely conscious of their centralism, were turned into "the heathen," while their religion, the last word of sweetness and light, now appeared as a synonym for hatred and darkness. To-day a Ghetto story—especially if laid in the Russo-Polish Pale—would reveal the war for righteousness as an incomprehensible nightmare

10 in which the Jew fervent to pour out his blood and his treasure for Russia finds himself hounded and tortured between the separate hates of the Russian and the Pole, and only saved by the conquering Kaiser bringing, like Napoleon, equal rights for all races. Even in England the Jew who won the Victoria Cross and was refused a

15 meal in a restaurant in one of our greatest Liberal centres—in Leeds to be precise—must have been somewhat bemused, the more so as he himself makes speeches on the Asquith model.

The angle at which the Jew sees the war can thus rarely be what the Censorship Bureau would consider a right angle—it is either

20 too obtuse or too acute. A Christian gunner—if that is not an Irish bull—wrote to the *Yorkshire Evening Post*: "I am a Britisher, home on seven days' leave, after being out in France for fifteen months ... What has surprised me as much as anything in this war of surprises is the great number of Jewish boys who are doing their

25 bit at the Front and doing it right. Most of them have enlisted under wrong names, hiding their proper names under English ones. Some of my best pals at the Front are Jews, whom anyone would welcome as pals and who are true as steel."

That the Christian gunner is not exaggerating let the story of

30 Private Sam Thomson illustrate—the young signaller of the Camerons who in a house at Loos killed single-handed three Germans and captured thirty, and whose real name was Sam Woolf. Sam was anxious to give his all for England, yet he felt it necessary to smuggle himself into her army. And it is a sad fact

35 that, despite the resounding cry for recruits, Jews have been

frequently refused or, if accepted, "chipped," as it is called, by their comrades. It is the same in the French trenches, where the Jewish Volunteers in the Foreign Legion are accused of enlisting for the food. Even a Jewish officer in an English regiment who gave up the
40 Bar to enlist found life almost unbearable.

And if this is so in free democracies, what must be the situation in Russia, where even the law is on the side of the mob, and what must have been the patriotism of those persecuted Jewish volunteers of the French Foreign Legion, who, being shot as mutineers
45 for demanding to be removed to another regiment, faced the firing squad with unbandaged eyes, crying "Vive la France! Vive la Russie!" Surely Jews are the only Christians nowadays.

(ii) from 'The Ruined Romantics' (1916)

"Glory of war," writes a colonial from the Dardanelles, "is a thing of the past." And, indeed, nearly every one of my own acquaintances at the Dardanelles was down with dysentery, which does not seem to be even counted in the casualties, unless death
5   lends it a little dignity.

Early in the war—through my perilous habit of "walking in war time"—I was captured by a British officer and made to address his men. The khaki congregation, young recruits in all the pride of life and limb, squatted in a meadow, and I stood, like Abraham of old,
10 in the door of a tent. It was a picturesque scene, growing more romantic as the light faded and my discourse soared to the stars that came out to listen. I spoke of national righteousness, of duty, and glory, and how they must shame the Goths by chivalry to their women and children. "Thank you, thank you," cried the captain,
15 fervently grasping my hand, when my heroic accents died on the perfumed darkness of the summer night. "You have saved me my eventing exhortation. I was about to address them on lice!" How many of these young knight-errants have since been infected with typhus by these unromantic insects I know not, but it is the *pediculi*
20 more than the Germans that have devastated Serbia. "They have practically taken possession of Serbia," wrote a doctor to *The Times*. "Rats and lice enjoy this warm weather," writes a British soldier from a front trench in Flanders.

[236]

"The lordliest life on earth"—or the lousiest— appears also to
25 lead to insanity—whether the madness of melancholia or of terror.
The Austrian asylum of Steinhof has had to be enlarged to receive
the patients from the front. And this lordly life has begotten new
diseases—now a novel form of neuritis, anon a trench fever
credited to the bites of body parasites, the real lordly livers. The
30 old diseases of course flourish more vigorously than ever; the list
reads like one of the passages Zola penned so unctuously in
"Lourdes": "Typhoid, tetanus, paratyphoid A and B, jaundice,
dysentery, spotted fever."

The marvel is that madness does not overtake whole battalions.
35 For not in Dante's "Inferno," nor in Poe at his most gruesome, nor
in all the literature of horror, nor in the wildest pictures of Wiertz,
can anything be found even to equal the simple statements of the
war reports. In the Artois, says Mr. Buchan, "the French parapets
are practically composed of dead Germans." We read of valleys
40 turning into volcanos, of "heads and limbs flying in all directions,"
of men wading through a sunlit blue sea that turns red, of chips of
Alpine granite blinding 70,000 Austrians in six months, of ravines
solidified with standing corpses. "There were bunches of corpses
caught upon our barbed wire defences," says a French war report.
45 There are all manner of wounds, writes Mr. Alfred Stead in the
Daily Express—"men without the bottom of their faces, men who
have lost noses, eyes and ears.... The smell of blood was heavy in
the church, the incense of the world to the God of War—that
sickening smell which affects even the surgeons more than the
50 most horrible wounds.... In the space before the altar were the
worst cases. When I went in, there were four dying in agony, the
cries, despite injections of morphia, being frightful, and the writh-
ing limbs and convulsed features unforgettable. They all died in
the night." [...]
55 "Shall we never shed blood?" wistfully wailed that incurable
romantic, Stevenson, comrade in letters of the author of "The Song
of the Sword," bedridden both. They dreamed of being soldiers
because they were invalids, and of being seamen because they were
not able-bodied. It is to be hoped the *manes* of these "literary gents"
60 are satisfied now. It would be no unfitting hell for these frivolous
romantics to be compelled to witness the measureless agony of this
war; the suffering of mules and horses, as well as of men, women,

[237]

and children; the illimitable carnage and bestiality, the insanities, suicides, hangings, shootings, crucifixions, buryings or burnings
65 alive; the diseases, exiles, and anguishes; to hear the innumerable moans of milkless infants, and see every gate to death open and besieged by agonizing queues. The only excuse one can find for Henley and Stevenson (and the school they created) is that they had no imagination. They lived remote from Mars and could see
70 only its ruddy splendour.

In the presence of the war itself our poets are dumb, or if they speak it is of its spiritual inspirations, its intellectual ironies, or its psychological incongruities. Of the old joy of battle there is not a trace. The poor ruined romantics! Even Kipling, who but for the
75 grace of God might have been Poet Laureate of Prussia, has not egged on the slaughter. Indeed, with the close of the South African war and the publication of his great pacificist poem "The Settler", his career as a Tyrtæus seems to have ended. That wonderful poem —of an Old Testament greatness—is Kipling's real "Recessional."
80 And his vilification of the "senseless bullet" and the "barren shrapnel" and his glorification of the "holy wars" of united mankind against the evils of Nature mark the public bankruptcy of the ruined romantics.

David Jones
1895–1974

extract from the 'Preface' to *In Parenthesis* (1937)

For biography, see Poetry Anthology, p. 150.

The Preface of *In Parenthesis* offers insights into Jones's idiosyncratic poetic methods, their source in his interpretation of war experience and his attempt to recover a sense of British identity through writing about that experience.

DISCUSSION: Chapter 2.
SOURCE: Jones 1937: ix, x–xi.

from the 'Preface' to In Parenthesis *(1937)*

This writing has to do with some things I saw, felt, & was part of. The period covered begins early in December 1915 and ends early in July 1916. The first date corresponds to my going to France. The latter roughly marks a change in the character of our lives in the

5 Infantry on the West Front. From then onward things hardened into a more relentless, mechanical affair, took on a more sinister aspect. The wholesale slaughter of the later years, the conscripted levies filling the gaps in every file of four, knocked the bottom out of the intimate, continuing, domestic life of small contingents of

10 men, within whose structure Roland could find, and, for a reasonable while, enjoy, his Oliver. In the earlier months there was a certain attractive amateurishness, and elbow-room for idiosyncrasy that connected with a less exacting past. The period of the individual rifle-man, of the 'old sweat' of the Boer campaign, the

15 'Bairnsfather' war, seemed to terminate with the Somme battle. There were, of course, glimpses of it long after—all through in fact—but it seemed never quite the same. The *We've Lived and*

Loved Together of the Devons was well enough for the Peninsula,
but became meaningless when companion lives were at such short
20 purchase. Just as now there are glimpses in our ways of another
England—yet we know the truth. Even while we watch the boatman
mending his sail, the petroleum is hurting the sea. So did we in 1916
sense a change. How impersonal did each new draft seem arriving
each month, and all these new-fangled gadgets to master. [...]
25   My companions in the war were mostly Londoners with an
admixture of Welshmen, so that the mind and folk-life of those
two differing racial groups are an essential ingredient to my theme.
Nothing could be more representative. These came from London.
Those from Wales. Together they bore in their bodies the genuine
30 tradition of the Island of Britain, from Bendigeid Vran to Jingle
and Marie Lloyd. These were the children of Doll Tearsheet.
Those are before Caractacus was. Both speak in parables, the wit
of both is quick, both are natural poets; yet no two groups could
well be more dissimilar. It was curious to know them harnessed
35 together, and together caught in the toils of 'good order and
military discipline'; to see them shape together to the remains of
an antique regimental tradition, to see them react to the few things
that united us—the same jargon, the same prejudice against 'other
arms' and against the Staff, the same discomforts, the same
40 grievances, the same maims, the same deep fears, the same pathetic
jokes; to watch them, oneself part of them, respond to the war
landscape; for I think the day by day in the Waste Land, the sudden
violences and the long stillnesses, the sharp contours and unformed
voids of that mysterious existence, profoundly affected the imagin-
45 ations of those who suffered it. It was a place of enchantment. It is
perhaps best described in Malory, book iv, chapter 15—that
landscape spoke 'with a grimly voice'.
    I suppose at no time did one so much live with a consciousness
of the past, the very remote, and the more immediate and trivial
50 past, both superficially and more subtly. No one, I suppose,
however much not given to association, could see infantry in tin-
hats, with ground-sheets over their shoulders, with sharpened pine-
stakes in their hands, and not recall

55   '... or may we cram,
            Within this wooden O ...'

[240]

But there were deeper complexities of sight and sound to make
ever present

'the pibble pabble in Pompey's camp'

60   Every man's speech and habit of mind were a perpetual showing:
now of Napier's expedition, now of the Legions at the Wall, now
of 'train-band captain', now of Jack Cade, of John Ball, of the
commons in arms. Now of *High Germany*, of *Dolly Gray*, of Bullcalf,
Wart and Poins; of Jingo largenesses, of things as small as the
65   Kingdom of Elmet; of Wellington's raw shire recruits, of ancient
border antipathies, of our contemporary, less intimate, larger
unities, of *John Barleycorn*, of 'sweet Sally Frampton'. Now of Coel
Hên—of the Celtic cycle that lies, a subterranean influence as a
deep water troubling, under every tump in this Island, like Merlin
70   complaining under his big rock.

Virginia Woolf
1882–1941

from *Three Guineas* (1938)

Woolf is best known as the author of the key modernist novels *Mrs Dalloway* (1925) and *To the Lighthouse* (1927), but her work also includes important contributions to feminist theory. *Three Guineas* (1938) is an extended essay on feminism, militarism and masculinity, and develops arguments for women's economic and cultural autonomy first expressed in *A Room of One's Own* (1929). The concern with the threat of war and the militarization of society is characteristic of many works of the late 1930s (it was published in the same year as Orwell's *Homage to Catalonia* and W. H. Auden's journey to the Sino-Japanese war, described in *Journey to a War* [1939]). However, Woolf's argument for a feminist neutrality marks her difference to the conventional leftist politics of the period and offers a radical development of the theories first put forward by pacifist feminists in the First World War.

Three Guineas is written as a reply to a letter from a middle-class barrister posing the question 'How can war be prevented?' In the extract Woolf is outlining the responsibilities of a new society of 'the daughters of educated men' in their attitudes to war.

DISCUSSION: Chapter 7.
SOURCE: Woolf 1943: 193–8.

from Three Guineas *(1938)*

Their first duty, to which they would bind themselves not by oath, for oaths and ceremonies have no part in a society which must be anonymous and elastic before everything would be not to fight with arms. This is easy for them to observe, for in fact, as the papers
5   inform us, "the Army Council have no intention of opening recruiting for any women's corps." The country ensures it. Next they would refuse in the event of war to make munitions or nurse the wounded. Since in the last war both these activities were mainly discharged by the daughters of working men, the pressure
10   upon them here too would be slight, though probably disagreeable. On the other hand the next duty to which they would pledge themselves is one of considerable difficulty, and calls not only for courage and initiative, but for the special knowledge of the educated man's daughter. It is, briefly, not to incite their brothers
15   to fight, or to dissuade them, but to maintain an attitude of complete indifference. But the attitude expressed by the word "indifference" is so complex and of such importance that it needs even here further definition. Indifference in the first place must be given a firm footing upon fact. As it is a fact that she cannot
20   understand what instinct compels him, what glory, what interest, what manly satisfaction fighting provides for him—"without war there would be no outlet for the manly qualities which fighting develops"—as fighting thus is a sex characteristic which she cannot share, the counterpart some claim of the maternal instinct which
25   he cannot share, so is it an instinct which she cannot judge. The outsider therefore must leave him free to deal with this instinct by himself, because liberty of opinion must be respected, especially when it is based upon an instinct which is as foreign to her as centuries of tradition and education can make it. This is a
30   fundamental and instinctive distinction upon which indifference may be based. But the outsider will make it her duty not merely to base her indifference upon instinct, but upon reason. When he says, as history proves that he has said, and may say again, "I am fighting to protect our country" and thus seeks to rouse her
35   patriotic emotion, she will ask herself, "What does 'our country' mean to me an outsider?" To decide this she will analyse the meaning of patriotism in her own case. She will inform herself of

the position of her sex and her class in the past. She will inform
40 herself of the amount of land, wealth and property in the possession
of her own sex and class in the present—how much of "England"
in fact belongs to her. From the same sources she will inform
herself of the legal protection which the law has given her in the
past and now gives her. And if he adds that he is fighting to protect
45 her body, she will reflect upon the degree of physical protection
that she now enjoys when the words "Air Raid Precaution" are
written on blank walls. And if he says that he is fighting to protect
England from foreign rule, she will reflect that for her there are no
"foreigners", since by law she becomes a foreigner if she marries a
50 foreigner. And she will do her best to make this a fact, not by forced
fraternity, but by human sympathy. All these facts will convince
her reason (to put it in a nutshell) that her sex and class has very
little to thank England for in the past; not much to thank England
for in the present; while the security of her person in the future is
55 highly dubious. [...]

    She will find that she has no good reason to ask her brother to
fight on her behalf to protect "our" country. "'Our country,'" she
will say, "throughout the greater part of its history has treated me
as a slave; it has denied me education or any share in its possessions.
60 'Our' country still ceases to be mine if I marry a foreigner. 'Our'
country denies me the means of protecting myself, forces me to
pay others a very large sum annually to protect me, and is so little
able, even so, to protect me that Air Raid precautions are written
on the wall. Therefore if you insist upon fighting to protect me, or
65 'our' country, let it be understood, soberly and rationally between
us, that you are fighting to gratify a sex instinct which I cannot
share; to procure benefits which I have not shared and probably
will not share; but not to gratify my instincts, or to protect either
myself or my country. For," the outsider will say, "in fact, as a
70 woman, I have no country. As a woman I want no country. As a
woman my country is the whole world." And if, when reason has
said its say, still some obstinate emotion remains, some love of
England dropped into a child's ears by the cawing of rooks in an
elm tree, by the splash of waves on a beach, or by English voices
75 murmuring nursery rhymes, this drop of pure, if irrational, emotion she will make serve her to give to England first what she
desires of peace and freedom for the whole world.

Edgell Rickword
1898–1982

(i) extract from 'Notes on Culture and the War' (1940)
(ii) extract from 'Poetry and Two Wars' (1941)

Rickword fought in the First World War and his war experiences affected both his political commitments in the 1930s and the literary judgements shown in 'Poetry and Two Wars'. Rickword edited the *Calendar of Modern Letters* and *Scrutinies*, two of the most influential literary journals of the 1920s and 1930s, and also wrote poetry, some of it provoked by the war (see Rickword 1976). After joining the Communist Party in 1934, he became editor of the leading left-wing periodical of the 1930s, *Left Review.* Unlike many thirties leftist intellectuals, Rickword remained a committed Marxist throughout the Second World War, and edited *Our Time*, a journal that preserved a commitment to political writing and popular culture in wartime.

'Notes on Culture and the War' was published in *Poetry and the People* (the original name of *Our Time*) in July 1940 and suggests the possibility of the revival of a radical popular culture in wartime. 'Poetry and Two Wars' provides a political analysis of the culture of wartime, offering a reassessment of the work of First World War poets. It appeared in *Our Time* in April 1941.

DISCUSSION: Chapters 3 and 4.
SOURCE: (i) Rickword 1978: 135–6.
　　　　　(ii) Rickword 1978: 157–9, 159–61.

(i) from 'Notes on Culture and the War' *(1940)*

Reading is a solitary act, it is often a means of escape from reality, but speech is necessarily social. So it may be a very good thing for us to be thrown on our own resources and unable to stuff our heads with the crudities and sentimentalities of the millionaire Press. Then the natural storytellers and poets will come into their own, making conscious the feelings of their group, be it large or small. They are the organisers of emotion, one of the factors directing the collective effort to a common aim. Round the camp-fires of the armies of freedom, on the steppes and on the sierras, many stories and ballads grew up celebrating popular heroes and staunch leaders of the people. During the Spanish war it is no exaggeration to say that thousands of such ballads were composed by "amateur" poets and circulated in the village or the regiment, whilst scores of them became popular throughout the country. So it has been, so it will be again with us. It is not want of paper but only lack of conviction which can hamper a popular revival of poetry.

But it would be foolish to overlook one of the many differences in the situation here. In Russia and in Spain, where the bulk of the population was a largely illiterate peasantry, oral poetry was a part of everyday life, the ballad singer was the radio and the newspaper of the countryside. A century of industrialism has broken the roots of our tradition and left us dependent on imported song, the anæmic product of commercialised inspiration (except for what we have lifted from the Negroes). But there is plenty of evidence—the popularity of Unity Theatre, the circulation of this paper—that the blood is beginning to flow again in the numbed limb. Everything now depends on the development of democratic initiative, on whether the people are really *roused* and not merely shepherded, and that involves political considerations which are too complex to discuss here. [...]

So we can expect that one day the lugubrious joviality of such official hand-outs as *Roll up the Barrel* will be superseded by songs that the other ranks have made for themselves. When that happens we shall know that a transformation has taken place in the English consciousness similar to that which enabled the people of Spain to stand up to their ordeal.

(ii) from 'Poetry and Two Wars' (1941)

An interesting exposition of part of the dilemma in which the confused progressives of yesterday find themselves is made by a natural Conservative, Lord David Cecil.

"Now that the clash has come" (between the forces of reaction
5 and progress, according to the critic) "these writers seem strangely dubious as to the part they should play in it. They seem equally incapable of Brooke's passionate fighting spirit or Owen's passionate pacifism.[1] It is understandable. The combatants in 1914 hoped they were fighting a war 'to end war.' In view of the events of the
10 last twenty years no one can be convinced that England's victory, however decisive, will certainly ensure a permanent peace." As a consolation and philosophy for writers in a world supposedly made safe for Anglo-American imperialism, Lord Cecil appropriately recommends a creed which accepts suffering as an inevitable
15 feature of a sinful world and which teaches "that it is in suffering, if properly understood, that we can achieve the intensest vision of God."

But the T.L.S. is not gratified at the notion of our writers setting out to achieve the Beatific Vision with Hitler threatening the Suez
20 Canal, and in an editorial comment it gently chides its aristocratic contributor for not setting them a task showing a more immediate return, such as the romanticisation of the present armed conflict. "The perils of our day," exclaims the leader writer, "demand primarily a literature that deals with war as it is, its brutality, its
25 incongruous interruption of life, its victimization, and the heroism of men and women who prefer death to submission to a dehumanising tyranny. And this, too, should lead to a literature of England as it is. Lack of themes, indeed!"

There in essence, substituting the word *life* for *war*, are the
30 characteristics of the literature which the working-class movement develops in its struggle to free itself from the cultural disabilities of a decadent civilisation. So why should *The Times*, which for so many years has been commending the elegant vapidities and fatuous experiments of secluded ladies and gentlemen to the
35 cormorant appetites of its leisured readers, and hushing down on the genuine things created under the most adverse conditions by

[247]

actual participants in the social struggle, suddenly call for a recognition of the brutality of existence and of the heroism of ordinary men and women?

40   Because it knows, the old fox of Printing House Square, that the misfortunes it enumerates would be laid, by the authors it trusted and boosted, to the charge of the external enemy, whereas in peace time they could not but be laid to a home account. Brutality in itself neither makes nor mars literature. A cult of brutality, in

45   subject-matter and technique, has been common, since the last war, to all countries where the anarchic play of forces fosters the growth of anti-social impulses. So the fact that scores of people are drowned in sewage through a bursting bomb does not provide a "nobler opportunity" for the writer, to use this unctuous journal-

50   ist's phrase, than the fact that scores of men are choked to death by fire-damp in a blocked working.

To the T.L.S. and its circle of readers, peace and war may be sharply distinguished, but to the majority of the inhabitants, war only accentuates miseries which are part and parcel of their daily

55   lives. Not to speak of conditions on far-away plantations, the brutality of industrial life can be reckoned by the fact that the output per worker per hour has nearly doubled since the last war; the "incongruous interruption of life" is a good description of the fate of the worker flung on to the scrap-heap of unemployment

60   when still in his prime; the threat of victimisation is always over the militant's head, whilst James Connolly's is only one name out of a great army who have "preferred death to a dehumanising tyranny." Lack of themes, indeed! [...]

War is the result of the same human will that condemns the

65   people to low and precarious standard of life whether engaged with an external foe or not. Lack of this understanding prevented Sassoon from developing in peace-time a poetry of indignant pity and keen satire such as he wrote out of his war experience. His latest book shows him now to be introspective and vaguely

70   mystical, whilst his satiric gift has sunk to the vulgar common-place of:

"The cultural crusade of Teuton tanks."

And the poet who wrote in *Attack*:

> "Then, clumsily bowed
75   With bombs and guns and shovels and battle gear,
> Men jostle and climb to meet the bristling fire.
> Lines of grey muttering faces, masked with fear,
> They leave their trenches, going over the top
> While time ticks blank and busy on their wrists,
80   And hope, with furtive eyes and grappling fists,
> Flounders in mud. O Jesu, make it stop...."

a passage which in its truth gives "courage" real meaning, in the last line of a new poem describes courage as

> "A kneeling angel holding faith's front line,"

85 which is emptily rhetorical.

Yet Sassoon came near to seeing the human motivation behind the seemingly cosmic disaster. Read any of the war section in his "Poems Newly Selected," particularly *To Any Dead Officer.*

> "Good-bye, old lad! Remember me to God,
90   And tell Him that our Politicians swear
> They won't give in till Prussian Rule's been trod
>
> Under the Heel of England.... Are you there? ...
> Yes ... and the War won't end for at least two years;
> But we've got stacks of men ... I'm blind with tears,
95   Staring into the dark. Cheero!
> I wish they'd killed you in a decent show."

Or consider this from *Reconciliation* (unfortunately omitted from the new selection) spoken to a mother standing by her son's grave:

> "Men fought like brutes; and hideous things were done:
100   And you have nourished hatred, harsh and blind.
> But in that Golgotha perhaps you'll find
> The mothers of the men who killed your son."

Reading that with its reflection of the real internationalism so strong in 1919, I feel it was one of the things he meant when he said
105 in another poem:

> "Look down, and swear by the slain of the War
>   that you'll never forget!"

And Owen, too, saw in national-political ambitions which the statesmen would not give up, the reason for the continuance of the
110 war which no longer inspired the faith of the soldiers of either side.

The true poets must be truthful, said Owen. There can be no more specific instruction today than that. But mere realism, how brutally factual, is not truth. The concrete experience, which must be the writer's starting-point, does not exist in isolation from the
115 complex of social relationships. A hungry woman in a Barcelona food-queue during the war of intervention and a hungry woman in a Liverpool food-queue (if Lord Woolton had not abolished food-queues) would at first glance appear to be objectively ident-ical as subject matter for a poem or story. But their hunger (if we
120 may be permitted to stretch the imagination so far in the case of the Liverpool woman) though due to the same ultimate cause, would have as immediate cause something quite different, one being a matter of the common interest, the other that of individual interests. Each would have its particular emotional expression
125 which it is the writer's job to clarify and represent in a vivid way. What brought out fortitude in Barcelona might provoke indigna-tion in Liverpool. So, as it is not hunger "in general" that provides the subject-matter for true poetry, so it is not war "in general", but the particular war in which the writer is involved. And to the extent
130 to which he can catch the peculiar emotional atmosphere of the war in his work will embody the truth about it. It is not necessarily a matter of torn bodies and blasted buildings. The *Good Soldier Schweik*, with its broad farce, slapstick even, exposes the corruption and oppression of the old Austrian Empire more vividly than a
135 straight-forward denunciation. It is a matter of being able to see what is under one's nose, not of any particular manner or approach to the subject; ridicule and indignation equally serve the truth. The only condition is to feel as the people feel, not as the journalists pretend they feel, nor as we abstractedly, might like them to feel.
140 Such writers can only come from among the people. The startling success of Sassoon, his sudden ability to speak out, must have been stimulated by his contact with the masses in uniform. Losing that, he has relapsed into mysticism and verbiage. All honour to those who from a privileged class-position found expression for the
145 wrongs of the suffering people, though they could do no more than protest at the inhumanity of war. But today the consciousness of

what war is is not confined to a handful of advanced industrial workers, it is widespread throughout the mass of the people themselves. The true poets of this war have a vast potential
150 audience, and the fact that they are bound up with the masses themselves will determine the significance of the war literature to come. These potential poets had passed through the stage of emotional protests before the war caught them, so that they see the war not as a temporary disease, but as the culminating criminality
155 of a system. They had already accepted the organisation of that emotional protest with the aim of altering the conditions that gave rise to it. So the emotions will not expend themselves in anger and pity, but, fusing these with understanding, forge instruments to free men's minds from false hatreds and bring out their underlying
160 confidence in their own ability to make the rebel songs come true.

Montagu Slater
1902–56

from 'Bless 'em All: A Piece About Army Songs' *(1941)*

Slater was active as a communist and writer throughout the 1930s and, after the Second World War, wrote the libretto for Benjamin Britten's opera *Peter Grimes*. His essay on soldiers' songs was written in 1941 for the journal *Our Time* to which he was a regular contributor. It celebrates the songs as representing a radical popular culture in opposition to the sanitized products of the wartime mass entertainment industries. In this extract Slater discusses the song 'Bless 'em All', originally an army song which was then adapted by commercial songwriters to become a hit in the early years of the war.

DISCUSSION: Chapter 3.
SOURCES: Slater 1941: 24–6.

from 'Bless 'em All: A Piece About Army Songs'
(1941)

"Bless 'em all" is a folk song that has grown up right under our noses. It is only recently that the dance bands have taken it up and plugged it in its bowdlerised form. Its history is known. It was written before the war by two airmen on a troopship. It is the song 5 of the pre-war services. And the first word of the chorus is not really "Bless," but a rude word, a word signifying the first of physical pleasures, but used in other contexts as a peculiarly contemptuous curse. I imagine it has nearly always been used in that sense. [...]

In any case, airmen don't care. There's not much homesickness 10 in their song. True it is about a troopship coming back from Bombay. But they're coming home on no long, long trail. God knows what has happened to the home fires. It's a song of a cold world. There's no tender and misremembered past to look back to, and the long, long trail back to the womb would not, this time, be among nightingales and white moonbeams. In fact, there's only one phrase to meet the situation seen very properly as a whole. They use it, tenderly, with a loving emphasis in the rhythm, lingering on the operative word:

"Bless 'em all" (you needn't read "Bless," though I'm bound to write it):

> "Bless 'em all, bless 'em all,
> The long and the short and the tall,
> Bless all the sergeants and double-u O ones [W.O.1's]
> Bless all the corporals and their blinkin' sons,
> 'Cos we're saying good-bye to them all,
> As back to their billets they crawl,
> You'll get no promotion this side of the ocean,
> So cheer up, my lads, BLESS 'EM ALL."

A word about the tune. It has been a usual habit of soldiers till now to go back to hymns, ancient and modern. This tune comes out of the "Blue Danube," a gay little dance—as was the "Carmagnole" and "Cà Ira." No dreary bleating of homesick hymns. We shall enjoy this. "Bless 'em all." (Only don't say "Bless," though I have to write it.):

> "There's a troopship just leaving Bombay,
> Bound for Old Blighty shore,
> Heavily laden with time-expired men,
> Bound for the land they adore.
> There's many an airman just finishing time,
> There's many a twirp signing on,
> You'll get no promotion this side of the ocean,
> So cheer up, my lads, bless 'em all."

They're bright-eyed, these song-makers, even shall we say, a little cynical:

> "If you work hard you'll get better pay!
> We've heard it all before;
> Clean up your buttons and polish your boots,
> Scrub out the barrack-room floor.
> There's many a rookie has taken it in,
> Hook, line and sinker and all...."

But not now. Somebody has found his specs. Joins in the chorus. "Bless 'em all." It goes on and on:

"The sergeant's a very nice chap,
Oh what a tale to tell;
55   Ask him for leave on a Saturday night,
He'll pay your fare home as well.
There's many an airman has blighted his life,
Through writing rude words on the door...."

But why write 'em? Isn't it even more satisfactory to sing 'em?

60   "Bless 'em all, bless 'em all,
The long and the short and the tall."

Who said rude words?
And who said there were no modern folk songs? Doesn't it start singing in your brain now? A tight-lipped, ironical joke. Isn't it the
65 man of the moment who sings it? Don't you know him? Isn't he you? I like this song. I like its jaunty tune. I like the words. I like it because it has action in it.

"Bless 'em all, bless 'em all,
Bless all the sergeants and double-u O ones,
70   Bless all the corporals and their blinkin' sons,
For we're saying good-bye to 'em all...."

Bless all the profiteers and the armament manufacturers, and the Bank Directors and Lord Stamp. Bless all the Blimps and the Ministers of Information. Bless the Censor with his steam-kettle
75 and the Special Branch with their midnight calls. Bless the gilded gorgers in grill rooms and the family lovers who think an Anderson upholds the Home, Sweet Home.

"We're saying good-bye to 'em all."
Not yet, but we will be.
80   "As back to their billets they crawl."
They will. Fou, fou, fou, fou.
"We'll get no promotion this side of the ocean,
So cheer up, my lads, — 'em all."

Keith Douglas
1920–44

from letter to J. C. Hall (1943)

For biography of Douglas, see Poetry Anthology, p. 202.
The letter of August 1943 to his friend and fellow-poet J. C. Hall is Douglas's
fullest statement of his ideas about poetry and his attitude to war.

DISCUSSION: Chapter 7.
SOURCE: Douglas 1979b: 124.

from a letter to J. C. Hall (1943)

To write on the themes which have been concerning me lately in
lyrical and abstract forms, would be immense bullshitting. In my early
poems I wrote lyrically, as an innocent, because I was an innocent: I
have (not surprisingly) fallen from that particular grace since then. I
5 had begun to change during my second year at Oxford. T. S. Eliot
wrote to me when I first joined the army, that I appeared to have
finished with one form of writing and to be progressing towards
another, which he did not think I has mastered. I knew this to be true,
without his saying it. Well, I am still changing: I don't disagree with
10 you if you say I am awkward and not used to the new paces yet. But
my object (and I don't give a damn about my duty as a poet) is to write
true things, significant things in words each of which works for its place
in a line. My rhythms, which you find enervated, are carefully chosen
to enable the poems to be *read* as significant speech: I see no reason to
15 be either musical or sonorous about things at present. When I do, I
shall be so again, and glad to. I suppose I reflect the cynicism and the
careful absence of expectation (it is not quite the same as apathy) with
which I view the world. As many others to whom I have spoken, not
only civilians and British soldiers, but Germans and Italians, are in the

20 same state of mind, it is a true reflection. I never tried to write about war (that is battles and things, not London can Take it), with the exception of a satiric picture of some soldiers frozen to death, until I had experienced it Now I will write of it, and perhaps one day cynic and lyric will meet and make me a balanced style. Certainly you will
25 never see the long metrical similes and galleries of images again. [...]

To be sentimental or emotional now is dangerous to oneself and to others. To trust anyone or to admit any hope of a better world is criminally foolish, as foolish as it is to stop working for it. It sounds silly to say work without hope, but it can be done; it's only a form of insurance; it doesn't mean work hopelessly.

Arthur Koestler
1905–83

from 'In Memory of Richard Hillary' (1943)

Koestler was born in Budapest. He joined the Communist Party in 1932 and worked as a journalist in Spain during the Civil War. He was sentenced to death by Franco's forces and imprisoned, an experience evoked in his novel *Darkness at Noon* (1940). After internment in occupied France, Koestler came to London in 1940. He became a novelist and political essayist.

The essay on Richard Hillary (1920–43) was originally published in *Horizon* in 1943 as 'The birth of a myth' and was reprinted as 'In memory of Richard Hillary' in the collection *The Yogi and the Commissar and Other Essays* (1945). Hillary was an RAF pilot who was shot down in 1940 and badly burned. He returned to active service and was killed in an accident. Hillary's autobiography, *The Last Enemy* (1942), is an account of his experiences and an analysis of his generation of RAF volunteers. Koestler's essay explores the nature of heroism in Second World War, using Hillary as an example of what he sees as a new kind of hero who is not motivated by conventional ideas of patriotism or masculinity.

> DISCUSSION: Chapter 7.
> SOURCE: Koestler 1945: 52–3, 63–4, 66–7.

from 'In Memory of Richard Hillary'

But why then, in God's name, did he go back? Was it vanity? 'I wonder if that is true of me, or whether, as some silly girl said, I am going back purely out of vanity. I think not; because implicit in my decision was the acceptance of the fact that I shall not come
5   through.' You can be clever and twist this around and say that the quotation does not disprove the charge, *qui s'excuse, s'accuse,* and so on. Granted; but then you have to find a more illuminating name for an urge which accepts destruction to get satisfied. Narcissus did not burn himself alive to preserve his image in the stream.

10 Urge of self-destruction, masochism, morbidity? ... 'My darling, I am like a man, who, travelling through a dark tunnel and seeing a pinpoint of light ahead, has shouted for joy, then hesitated, stricken for fear it may be a mirage. Reassured, he presses forward, silent, his heart hammering, and it is only when he stumbles out into the

15 light that he relaxes and, weeping for joy, pours out his heart. Richard.' A boy who writes this kind of love-letter does not seem a morbid masochist. But again one may argue that the one does not exclude the other, *les extrêmes se touchent*, etc.; and again granted.

Fanatical devotion to a cause? ... 'I could not immediately

20 disabuse my sympathizers of their misplaced pity without appearing mock-modest or slightly insane. And so I remained an imposter. They would say, "I hope someone got the swine who got you: how you must hate those devils!" and I would say weakly, "Oh, I don't know", and leave it at that. I could not explain that I had not been

25 injured in their war, that no thoughts of "our Island Fortress" or of "making the world safe for democracy" had bolstered me up when going into combat. I could not explain that what I had suffered I in no way regretted; that I welcomed it; and that now that it was over I was in a sense grateful for it and certain that in time it would help

30 me along the road of my own private development.' But perhaps this too is just modesty after all, or inverted pride; the young Englishman's love to overstate his understatements. [...]

As it is, his place in literature can only be marked by a blank; and yet we can at least define with some probability the position

35 of that blank on the map. With the 'bourgeois' novel getting more and more exhausted and insipid as the era which produced it draws to its close, a new type of writer seems to take over from the cultured middle-class humanist: airmen, revolutionaries, adventurers, men who live the dangerous life; with a new operative

40 technique of observation, a curious alfresco introspection and an even more curious trend of contemplation, even mysticism, born in the dead centre of the hurricane. St. Exupéry, Silone, Traven, Hemingway, Malraux, Scholochow, Istrati may be the forerunners; and Hillary might have become one of them. But one slim volume,

45 a packet of letters, two short stories are all that is left; and that is not enough to fill in the blank.

Thomas Mann says somewhere that to leave a trace behind him a writer must produce not only quality but bulk; the sheer bulk of

the *œuvre* helps its impact on us. It is a melancholy truth; and yet
50 this slim volume of Hillary's seems to have a specific weight which
makes it sink into the depth of one's memory, while tons of printed
bulk drift as flotsam on its surface. [...]

What meticulous efforts to keep a clean head and dodge *la gloire*!
There are those who die with their boots clean, and those who die
55 with their minds clean. For the former it is easier—their life and
death are ruled by exclamation marks. For the Hillarys it is harder;
their curriculum is punctuated by question-marks which they have
to unbend, straighten, point all by themselves.

But the aim at which they point we can only guess. We can guess
60 it, not from his formulations and ratiocinations, but from those
parts in his writings where he is un-selfconscious and inarticulate.
'In an age when to love one's country is vulgar, to love God archaic,
and to love mankind sentimental, you do all three', he says to Peter
Pease—to the same Peter whom he admires most of all his friends,
65 whose death he sees in a vision under the anaesthetic and whose
memory becomes a cult and an obsession for him. And through
that one sentence with its three disparaging adjectives, we get a
glimpse into the concealed nostalgia, the *mal du siècle* of those who
die with their minds clean.

70 For, in spite of all intellectual camouflage and nimbleness of
formulation, one does not let one's body go up in flames thrice out
of sheer 'dislike of organized emotion and patriotism'. It sounds all
very well, and it is not true. But one does it– perhaps, if one is
exceptionally sensitive and exceptionally brave, and if one caught
75 the bug of the great nostalgia of one's time—in search of a
redeeming emotion; of a credo, neither sentimental, vulgar nor
archaic, whose words one could say without embarrassment or
shame. When all isms become meaningless and the world an alley
of crooked query-marks, then indeed a man's longing for the Holy
80 Grail may become so strong that he flies back like a moth into the
flame; and having burned his wings, crawls back into it again. But
this, of course, is the one instinct in man's condition which he
cannot rationalize.

Richard Hillary was burnt thrice. After the first time they
85 brought him back and patched him up and made him a new face.
It was wasted, for the second time his body was charred to coal.
But to make quite sure that the pattern be fulfilled, it was his wish

to be cremated; so they burned him a third time, on the twelfth of January, 1943, in Golders Green; and the coal became ashes and
90 the ashes were scattered into the sea. There the man ends and the myth begins. It is the myth of the Lost Generation—sceptic crusaders, knights of effete veneer, sick with the nostalgia of something to fight for, which as yet is not. It is the myth of the crusade without a cross, and of desperate crusaders in search of a
95 cross. What creed they will adopt, Christ's or Barrabas', remains to be seen.

Stephen Spender
1909–

from *Citizens in War – and After* (1945)

Stephen Spender was an associate of W. H. Auden and himself one of the leading poets of the 1930s. Spender actively supported the Republican cause in the Spanish Civil War and was briefly a member of the Communist Party. As with many left-wing intellectuals, the outbreak of war caused a re-evaluation of political commitments (see Spender 1978 for essays from this period). In 1939 he helped found the periodical *Horizon* and wrote a great deal of poetry, criticism and journalism during the war. He was also a member of the Auxiliary Fire Service and drew upon his experiences in Civil Defence to write *Citizens in War – and After* (1945). The book is both a record of the contribution of the civilian Civil Defence (CD) organizations to the war effort and a political argument for a collectivist post-war reconstruction programme based on the CD principles of local organization. The extracts show Spender returning to favourite 1930s themes of popular culture and definitions of Englishness. He also experiments with the highly rhetorical language of the new Romantic movement in the sections of poetry. Spender's autobiography *World Within World* (1951) and his *Journals 1939–1983* (1985) give a full account of the war years.

DISCUSSION: Chapter 3.
SOURCE: Spender 1945: 15, 53–4, 71.

from Citizens in War – and After *(1945)*

Civil Defence workers would probably agree that they have shared many experiences which they do not want to lose after the war. One such experience is the breakdown of social barriers among neighbours: the discovery that at the wardens' post, or the
5   depot, or the fire station, men and women leading entirely different lives can become friends and respect each other. In the units of Civil Defence people have been able to apply the disciplined co-operation and courage necessary for war to some of the problems

which are always with us. Civil Defence is not just a war service.
It is a vast social movement in which civilians have become aware
that they are citizens, that they have neighbourly responsibilities
extending beyond the defence of cities during air raids, that they
can educate themselves and help each other in numerous ways.
Civil Defence workers feel vividly that it would be a misfortune if
the local patriotism, the neighbourliness, the social tasks under-
taken during these years, should be forgotten and dissolved with
the peace. Of course, the main experience of Civil Defence is actual
Blitz experience. Men and women in these services have witnessed
the growth of myths. They have seen devastating, terrible and
inspiring sights, and they have emerged with the feeling of having
been reborn into a new community.

Wherever I have travelled in England during the past months,
I have been enormously impressed by the growth of local myths,
which are going to play a pervasive though impalpable part in the
spiritual development of men and women living after this war. For
the myth—the bomb story, the heroic episode, in which people
forgot themselves and acted disinterestedly—provides us with a
standard of behaviour by which we shall judge ourselves after the
war. Local patriotism and an increased interest in local government
are likely to result from these experiences, and the local Civil
Defence organizations, in whatever form they exist, are bound to
play a part in this revival of regionalism. [...]

DAWN

At the end of a night of blitz, light trickles drop by drop like
water into the great tank of fire and smoke and broken glass and
rubble which is a city. Gradually the whole sky fills with pale
watery light. And through the pale strained dawn there comes a
sigh of steam, the relieved cry of a battered machine-made world
like a giant regaining consciousness. This almost human utterance
is the all-clear. People who have not slept turn over and sleep for
an hour. The firemen and rescue workers raise a cheer, as tired and
mechanical almost as the utterance of the sirens, and then they go
on digging through the rubble and putting out the fires, until either
the job is done, or they are relieved by the next watch which comes
on duty in the morning.

The city workers walk through the streets full of debris to their

work. The traffic roars, fainter perhaps than usual, but remarkable, really, in its volume. A city is like a human body whose life blood, when one vein becomes bruised, can flow through other veins.
50 Barriers are put up round places where there are unexploded bombs, and the Bomb Disposal Squads arrive, and, like skilled surgeons, operate on each case.

The people who carry on take a vague æsthetic interest in the appearance of the morning's ruins, in the visible news of de-
55 struction, just as in time of peace they took a vague interest in the progress of some new store that was being built in Oxford Street.

ABYSS

When the foundations quaked and the pillars shook,
I trembled, and in the dark I felt the fear
60 Of the photograph my skull might take
Through the eye sockets, in one flashlit instant,
When the crumbling house would obliterate
Every impression of my sunlit life
With one impression of black final horror
65 Covering me with irrecoverable doom.

But the pulsation passed, and glass lay round me,
And I rose from acrid dust, and in the night
I walked through the clattering houses
A prophet seeking tongues of flame.

70 Against a background of cloud, I saw
The houses kneel, exposed in their abject
Centennial human prayer: "O Fate,
Spare us from grief that punishes our neighbours!"
And the heads of all men living, cut open,
75 Revealed the same shameless entreaty.

Then in the icy night, indifferent to our
Sulphurous nether fate, I saw
The dead of all time float on one calm tide
Uplifted on the spears of stars, above
80 This town whose walls of brick and flesh
Are transitory dwellings of the spirit
Which flows into that flooding sky of death.

The streets were filled with London prophets,
Saints of Covent Garden, Parliament Fields,
85   The Heath, Lambeth, and Saint John's Wood Graveyard,
Who cried in Cockney fanatic voices:
"In the midst of loif is death." And they all kneeled
And prayed against the misery manufactured
In factories, the pride of houses,
90   Ambition of palaces, vain hope of Churches,
And they worshipped children and enamelled flowers,
They opened slum windows on to angels
Who climbed up all the sooty steeples,
Like steeple jacks or poor chimney-sweeps.

95   And they sang: "We souls of the abyss,
Dancing in frozen peace of upper air,
Naively familiar with the stars and angels,
We say: 'Rejoice in the abyss,'
For hollow is the centre of the skull, the vacuum
100   Drifting under pale gold of Saint Paul's Cross.
Unless your lives accept the space of death,
At the centre of your building and your loves,
Within the bells of flowers and bells of towers,
All human aims are hatred and denial,
105   Each life is lived upon the death of others,
And the terrible averted face
Of every man and woman, cuts, like a sword,
The smile from every neighbour's face."

[...] It is unlikely that, outside kindergartens, you would make
110 surprising artistic discoveries amongst workers and farm labourers
in England.

It is difficult to explain why this is, though it is easy enough to
hint at a superficial reason. It is certainly not because the English
are an inartistic, unimaginative race, indifferent to beauty. Their
115 humour often shows a rich imagination which leaves the poets
feeling that it is they rather than the workers who lack imagination.
Moreover, a scarcely expressed poetry often emerges in their lives.

The obstruction which prevents their entering the world of art
seems to lie largely in their education, in their lack of leisure, and,

120 above all, in the sense of social impotence which I have already marked. Art is, in its own sphere, an exercise of power, and only those who secretly exult in their own power, however hidden this may be, can enter into its world. The workers observe beauty in Nature, their lives are often illuminated with tenderness, and with
125 moments of poetry. All this is inexpressible because the confidence which can allow it to break forth is not there. Their own moments of poetry they regard as moments of weakness.

As a matter of fact, poetry is probably nearer to them than the other arts. A surprising amount of poetry is read. But it is read
130 under difficult conditions produced by their education. One day, where I was stationed, a group of men asked me to explain to them a poem of mine which they had found in a magazine. I decided that it was best to let them have their laugh, so I read it. However, they did not laugh, and one of them said, "We understand it now. The
135 meaning goes on from line to line. You see, we were taught always to read poetry stopping at the end of every line." In Civil Defence we see the socially conscious world of the future in miniature; and one is led, at every point, to the conclusion that the central problem is education, firstly, in the technical and political knowledge
140 necessary to a citizen of a better-planned society; and secondly, in those values of appreciation and imagination, learned perhaps through art, without which the post war world, however planned, will really become an enlargement and distortion on an enormous scale of the ignorance, vulgarity, and greed of individuals before
145 the war.

G. S. Fraser
1915–80

from 'Recent Verse: London and Cairo' (1944)

For a biography of Fraser, see Poetry Anthology, p. 209.

Fraser's article on Cairo poetry was written for the magazine *Poetry London*. The editor of *Poetry London*, M. J. Tambimuttu, was a leading supporter of the 'new romantic' poetry that Fraser sees as characteristic of verse written in England during the war. Fraser suggests the effects of the different wartime culture of Egypt on the development of a distinctive 'neo-classicism' in the work of poets like Terence Tiller and Fraser himself.

DISCUSSION: Chapter 6.
SOURCE: Fraser 1944: 8–9, 9–10, 11–12.

from 'Recent Verse: London and Cairo' *(1944)*

Cairo's poetry that is worth considering is … that of the English public servant: a civilian, a person in comfortable circumstances, a man with an assured social station (in all these things differing, for instance, from an English romantic poet, like my friend Tom
5 Scott). What is even more important is that he is a man who has been living in Greece, or Egypt, or Jugoslavia, or somewhere on the Mediterranean seaboard since some years before the war, and that he fits far more aptly into the static but sometimes gracious patterns of Mediterranean civilisation than into any imaginable
10 contemporary English background. He has acquired some of the qualities of that civilisation: which is serene, taciturn, unchanging and sad. …

Because the war is world-wide in its material aspect, there is a tendency to suppose that it must be world-wide in its spiritual
15 impact, too. But to visit Luxor and consider, in the brilliant air of Upper Egypt, the fallen basalt head of Rameses II, the serene, indifferent smile, or to watch an ox pulling a water wheel,

[266]

20   eyes from the mud and laughing
          filth and hunger steady as the sun. And sunk
          somewhere in all a patience of this ground
          like the blind ox's round,

is to realise that there do indeed exist ancient and indifferent civilisations in which all our excitements have somewhat of an air of intrusion. The intruder, the barbarian invader, the danger from outside, is nothing new in Greek or Egyptian history; and, indeed, it is a danger which a great, corrupt magnificent city like Cairo feels perfectly capable of being able to absorb. The spiritual crisis in Cairo is getting up in the morning and living through another day: it is not anything so transitory as a war. The spiritual solution is to have enough money and friends for wine and conversation in the evening: it is not anything so fatiguing, in a hot climate, as a scheme of redemption. The problem of the poet is not his content (scene, faces, incidents throng on one in that cosmopolitan city) but his form: it is elimination. 'I don't want experience,' said Terence Tiller, fretfully, to me in a Cairo tramcar, 'experience is a distraction....' [...]

We can expect, then, that the verse written in Cairo (under the sense, more or less conscious, that civilisation is something static, which suffers occasional brutal intrusions from outside) will be quite different from the verse written in London (under the sense that history is a process of painful development which has reached a crisis, and that this crisis makes universal moral claims). Cairo's best poetry will be placid and patient, rather than urgent in its tone, sad rather than tragic, persuasive rather then minatory moral rather than prophetic.

Robin Fedden
1908–77

extract from 'An Anatomy of Exile' (1946)

Robin Fedden was co-editor, with the poets Bernard Spencer and Lawrence Durrell, of the magazine *Personal Landscape*, which was published in Cairo in the Second World War. Fedden was a writer on the Middle East and later became the Historic Buildings Secretary of the National Trust.

The extract is taken from his introduction to an anthology of writing from *Personal Landscape*. He describes the particular cultural and political conditions that formed the context of wartime writing in the Middle East, and, like Fraser, contrasts the experience of wartime exile with that of war in England.

DISCUSSION: Chapter 6.
SOURCE: Fedden 1945 7–11.

from 'An Anatomy of Exile' *(1946)*

For a variety of reasons many people find exile in Egypt difficult out of all proportion to the trials which at first appear to be tangibly involved, and it is perhaps therefore worthwhile making a very brief Anatomy of this Exile. It may at any rate show what many of
5   the writers in *Personal Landscape* shared owing to their common geographical background, and in spite of the most disparate ideas on, and approaches to, life.

First of all there are the difficulties of climate. Egypt was designed for Northern Europeans to visit, not to live in. The winter
10   is incontestibly perfect, like an ideal English summer; but when one outstays what was once the tourist season and drags on for three or four years, as is inevitable in war-time, the disadvantages of having no real winter become all too apparent. It is not that Egyptian summers are intolerably hot, though 110 in the shade is
15   not exceptional, but that the Northerner comes terribly to lack

definite *changes* of season and the recurring stimuli that they offer. Where it is always relatively hot, where trees do not shed their leaves, the rhythm of the seasons to which he is innately accustomed is broken. The year is flaccid. The wheel of the months
20 ceases to turn with any vitality. Milton said that he could write only in the winter: what is a poet to do in a country where spring and autumn are indistinguishable to all except the trained naturalist?

The landscape too, though beautiful in its own relaxed way, is as flaccid as the year. Except for the deserts where only the soldiers
25 have lived, it is boneless and unarticulated. No rock, no gesture on the part of the earth, disturbs the heavy Nilotic mould which is cultivated Egypt. Everything is muffled. Flat, alluvial and spineless, the fields turn out their bumper crops month after month: but the Northerner tends to turn out nothing. It is all too rich, too
30 unresistant; he can get no purchase for eye or foot or mind in this loose accumulating silt. [...]

Not the least curious thing about a country with so much "past", is that the stranger finds no historical continuity. Upon the black alluvial soil stand pharoanic temples and concrete apartment
35 houses, and nothing links them. Hypostyle halls and mediæval mosques are well enough to visit and admire, but they don't connect up with the way one thinks. What is missed and missing is the middle distance: where there should be an eighteenth century, there is the Turkish hiatus. Saladin is juxtaposed to
40 cinemas, and To-day, having no ancestry, is ridiculously isolated and uncertain of itself. For the average cultured European with his seventeenth and eighteenth centuries, from which his taste may wander but to which it inevitably returns, a recent historical continuity is the very ground he stands on and this lacuna, which
45 afflicts Egypt and most of the Levant, seems almost indecent. The rootless present wobbles like an ill-made table. In savage and colonial places, Kenya or the Solomon Islands, one expects such discontinuity and adjusts oneself accordingly, but the innocent exile coming to the "cradle of civilization" is taken aback. [...]
50 Finally, the war, which elsewhere would probably have given meaning to a banishment for which it was directly responsible, has in the Middle East lacked poetic, if not practical, urgency for all but the minority who actually fought through the desert. Most of the inconveniences of war as they affect the non-combatant have

55 been present—black-outs, restrictions, parades, long working hours, rationing, rocketing prices, and a vast ubiquitous black-market—yet at the same time its tonic qualities have been absent. It has been difficult to feel the stimulus of danger or of participation in a common effort for a common end, when living in a country

60 that has preserved at any rate a paper neutrality and where the vast majority of the inhabitants have had no knowledge of, and no interest in, the issues at stake. The desert is not the sown and is indeed so sharply divided from it that it was not easy either for Englishmen in Egypt, or for the minority of educated Egyptians,

65 to achieve any sense of danger and tension from the desert campaign, or to translate their feelings about it into a source of emotional energy. Only when Rommel, advancing on Alamein, was almost in sight of the green belt (or alternatively when an occasional raid seemed to justify A.R.P. lectures), did the war

70 suddenly become a tonic and effect just that stepping-up of emotional tempo which lends events immediate significance and obscures the day-to-day dreariness of a state of semi-hostility. War in a neutral country like Egypt is war at its most sterile; expatriates of all nations have felt here the length and inconvenience rather

75 than the inspiration of the struggle.

Further Reading

There are several useful anthologies of both First and Second World War writing. Ferguson 1972 and Fussell 1991 provide wide ranging selections. Silkin's *Penguin Book of First World War Poetry* is the most accessible collection of First World War poetry (Silkin 1979), and Gardener 1964 and Parsons 1965 are useful supplements. Hibberd and Onions' anthology offers a good cross section of First World War poetry which goes beyond the canon and has an excellent introduction (Hibberd and Onions 1986). Cross's selection includes many European poets in translation (Cross 1988) and Stallworthy's Oxford anthology sets the poetry of both wars in a longer historical perspective (Stallworthy 1988). Reilly 1981 remains the standard anthology of women's poetry of the First World War.

The canon of Second World War writing is less well-established than that of the First World War and this is reflected in the anthologies. Blythe 1982 is perhaps the best overview and has a stimulating introduction; however, its main emphasis is on prose. Hamilton 1965, Gardener 1966 and Hamblett 1966 assemble a wide range of writing, and Skelton's Penguin anthology of 1940s poetry provides a wider context for the poetry of the war (Skelton 1968). Reilly 1984 is an anthology of women's poetry of the war.

There are numerous critical works, especially on First World War writing. Silkin 1972 and Fussell 1975 are crucial to any study of war writing (see Chapter 1). Other influential works include Johnston 1964 and Bergonzi 1965. More recently, Hynes 1990 provides a thorough survey of First World War writing. Hibberd 1981 is a useful collection of critical essays. Ross 1967 remains a good account of Georgianism, and Millard 1991 deals with several neglected, but influential, poets of the pre-First World-War period. Khan 1988 is the only book-length study of women's poetry, though Tylee 1990 provides an excellent account of the context for women's writing in the period. Hibberd 1990 is a chronological anthology of literary, political and social writing with a clear explanation of the progress of the war.

Shires 1985 and Scannell 1976 are general studies of Second World War poetry, and Sinclair 1989 provides a detailed account of mainly London-based literary life during the war. Hewison 1977 is an excellent survey of wartime culture, as is Paul Fussell's sequel to *The Great War and Modern Memory, Wartime* (Fussell 1989). Longley 1986 contains essays on poets connected with the First and Second World Wars, as well as other conflicts.

Bibliography

ADAMS, A. (ed.) (1968) *Explorations: War*, Oxford: Pergamon Press.

BANERJEE, A. (1976) *Spirit Above Wars: A Study of English Poetry of the Two World Wars*, London: Macmillan.

BAUDRILLARD, J. (1991) 'The reality gulf', *Guardian*, 11 January: 25.

BENSTOCK, SHARI (1987) *Women of the Left Bank: Paris, 1900–1940*, London: Virago Press.

BENTON, M. G. and P. (eds) *Touchstones 3*, London: English University Press.

BERGONZI, B. (1965) *Heroes' Twilight: A Study of the Literature of the Great War*, London: Constable & Co.

BEST, G. (1975) 'Militarism and the Victorian public school', in B. Simon and I. Bradley (eds) *The Victorian Public School*, London: I. Gill and Macmillan.

BLAMIRES, D. (1971) *David Jones: Artist and Writer*, Manchester: Manchester University Press.

BLYTHE, R. (ed.) (1982) *Writing in a War*, Harmondsworth: Penguin.

BOLD, A. (1988) *MacDiarmid-Christopher Murray Grieve: A Critical Biography*, London: John Murray (Publishers).

BOWEN, R. (1980) 'The edge of a journey: notes on Bernard Spencer', *London Magazine* 19 (9–10): 88–102.

—— (1982–3) 'Monologue for a Cairo evening', *London Magazine* December 1982–January 1983: 22 (12): 50–60.

BROOKE, R. (1918) *Collected Poems*, London: Sidgwick & Jackson.

BROPHY, J. and PARTRIDGE, E. (eds) (1965) *The Long Trail: What the British Soldier Sang and Said in the Great War of 1914–18*, London: André Deutsch.

BURNETT, G. (1987–8) 'A Poetics out of war: H.D.'s responses to the First World War', in *Agenda* 25 (3–4): 54–63.

CALDER, A. (1971) *The People's War: Britain 1939–1945*, London: Panther.

CALDER, A. and SHERIDAN, D. (eds) (1984) *Speak for Yourself: A Mass Observation Anthology 1937–49*, London: Jonathan Cape.

CEADEL, M. (1980) *Pacifism in Britain 1914–1945: The Defining of a Faith*, Oxford: Clarendon Press.

CLARKE, I. F. (1966) *Voices Prophesying War, 1765–1984*, Oxford: Oxford University Press.

COHEN, J. (1975) *Journey to the Trenches: The Life of Isaac Rosenberg*, London: Robson Books.

COLLECOTT, D. (1981) 'Isaac Rosenberg (1890–1918): a cross cultural case study', in A. Newman (ed.) *The Jewish East End 1840–1939*, London: The Jewish Historical Society.

COLLS, R. and DODD, P. (eds) (1986) *Englishness: Politics and Culture 1880–1920*, Beckenham: Croom Helm.

CROSS, T. (1988) *The Lost Voices of World War One*, London: Bloomsbury Publishing.

CUTBILL, J. (1987) 'The truth untold', *New Statesman* 16 January: 22–4.

DALLAS, K. (ed.) (1972) *The Cruel Wars: 100 Soldiers' Songs from Agincourt to Ulster*, London: Wolfe Publishing.

DANGERFIELD, G. (1966) *The Strange Death of Liberal England*, London: Mac-Gibbon and Kee.

DAVIE, D. (1983) 'Editorial', *PN Review 34* 10 (2): 1–2.

—— (1989) *Under Briggflatts: A History of Poetry in Great Britain, 1966–1989*, Manchester: Carcanet Press.

DAVIES, A. (1984) *Where Did the Forties Go? A Popular History*, London: Pluto Press.

DAWSON, G. (1990) 'Playing at war: an autobiographical approach to boyhood fantasy and masculinity', *Oral History* (18) 1: 44–53.

DELANY, P. (1987), *The Neo-pagans: Friendship and Love in the Rupert Brooke Circle*, London: Macmillan.

DIAMOND, M. (1990) 'Political heroes of the Victorian music hall', *History Today*, 40: 33–9.

DOUGLAS, K. (1979a) *Alamein to Zem Zem*, ed. D. Graham, Oxford: Oxford University Press.

—— (1979b) *The Complete Poems of Keith Douglas*, ed. D. Graham, Oxford: Oxford University Press.

—— (1985) *A Prose Miscellany*, ed. D. Graham, Manchester: Carcanet Press.

DUNCAN, R. (1944) *Journal of a Husbandman*, London: Faber & Faber.

DUPLESSIS, R. BLAU (1986) *H.D.: The Career of That Struggle*, Brighton: Harvester.

DURRELL, L. (1944) 'Airgraph on refugee poets in Africa', *Poetry London* 2 (10): 212–15.

EKSTEINS, M. (1989) *Rites of Spring: The Great War and the Birth of the Modern Age*, London: Bantam Press.

FEDDEN, R. (ed.) (1945) *Personal Landscape: An Anthology of Exile*, London: Editions Poetry London.

—— (1966) 'Personal Landscape', *London Magazine* March: 63–5.

FERGUSON, J. (ed.) (1972) *War and the Creative Arts*, London: Macmillan/Open University Press.

—— (1980) *The Arts in Britain in World War 1*, London: Stainer & Bell.

FISHMAN, W. (1975) *East End Jewish Radicals*, London: Gerald Duckworth & Co.

FLORENCE, M. S., MARSHALL, C. and OGDEN, C. K. (1987) *Militarism Versus Feminism: Writings on Women and War*, eds M. Kamester and J. Vellacott, London: Virago Press.

FRASER, G. S. (1944) 'Recent verse: London and Cairo', in *Poetry London* 2 (10): 215–19.

—— (1981) *The Collected Poems of G. S. Fraser*, Leicester: Leicester University Press.

—— (1983) *A Stranger and Afraid*, Manchester: Carcanet Press.

FULLER, J. G. (1990) *Troop Morale and Popular Culture in the British and Dominion Armies 1914–1918*, Oxford: Clarendon Press.

FUSSELL, P. (1975) *The Great War and Modern Memory*, New York & London: Oxford University Press.

—— (1980) *Abroad: British Literary Traveling Between the Wars*, New York & London: Oxford University Press.

—— (1989) *Wartime: Understanding and Behaviour in the Second World War*, New York & Oxford: Oxford University Press.

—— (1990) *Killing in Verse and Prose and Other Essays*, London: Bellew Publishing.

—— (ed.) (1991) *The Bloody Game: An Anthology of Modern War*, London and Sydney: Scribners.

—— (1992) 'War poetry: the Great War to Viet-Nam,' Anglia Polytechnic University, Cambridge, 14 May.

GARDNER, B. (ed.) (1964) *Up the Line to Death: The War Poets 1914–1918*, London: Methuen.

—— (ed.) (1966) *The Terrible Rain: The War Poets 1939–45*, London: Methuen.

GARNETT, S. (1990) *Salute to the Soldier Poets*, Cheltenham: This England Books.

GILBERT, S. and GUBAR, S. (1989) *No Man's Land, Volume 2: Sex Changes*, New Haven & London: Yale University Press.

GLASS, S. T. (1966) *The Responsible Society: The Ideas of the English Guild Socialist*, London: Longman.

GRAHAM, D. (1974) *Keith Douglas 1920–1944: A Biography*, London: Oxford University Press.

—— (1984) *The Truth of War: Owen, Blunden, Rosenberg*, Manchester: Carcanet Press.

GRAVES, R. P. (1986) *Robert Graves: The Assault Heroic 1895- 1926*, London: Weidenfeld & Nicolson.

GRAVES, R. (1925) *Poetic Unreason and Other Studies*, London: Cecil Palmer.

—— (1949) *The Common Asphodel*, London: Hamish Hamilton.

—— (1988) *Poems About War*, London: Cassell.

GRAY, N. (1989) *The Paintings of David Jones*, London: Lund Humphries Publishers/Tate Gallery.

GUEST, B. (1985) *Herself Defined: The Poet H.D. and Her World*, London: Collins.

GURNEY, I. (1954) *Poems by Ivor Gurney* ed. E. Blunden, London: Hutchinson.

—— (1984) *Collected Poems of Ivor Gurney*, ed. P. J. Kavanagh, Oxford & New York: Oxford University Press.

—— (1991) *Collected Letters*, ed. R. K. R. Thornton, Ashington & Manchester: Mid-Northumberland Arts Group/Carcanet Press.

H.D. (Hilda Doolittle) (1984a) *Bid Me To Live*, London: Virago Press.

—— (1984b) *Collected Poems 1912–1944*, ed. L. L. Martz, Manchester: Carcanet Press.

—— (1987–8a) 'Letter to Norman Pearson', *Agenda* 25 (3–4): 71–6.

—— (1987–8b) 'Responsibilities', *Agenda* 25 (3–4): 51–3.

HAGUE, R. (1975) *David Jones*, Cardiff: University of Wales Press/Welsh Arts Council.

HAMBLETT, C. (ed.) (1966) *I Burn for England: An Anthology of the Poetry of World War Two*, London: Leslie Frewin.

HAMILTON, I. (ed.) (1965) *The Poetry of War 1939–45*, London: Alan Ross.

HARRISSON, T. and MADGE, C. (1940) *Mass Observation: War Begins at Home*, London: Chatto & Windus.

HARVIE, C. (1981) *No Gods and Precious Few Heroes*, London: Edward Arnold.

HASSALL, C. (1959) *Edward Marsh, Patron of the Arts: A Biography*, London: Longman.

HENDERSON, H. (1950) *Ballads of World War II*, Glasgow: Lili Marlene Club.

—— (1986–7) 'The poetry of the war in the Middle-East, 1939–1945', *Aquarius* 17–18: 64–73.

—— (1990) *Elegies for the Dead in Cyrenaica*, Edinburgh: Polygon.

—— (1992) *Alias MacAlias* Edinburgh: Polygon.

HEWISON, R. (1977) *Under Siege: Literary Life in London 1939–45*, London: Weidenfeld & Nicolson.

HIBBERD, D. (ed.) (1981) *Poetry of the First World War: A Casebook*, London: Macmillan.

—— (1986) *Owen the Poet*, London: Macmillan.

—— (1990) *The First World War*, Basingstoke: Macmillan.

—— (1992) *Wilfred Owen: The Last Year 1917–1918*, London: Constable & Co.

HIBBERD, D. and ONIONS, J. (eds) (1986) *Poetry of the Great War: An Anthology*, London: Macmillan.

HILL, G. (1964–5) '"I in another place", homage to Keith Douglas', *Stand* 6 (4): 6–13.

—— (1984) 'Gurney's hobby', *Essays in Criticism* 34 (2): 97–128.

HILLARY, R. (1942) *The Last Enemy*, London: Macmillan.

HINTON, J. (1989) *Protests and Visions: Peace Politics in 20th Century Britain*, London: Hutchinson Radius.

HOBDAY, C. (1989) *Edgell Rickword: A Poet at War*, Manchester: Carcanet Press.

HOBHOUSE, L. T. (1974) *Liberalism*, London: Oxford University Press.

HOWARD, M. (1978) *War and the Liberal Conscience*, London: Temple Smith.

HOWELL, D. (1986) *A Lost Left: Three Studies in Socialism and Nationalism*, Manchester: Manchester University Pres.

HOWKINS, A. (1986) 'The discovery of rural England', in R. Colls and P. Dodd (eds.) *Englishness: Politics and Culture 1880–1920*, Beckenham: Croom Helm.

HUGHES, C. (1979) *David Jones: The Man Who Was on the Field*, Manchester: David Jones Society.

HUGHES, T. (1963) 'The poetry of Keith Douglas', *Critical Quarterly* 5 (1): 43–8.

HULME, T. (1924) *Speculations: Essays on Humanism and the Philosophy of Art*, ed. H. Read, London: Kegan Paul, Trench, Trubner & Co.

HURD, M. (1978) *The Ordeal of Ivor Gurney*, Oxford & New York: Oxford University Press.

HYNES, S. (1972) *Edwardian Occasions: Essays on English Writing in the Early Twentieth Century*, London: Routledge.

—— (1990) *A War Imagined: The First World War and English Culture*, London: Bodley Head.

ISHERWOOD, C. (1979) *Lions and Shadows: An Education in the Twenties*, London: Magnum Books.

JOHN, A. (1970) *Alun Lewis*, Cardiff: University of Wales Press.

JOHNSTON, J. H. (1964) *English Poetry of the First World War*, Princeton NJ: Princeton University Press.

JONES, D. (1937) *In Parenthesis*, London: Faber & Faber.

—— (1973) *Epoch and Artist: Selected Writings*, ed. H. Grisewood, London: Faber & Faber.

—— (1974) *The Sleeping Lord and Other Fragments*, London: Faber & Faber.

—— (1978) *The Dying Gaul and Other Writings*, ed. H. Grisewood, London & Boston: Faber & Faber.

—— (1980) *Dai Greatcoat: A Self-Portrait of David Jones in His Letters*. ed. R. Hague, London: Faber & Faber.

—— (1989) *David Jones: Paintings, Drawings, Inscriptions, Prints*, London: South Bank Centre.

JONES, G. S. (1974) 'Working-class culture and working-class politics in London, 1870–1900: notes on the remaking of a working class', *Journal of Social History* 7 (4): 460–508.

KHAN, N. (1988) *Women's Poetry of the First World War*, Hemel Hempstead: Harvester Wheatsheaf.

KING, J. (1990) *The Last Modern: A Life of Herbert Read*, London: Weidenfeld & Nicolson.

KOESTLER, A. (1945) *The Yogi and the Commissar and Other Essays*, London: Jonathan Cape.

KROPOTKIN, P. (1942) *Selections*, ed. H. Read, London: Freedom Press.

LARKIN, P. (1983) *Required Writing: Miscellaneous Pieces 1955–1982*, London: Faber & Faber.

LAWRENCE, T. E. (1939) *Seven Pillars of Wisdom*, London: Reprint Society/ Jonathan Cape.

LEAVIS, F. R. (1963) *New Bearings in English Poetry*, Harmondsworth: Penguin.

LEED, E. (1979) *No Man's Land: Combat and Identity in World War One*, Cambridge: Cambridge University Press.

LEFTWICH, J. (1957) *Israel Zangwill*, London: James Clarke & Co.

LEHMANN, J. (1980) *Rupert Brooke: His Life and Legend*, London: Weidenfeld & Nicolson.

LEVENSON, M. H. (1984) *A Genealogy of Modernism: A Study of English Literary Doctrine 1908–1922*, Cambridge: Cambridge University Press.

LEWIS, A. (1942) *Raiders' Dawn and Other Poems*, London: Allen & Unwin.

—— (1945) *Ha! Ha! Among the Trumpets: Poems in Transit*, London: Allen & Unwin.

—— (1981) *Selected Poems*, eds J. Hooker and G. Lewis, London: Unwin Paperbacks.

—— (1982) *Alun Lewis: A Miscellany of His Writings*, ed. J. Pikoulis, Bridgend: Poetry Wales Press.

—— (1989) *Alun Lewis: Letters to My Wife*, ed. G. Lewis, Bridgend: Seren Books.

—— (1990) *Collected Stories*, ed. C. Archard, Bridgend: Seren Books.

LIDDIARD, J. (1975) *Isaac Rosenberg: The Half Used Life*, London: Victor Gollancz.

LLOYD, A. L. (1975) *Folk Song in England*, London: Paladin.

LONGLEY, E. (1986) *Poetry in the Wars*, Newcastle upon Tyne: Bloodaxe Books.

MACCARTHY, F. (1989) *Eric Gill*, London: Faber & Faber.

MACDOUGALL, H. A. (1982) *Racial Myth in English History*, Montreal & London: Harvest House/University Press of New England.

MACKENZIE, J. M. (ed.) (1984) *Propaganda & Empire: The Manipulation of British Public Opinion 1880–1960*, Manchester: Manchester University Press.

—— (ed.) (1986) *Imperialism and Popular Culture*, Manchester: Manchester University Press.

—— (ed.) (1992) *Popular Imperialism and the Military, 1850–1950*, Manchester: Manchester University Press.

MCLEAN, I. (1983) *The Legend of Red Clydeside*, Edinburgh: John Donald Publishers.

MACLEAN J. (1978) *In the Rapids of Revolution: Essays, Articles and Letters 1902–23*, ed. N. Milton, London: Allison & Busby.

MACLEAN, S. (1985) *Ris a' Bhruthaich: The Criticism and Prose Writings of Sorley MacLean*, ed. W. Gillies, Stornaway: Acair.

—— (1989) *From Wood to Ridge/O Choille gu Bearradh: Collected Poems in Gaelic and English*, Manchester: Carcanet Press.

—— (1991) 'An interview with Sorley MacLean', *Chapman 66*: 1–8.

MCNAUGHTON, A. (1985) 'Hamish Henderson – Folk Hero', *Chapman* 42, 8 (5): 22–9.

MANGAN, J. A. (1981) '"The grit of our forefathers": invented traditions, propaganda and imperialism', in J. M. MacKenzie (ed.) *Imperialism and Popular Culture*, Manchester: Manchester University Press.

MANNING, O. (1944) 'Poets in exile', *Horizon* 10 (58): 270–9.

MARWICK, A. (1967) *The Deluge: British Society and the First World War*, Harmondsworth: Penguin.

—— (1977) *Women at War 1914–1918*, London: Fontana/ Imperial War Museum.

MASS OBSERVATION (1940) *War Begins at Home*, eds T. Harrisson and C. Madge, London: Chatto & Windus.

MATHIAS, R. (1980) 'The black spot in the focus': a study of the poetry of Alun Lewis', *Anglo-Welsh Review,* 67: 43–78.

MIDDLETON MURRY, J. (1952) *Community Farm*, London: Peter Nevil.

MILLARD, K. (1991) *Edwardian Poetry,* Oxford: Clarendon Press.

MITCHELL, J. (1966) 'Hamish Henderson and the folk-song revival', in *Essays in Honour of William Gallacher,* Berlin: Humboldt Universität zu Berlin.

MOOREHEAD, C. (1987) *Troublesome People: Enemies of War: 1916–1986*, London: Hamish Hamilton.

MORGAN, E. (1990) *Crossing the Border,* Manchester: Carcanet Press.

MURDOCH, B. (1990) *Fighting Songs and Warring Words: Popular Lyrics of Two World Wars*, London: Routledge.

NAIRN, T. (1981) *The Break-Up of Britain*, London: Verso.

NETTLEINGHAM, F. T. (1917) *Tommy's Tunes*, London: Erskine MacDonald.

—— (1918) *More Tommy's Tunes*, London: Erskine MacDonald.

NEWMAN, A. (1981) *The Jewish East End 1840–1939*, London: The Jewish Historical Society of England.

NORRIS, C. (1992) *Uncritical Theory: Intellectuals and the Gulf War*, London: Lawrence & Wishart.

NOYES, SIR ALFRED (1920) *Collected Poems of Alfred Noyes. Volume 3,* London & Edinburgh: W. Blackwood.

ORAGE, A. R. (1907) *Nietzsche in Outline and Aphorism*, Edinburgh & London: T. N. Foulis.

—— (1974) *Orage as Critic*, ed. W. Martin, London & Boston: Routledge.

ORR, P. (ed.) (1966) *The Poet Speaks*, London: Routledge.

ORWELL, G. (1942) 'Thomas Hardy looks at war', *Tribune*, 18 September 1944: 13.

—— (1968) *Collected Essays, Journalism and Letters* (4 vols), eds I. Angus and S. Orwell, London: Secker and Warburg.

OSBORNE, C. (1980) *W. H. Auden: The Life of a Poet*, London: Macmillan.

OWEN, H. (1963–5) *Journey from Obscurity: Wilfred Owen 1893–1918*, London: Oxford University Press.

OWEN, W. (1967) *Collected Letters*, eds H. Owen and J. Bell, London: Oxford University Press.

—— (1973) *War Poems and Others*, ed. D. Hibberd, London: Chatto & Windus.

—— (1983) *The Complete Poems and Fragments*, ed. J. Stallworthy, London: Chatto & Windus, Hogarth Press, Oxford University Press.

—— (1988) *Selected Poetry and Prose*, ed. J. Breen, London: Routledge.

—— (1990) *The Poems of Wilfred Owen*, ed. J. Stallworthy, London: Chatto & Windus.

PAGE, M. (1975) *The Songs and Ballads of World War Two*, London: Granada.

PALMER, R. (1988) *The Sound of History: Songs and Social Comment*, Oxford & New York: Oxford University Press.

—— (1990) *'What a Lovely War': British Soldiers' Songs from the Boer War to the Present Day*, London: Michael Joseph.

PARFITT, G. (1990) *English Poetry of the First World War: Contexts and Themes*, London & New York: Harvester Wheatsheaf.

PARSONS, I. M. (1965) *Men Who Marched Away*, London: Chatto & Windus.

PIKOULIS, J. (1972) 'Alun Lewis: the way back', *Critical Quarterly* 14 (2): 145–66.

—— (1978) '"East and east and east": Alun Lewis and the vocation of poetry', *Anglo-Welsh Review*, 63: 39–65.

—— (1984) *Alun Lewis: A Life*, Bridgend: Poetry Wales Press.

PRIESTLEY, J. B. (1940) *Postscripts*, London: William Heinemann.

READ, H. (1916) 'Sorel, Marx, and the War.', *New Age* 8 June, 128–9.

—— (1938) *Poetry and Anarchism*, London: Faber & Faber.

—— (1941) *To Hell with Culture*, London: Kegan Paul, Trench, Trubner & Co.

—— (1943) *The Politics of the Unpolitical*, London: Routledge.

—— (1944) *A World Within a War*, London: Faber & Faber.

—— (1963) *The Contrary Experience: Autobiographies*, London: Faber & Faber.

—— (1968) *The Cult of Sincerity*, London: Faber & Faber.

—— (1992) *Collected Poems*, London: Sinclair-Stevenson.

REILLY, C. W. (1978) *English Poetry of the First World War: A Bibliography*, London: Prior.

—— (ed.) (1981) *Scars Upon My Heart: Women's Poetry and Verse of the First World War*, London: Virago Press.

—— (ed.) (1984) *Chaos of the Night: Women's Poetry and Verse of the Second World War*, London: Virago Press.

—— (1986) *English Poetry of the Second World War: A Bibliography*, London: Mansell Publishing.

RICKARDS, M. and MOODY, M. (1975) *The First World War: Ephemera, Mementoes, Documents*, London: Jupiter Books.

RICKWORD, E. (1976) *Behind the Eyes: Collected Poems and Translations*, Manchester: Carcanet New Press.

—— (1978) *Literature in Society: Essays and Opinions Volume 2*, Manchester: Carcanet Press.

ROBERTS, R. (1973) *The Classic Slum: Salford Life in the First Quarter of the Century*, Harmondsworth: Penguin.

ROBINSON, J. S. (1982) *H.D.: The Life and Work of an American Poet*, Boston: Houghton-Mifflin.

ROCKER, R. (1956) *The London Years*, tr. J. Leftwich, London: R. Anscome.

ROSENBERG, I. (1979) *The Collected Works of Isaac Rosenberg*, ed. I. Parsons, London: Chatto & Windus.

ROSS, R. H. (1967) *The Georgian Revolt: Rise and Fall of a Poetic Ideal 1910–1922*, London: Faber & Faber.

ROSS, R. J. (1986) 'Marx, MacDiarmid and MacLean', in R. J. Ross and J. Hendry (eds) *Sorley MacLean: Critical Essays*, Edinburgh: Scottish Academic Press.

—— (1985 'Hamish Henderson: in the midst of things', *Chapman 42*, 8 (5): 11–18.

ROSS, R. J. and HENDRY, J. (eds) (1986) *Sorley MacLean: Critical Essays*, Edinburgh: Scottish Academic Press.

ROYLE, T. (ed.) (1990) *In Flanders Field: Scottish Poetry and Prose of the First World War*, Edinburgh: Mainstream Publishing Co.

RUSSELL, B. (1916) *Principles of Social Reconstruction*, London: Allen & Unwin.

—— (1968) *The Autobiography of Bertrand Russell 1914–1944 (Volume II)*, London: Allen and Unwin.

RUSSELL, D. (1992) '"We carved our way to glory": the British soldier in music hall song and sketch circa 1880–1914', in J. MacKenzie (ed.) *Popular Imperialism and the Military, 1850–1950*, Manchester: Manchester University Press.

SAID, E. (1978) *Orientalism*, London: Routledge.

SASSOON, S. (1937) *The Complete Memoirs of George Sherston*, London: Faber & Faber.

—— (1942) '*The Dynasts* in war time', *Spectator*, 6 February 1942: 127–8.

—— (1945) *Siegfried's Journey 1916–1920*, London: Faber & Faber.

—— (1981) *Diaries 1920–1922*, ed. R. Hart-Davis, London: Faber & Faber.

—— (1983) *Diaries 1915–1918*, ed. R. Hart-Davis, London: Faber & Faber.

—— (1983) *The War Poems of Siegfried Sassoon* ed. R. Hart-Davis, London: Faber & Faber.

SCAMMELL, W. (1988) *Keith Douglas: A Study*, London: Faber & Faber.

SCANNELL, V. (1976) *Not Without Glory: Poets of the Second World War*, London: The Woburn Press.

SELWYN, V. (ed.) (1989) *More Poems of the Second World War*, London: Dent/Salamander Oasis Trust.

SELWYN, V., DE MAUNY, E., FLETCHER, I., FRASER, G. S., and WALLER, J. (eds) (1980) *Return to Oasis: War Poems and Recollections from the Middle East 1940–1946*, London: Shepheard Walwyn (Publishers)/Editions Poetry London.

—— (eds) (1983) *From Oasis into Italy: War Poems and Diaries from Africa and Italy, 1940–1946*, London: Shepheard-Walwyn (Publishers).

SEYMOUR SMITH, M. (1982) *Robert Graves: His Life and Work*, London: Hutchinson.

SHARP, C. (1907) *English Folk-Song: Some Conclusions*, London: Simpkin/Novello.

SHAYER, D. (n.d.) 'Alun Lewis – the poet as combatant', *Poetry Wales* 10 (3): 79–83.

SHELDEN, M. (1989) *Friends of Promise: Cyril Connolly and the World of 'Horizon'*, London: Hamish Hamilton.

SHERIDAN, D. (ed.) (1990) *Wartime Women: An Anthology of Women's Wartime Writing for Mass-Observation 1937–45*, London: William Heinemann.

SHIRES, L. (1985) *British Poetry of the Second World War*, London: Macmillan.

SHOWALTER, E. (1987) *The Female Malady: Women, Madness and English Culture, 1830–1980*, London: Virago Press.

SILKIN, J. (1972) *Out of Battle: The Poetry of the Great War*, Oxford: Oxford University Press.

—— (ed.) (1979) *The Penguin Book of First World War Poetry*, Harmondsworth: Penguin.

—— (1981) 'Keith Douglas', *Agenda* 19 (2–3): 49–58.

SIMON, B. and BRADLEY, I. (eds) (1975) *The Victorian Public School*, London: Gill and Macmillan.

SINCLAIR, A. (1989) *War Like a Wasp: The Last Decade of the Forties*, London: Hamish Hamilton.

SKELTON, R. (ed.) (1968) *Poetry of the Forties*, Harmondsworth: Penguin.

—— (ed.) (1970) *Herbert Read: A Memorial Symposium*, London: Methuen.

SLATER, M. (1941) 'Bless 'em all: a piece about army songs', *Our Time* I (I): 21–6.

SMYTH, W. M. (ed.) (1957) *Poems of Spirit and Action*, London: Edward Arnold.

SOREL, G. (1916) *Reflections on Violence (Réflexions sur la Violence)*, tr. T. E. Hulme, London: Allen & Unwin.

SPENDER, S. (1944) 'War poetry between the wars', *Tribune* 22 September 1944: 13–14.

—— (1945) *Citizens in War – and After*, London: George Harrap.

—— (1951) *World Within World*, London: Hamish Hamilton.

—— (1978) *The Thirties and After: Poetry, Politics, People (1933–1975)* London: Fontana.

—— (1985) *Journals 1939–1983*, ed. J. Goldsmith, London: Faber & Faber.

STALLWORTHY, J. (1974) *Wilfred Owen*, London: Oxford University Press/ Chatto & Windus.

—— (1988) (ed.) *The Oxford Book of War Poetry*, London: Oxford University Press.

STEELE, T. (1990) *Alfred Orage and the Leeds Arts Club 1893–1923*, Aldershot: Scolar Press.

SUMMERFIELD, P. (1981) 'The Effingham Arms and the Empire: deliberate selection in the evolution of the music hall in London', in E. and S. Yeo (eds) *Popular Culture and Class Conflict 1590–1914*, Brighton: Harvester.

—— (1986) 'Patriotism and Empire: music hall entertainment 1870–1914', in J. M. MacKenzie (ed.) *Imperialism and Popular Culture*, Manchester: Manchester University Press.

TERRAINE, J. (1980) *The Smoke and the Fire*, London: Sidgwick & Jackson.

THOMAS, E. (1915) *This England: An Anthology from Her Writers*, London: Oxford University Press.

—— (1981) *A Language Not to Be Betrayed: Selected Prose of Edward Thomas*, ed. E. Langley, Manchester & Ashington: Carcanet Press/Mid-Northumberland Arts Group.

TILLER, T. (1943) *The Inward Animal*, London: Hogarth Press.

—— (1947) *Unarm, Eros*, London: Hogarth Press.

TINKER, D. (1982) *A Message from the Falklands: the Life and Gallant Death of David Tinker, Lieutenant R. N.*, ed. H. Tinker, London: Junction Books.

TOLLEY, A. T. (1985) *The Poetry of the Forties*, Manchester: Manchester University Press.

TREECE, H. (ed.) (1944) *Herbert Read: An Introduction to His Work by Various Hands*, London: Faber & Faber.

TSUZUKI, C. (1980) *Edward Carpenter 1844–1929: Prophet of Human Fellowship*, Cambridge: Cambridge University Press.

TYLEE, C. M. (1990) *The Great War and Women's Consciousness: Images of Militarism and Womanhood in Women's Writings, 1914–64*, London: Macmillan.

VAN WYK SMITH, M. (1978) *Drummer Hodge: The Poetry of the Anglo-Boer War (1899–1902)*, Oxford: Clarendon Press.

WALLACE, S. (1988) *War and the Image of Germany: British Academics 1914–1918*, Edinburgh: John Donald Publishers.

WARD, E. (1983) *David Jones: Myth-Maker*, Manchester: Manchester University Press.

WEBB, J. (1976) *The Occult Establishment*, La Salle, IL: Open Court.

WELLAND, D. S. R. (1960) *Wilfred Owen: A Critical Study*, London: Chatto & Windus.

WELLER, K. (1985) *'Don't be a Soldier': The Radical Anti-War Movement in North London 1914–1918*, London: The Journeyman Press History Workshop Centre.

WIENER, M. J. (1985) *English Culture and the Decline of the Industrial Spirit 1850–1980*, Harmondsworth: Penguin.

WILLIAMS, J. S. (1964) 'The poetry of Alun Lewis', *Anglo-Welsh Review* 14 (33): 59–71.

WILSON, J. M. (1975) *Isaac Rosenberg: Poet and Painter*, London: Cecil Woolf.

WOODCOCK, G. (1972) *Herbert Read – The Stream and the Source*, London: Faber & Faber.

WOOLF, V. (1943) *Three Guineas*, (1st edition 1938) London: Hogarth Press.

WRIGHT, D. G. (1978) 'The Great War, government propaganda and English "men of letters" 1914–16', *Literature and History* 7: 70–100.

YEO, E. and YEO, S. (eds) (1981) *Popular Culture and Class Conflict 1590–1914*, Brighton: Harvester Press.

ZANGWILL, I. (1916) *The War for the World*, London: Heinemann.

Index